P9-AOA-700

A DARING BLUEPRINT
FOR REVITALIZING
AMERICAN BUSINESS

Emmett C. Murphy

PRENTICE HALL
Englewood Cliffs, New Jersey 07632

Prentice-Hall International (UK) Limited, *London*
Prentice-Hall of Australia Pty. Limited, *Sydney*
Prentice-Hall Canada, Inc., *Toronto*
Prentice-Hall Hispanoamericana, S.A., *Mexico*
Prentice-Hall of India Private Limited, *New Delhi*
Prentice-Hall of Japan, Inc., *Tokyo*
Simon & Schuster Asia Pte. Ltd., *Singapore*
Editora Prentice-Hall do Brasil, Ltda., *Rio de Janeiro*

10   9   8   7   6   5   4   3   2   1

Library of Congress Cataloging-in Publication Data

Murphy, Emmett C.
    Forging the heroic organization : a daring blueprint for
revitalizing American business / Emmett C. Murphy, Michael Snell.
        p.   cm.
    Includes bibliographical references and index
    ISBN 0-13-100793-9
    1. Organizational effectiveness—United States. 2. Strategic
planning—United States. 3. Industrial management—United States.
I. Snell, Michael. II. Title.
HD58.9.M87   1994   94-34165
658.4'063—dc20   CIP

ISBN 0-13-100793-9

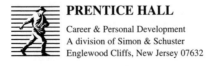

PRENTICE HALL
Career & Personal Development
A division of Simon & Schuster
Englewood Cliffs, New Jersey 07632

Printed in the United States of America

To Carol

ACKNOWLEDGMENTS

Like forging the Heroic Organization, this book came into being as the result of a shared vision of service, and I'd like to thank all the heroic partners who have shared this vision with me.

First, many thanks to my friend and creative partner Mike Snell, whose encouragement and good offices have enabled me to share the insights my associates and I at E. C. Murphy, Ltd., have gained while working with heroic leaders in the frontlines of organizational life.

I owe a great debt to Tom Power, senior editor at Simon & Schuster/Prentice Hall, who has supported our work from our first book, *The Genius of Sitting Bull: Thirteen Heroic Strategies for Today's Business Leaders.* Julie Felix has also worked with us from the beginning, providing research, incisive copy editing, and a special talent for bringing order out of chaos. Mark Murphy drafted the CEO and Frontline Manager chapters, synthesizing research from the national databases at E. C. Murphy, Ltd., and the American Society for Work Redesign. He also redesigned key consulting tools for the Heroic Guide to Action. I'm very grateful to Mark, as both his colleague and father, for the seminal insight he brought to the book in recommending St. James's great admonition that "faith, if it has no works, is dead" as a starting point. Mark and I have had a unique opportunity to share a continuing journey of faith in the development of this book.

Finally, I'm especially grateful to my wife Carol, to whom I dedicate this book, for her love and faith in our journey together, and to the other member of our personal heroic quartet, our daughter, Marissa, for exuberance and interest in the Medicine Circle of life, which is the heart of the Heroic Organization.

CONTENTS

v

PART THREE

THE HEROIC GUIDE TO ACTION: TOOLS FOR FORGING THE HEROIC ORGANIZATION • 243

INTRODUCTION
The Heroic Organization:
from Faith to Action

Faith, if it has no works, is dead

ST. JAMES

When Neil Armstrong set foot on the surface of the moon in 1969 and declared "That's one small step for man, one giant leap for mankind," an entire nation stepped with him. More than a single man's accomplishment or that of the Apollo 11 flight crew or even the National Aeronautics and Space Administration, Armstrong's step fulfilled an act of faith in the heroic capabilities of the United States government, its society and its institutions. Over twenty-five years later, America faces a crisis of faith in those same institutions, a crisis that affects virtually every citizen in every walk of life. As the aging Apollo 11 astronauts celebrate the twenty-fifth anniversary of their historic flight, the President sets up a legal defense fund to fight allegations of sexual misconduct; tobacco company executives stand accused of lying to Congress and the public; the media fabricates stories in their search for sensational headlines; the most democratic—and expensive—health-care system in the world does not provide basic services to nearly forty million citizens; record numbers of workers stand in unemployment lines seeking low-paying jobs in the wake of massive corporate downsizing, and even those who remain employed often have lost their faith in, and feel disconnected from, their organizations.

The landing on the moon fulfilled an unparalleled leap of faith by President John F. Kennedy, who, in 1963, declared that America would achieve that goal within the decade. His vision tapped a well-spring of energy that propelled the nation to achieve a goal of truly heroic proportions. Ironically, the effort occurred during the Vietnam War, a military venture that signaled the beginning of a cycle of social uncertainty and loss of national focus that has stalled history's greatest experiment in pluralistic democracy. In his book, *The Spirit of Community*, Amitai Etzioni offers this relevant observation:

> Since the Sixties, the [faith] that combined all the plurals into one mosaic—one society and one nation— [has] waned. The notion of a shared community or public interest which balances but does not replace the plurality of particular interest, has been eroded . . . As rights exploded and responsibilities receded, as the moral infrastructure crumbled, so did the public interest.

That observation connects with the words of St. James, who wrote, "Faith, if it has no works, is dead." Whether it's a religious belief, dedication to the ideals of democracy, or a commitment to serve the customer, rhetoric without action is hypocrisy. As Etzioni noted, America has been on a slide from faith since the Sixties, with the result that the very core of our culture lies in danger of a meltdown. Nowhere does this slide appear more evident than in the everyday commerce of organizational life.

Whether it's the deceitful practices of the tobacco companies, the self-serving plans of politicians, the manipulation by the media, or the unresponsiveness of our health-care and educational systems, narrow self-interest undermines the welfare of the larger community, sapping its energy and draining the reservoir of faith. As America moves toward a new millennium, its organizations face the challenge of redressing the excesses of self-interest that have undermined faith in America's pluralistic traditions, to forge a new bond of faith that restores the balance between rights and responsibilities.

Fortunately, a new generation of American organizations have already begun translating faith into action as they and their leaders accept the responsibility to redress the excesses of selfishness and forge a new order based on the timeless principles of heroic action.

Looking beyond immediate self-interest to the greater reward and power found in serving others, Heroic Organizations have begun retapping the tidal force of human energy that drives pluralistic democracy and thereby spurring a Renaissance in American organizational life. This book delivers a report on their success and distills from their efforts a leadership manual any organization can use to translate faith into practice.

THE NEED FOR HEROISM

Heroism is the driving force behind human progress. It is the great integrating force in human endeavor, and the need for it has been the dominant theme in human history. Heroism brings all the pieces of organizational life together to create a whole greater than the sum of its parts. Motivated by a deep faith in the worth and dignity of others and by the practical benefits of shared commitment, organizational heroes reach beyond narrow self-interest to secure the welfare of all. As Joseph Campbell noted, "Heroism is neither release nor ecstasy for oneself, but the wisdom and power to serve others."

The idealized definition of a hero describes a legendary or divine figure who possesses great strength, skill, and courage. This figure, like Superman, can leap tall buildings in a single bound and can outrun a speeding locomotive. In our all-too-real world, however, even Superman will stumble, fall to temptation, and find Mike Wallace knocking on his door with a *60 Minutes* video camera whirring behind his shoulder. Dwight D. Eisenhower, Franklin Delano Roosevelt and Harry Truman all loomed larger than life over a pre-exposé American landscape. But, could any of these presidents have fared better than George Bush or Bill Clinton under the unforgiving eye of today's media?

If you can judge the strength of a society by its heroes, then our contemporary culture often seems weak indeed. Who shoulders the blame, the public with its twin appetites for mass-marketed icons and the sordid details of their personal lives, or the media masters who erect these icons one day then shatter their clay feet the next? Whether you blame the public for seeking their heroes on Boston Garden's parquet basketball court or on MTV's music videos, or you bemoan the yellow journalism practiced by the producers of *Hard*

Copy and *A Current Affair*, doing so begs the real question: What constitutes authentic heroism, and how do we build authentic heroism into our society?

Behind those questions, of course, lies an even more fundamental question: Do we need heroes at all? If the hero creates order out of confusion and chaos, if the hero gives direction and leadership to those who have lost their way, if the hero provides a standard and a role model with which others can improve their lives, then the answer is yes. Who can argue that America in the late twentieth century does not need more order, more direction, more leadership, better models of behavior? Watergate, the Iran-Contra affair, Whitewater, and a continuing parade of political scandals have rocked our faith in our political system. Ivan Boesky, Michael Milken, and Charles Keating have undermined our confidence in our economic system. Drugs and automatic weapons have turned inner-city playgrounds into battlefields; our schools fail our students; our rivers run foul with pollution; our health-care system grows sicker every day.

Americans desperately need heroes, but not the idealized heroes of yesterday—they need the authentic heroes of tomorrow.

AUTHENTIC HEROISM

What does heroic behavior really involve and what specific role can it play in meeting the needs and realities of a dramatically and continuously reshaping world? To answer this question, we propose a new definition for what we call authentic heroism. The philosopher Georges Simenon put it well when he said, "The hero is a person who has the courage to make a good thing of his whole life." The authentic hero is not perfect but strives to do well in every endeavor. The hero sheds the cowardice of moral indifference and wears the badge of moral responsibility. Like the conventional hero, the authentic hero fashions a legend of accomplishment, but also admits and learns from mistakes; possesses great strength, but also acknowledges and works to overcome weaknesses; displays skill, but continually develops new skills; acts courageously, but realizes that fear always accompanies change. Authentic heroes are ordinary people who accept extraordinary responsibility to meet extraordinary challenges, and they do so by following three age-old principles of action.

First, authentic heroes *practice strategic humility*. Though confident in their own abilities, they recognize that they cannot go it alone. Instead, they channel their efforts to harnessing the energy of others. They *build heroic partnerships* that tap the tidal force of cooperation and trust that have propelled human achievement since the beginning of time. Finally, and most important, they *walk in a sacred manner*, following a disciplined protocol for translating faith into action.

In the first book in this series, *The Genius of Sitting Bull: Thirteen Heroic Strategies for Today's Business Leaders*, we applied the heroic concept to individual leaders and the personal skills they need in order to become authentic heroic leaders. Those skills included, among others, the ability to create commitment and build trust, to communicate on many levels, to think strategically and rightsize forces, to welcome crisis, and to measure results. In this second book, we apply these skills and our definition of authentic heroism to organizations, which, like individuals, must muster the courage and commitment to "make a good thing of their whole life."

THE HEROIC ORGANIZATION

A handful of organizations have already begun to grapple with the realities of a new economic world and to create order out of chaos. From large multinationals to small entrepreneurial companies, from complex teaching hospitals to neighborhood health clinics and not-for-profit public service and governmental agencies, these Heroic Organizations will write the next chapter of the American dream. This book chronicles their success and offers an operational plan for translating authentic heroism into action in organizational life. Borrowing as its metaphor the timeless heroic vision of *Cangleska Wakan* (CHON-GLESHKA WAH-KAHN)—the Native American Sacred Hoop, or Medicine Circle, which stresses the interrelatedness of everything in the world—the book explains how bold organizations are already creating a better future for themselves and all their stakeholders. From global visionaries such as General Electric and Intel, to regional and local organizations such as Hamot Medical Center and North American Tool and Die, a new generation of organizational leadership has begun proving how a commitment to the wholeness of an enterprise—organizational *Cangleska Wakan*—can transform disconnected and fractious organizational stakeholders into integrated and synergistic teams.

Organizational Medicine Circle

The integrated and synergistic organizations profiled in the pages ahead demonstrate the power of a process that both keys into the energy sources that drive our culture and respects the new global and domestic marketplace. They reveal that legendary achievement arises from authentic heroism: the willingness to learn from mistakes, overcome weaknesses, welcome change, lift others, and forsake self-interest for the benefit of the group—the ability, in short, to put works back into faith.

A BLUEPRINT FOR HEROIC ACTION

Authentic heroism in organizational life follows a seven-step process whereby the whole becomes greater than the sum of its parts. Applied to every aspect of an organization, the process allows leaders to fashion the organizational equivalent of the Sacred Hoop of sioux lore, an entity that respects the interrelatedness of all those whose lives depend on its success. People at any level in virtually every type of setting can use the harmony of *Cangleska Wakan* to revitalize their organizations.

THE SEVEN-STEP HEROIC PROCESS

1. Establish a Context for Action

2. Measure Mission Effectiveness

3. Identify Opportunities for Improvement

4. Mobilize Support

5. Take Action

6. Evaluate Results

7. Repeat the Process Continuously

Establishing a context for action both defines the challenge an organization must meet and creates the vision that should drive the organization's actions as it strives to meet the challenge. In a pluralistic culture such as ours, stakeholders will not follow leaders or support organizations that do not openly define their purposes and offer themselves up for public scrutiny. Authority comes from open negotiation among all stakeholders on the accuracy and validity of the vision. John Malone, CEO of Hamot Medical Center in Erie, Pennsylvania, established context when he invited all stakeholders, from patients to physicians, employees, the board, and the community to participate in transforming the bureaucratically hidebound medical center into a truly patient-focused institution. Malone challenged stakeholders to look beyond immediate self-interest and address Hamot's financial crisis by identifying the sources of waste and inefficiency that could impair patient care and threaten the organization's welfare. By establishing a patient-focused context for action, he defined a challenge and created a vision that unified all stakeholders in the pursuit of an organizational mission they could agree upon and support.

Establishing context creates a baseline against which the organization measures itself as it proceeds, which leads to step two, *measuring mission effectiveness*. The development of mission translates the faith embodied in the vision into a practical plan of action. The mission is a contract between stakeholders that bonds them together in the pursuit of specific goals and objectives. By measuring mission effectiveness, an organization measures its authenticity as an heroic organization and enforces the organization's social contract for openness and accountability. It also keeps the stakeholders in the Sacred Medicine Circle connected to one another by fueling negotiation, debate, and constant reassessment to ensure that the mission, and thus, the contract, is updated continuously to meet emerging challenges. Jack Welch measured mission effectiveness and made sure no one at GE was operating in the dark when he set crystal-clear goals—gaining #1 or #2 market position—and assiduously followed up on each division's progress. The goals proved both attainable and effective, and given the always changing demands of the market, they remain a strong challenge for GE's people, who have learned to measure their mission effectiveness constantly and stay on top.

Continuous reassessment naturally leads to step three, *identifying opportunities for improvement*. Identifying opportunities to eliminate waste and increase quality, and sharing this information with stakeholders, constantly reinforces the stated priorities of the organization and provides a platform for effective action. Thermos Corporation successfully used this strategy when it turned to its stakeholders to diagnose opportunities for improvement in the electric grill market. A cross-functional team of employees representing every department pounded the pavement performing hands-on market research. Innovation finally arose from a shared diagnosis of market opportunities and ways Thermos could exploit them, resulting in the hottest-selling electric grill ever to hit the market.

Pinpointing opportunities for improvement sets the stage for *mobilizing support*, then *taking action*. The heroic process gains its strength from the bonding of all stakeholders, mobilizing the entire Medicine Circle, and creating an unparalleled source of power to support concerted action. Effective action must be comprehensive, efficient, and rapid, the product of a collaborative effort and unified vision. It embodies the sort of "we're all in this together" enthusiasm that fueled success at Southwest Airlines, the most successful company in its turbulent industry. At Southwest, workers share ownership and pride in the company's accomplishments, and they act collectively to make their airline the best. This heroic upstart has bigger airlines scrambling to keep up. While other airlines creak under heavy burdens of debt and wrestle with crippling strikes, Southwest posts glowing financials, and its famous friendly service (one airline employee volunteered to take care of a passenger's dog for two weeks because the airline didn't allow dogs on the plane) wins kudos and ticket sales from customers nationwide.

Finally, *evaluating results* and *repeating the process continuously* seal the heroic commitment to continuous progress and improvement. The heroic organization does not strive for certainty, for certainty signals stagnancy, and stagnancy invites failure. Rather, the heroic organization strives for strength and flexibility—continually progressing under constantly changing circumstances. Lawrence Bossidy, CEO of Allied Signal, has been creating an organization that pays attention to the need for continuous progress. After evaluating a comprehensive restructuring effort in which stakeholders had mapped out the company's work and redesigned that work to improve quality and productivity, Bossidy found that the evaluation process itself yielded still more opportunities for the company. By establishing such a process of self-renewal, Allied Signal made a heroic commitment: to improve continuously, to reach out continuously to stakeholders, and to aspire continuously to the balance of *Cangleska Wakan.*

HOW TO USE THE BOOK

The Heroic Organization provides a blueprint for building an integrated organization that leaders at any level in virtually every type of setting can use to revitalize their organizations.

FOR BUSINESS—any manager in any business, large or small, can benefit from applying the principles of *Cangleska Wakan* and the seven heroic steps to building stronger stakeholder relationships. In an increasingly chaotic domestic and international marketplace, mission focus and stakeholder commitment provide the keys to success. Constant and abrupt changes will characterize the marketplace, confusing the unfocused and draining limited resources of energy, money, and time. Managers who master the seven steps to building an Heroic Organization will harness the competitive advantage of *Cangleska Wakan,* uniting all the stakeholders who can help their organizations respond with flexibility and speed to opportunities for growth, new product development, and all the innumerable crises that occur in organizational life, from sales and market-share decline to employee dissatisfaction, from government regulation to international competition.

America's businesses have reached a crossroads in their relationship with stakeholders. By abandoning the old shark mentality of "eat or be eaten," America's businesses can become full partners in the democratic process, committing themselves fully to developing relationships based on reciprocity, not on exploitation, on inclusion, not on exclusion. *The Heroic Organization* shows managers in all types of businesses how they can convert an investment in *Cangleska Wakan* into stability, growth, and a healthier bottom line.

FOR HEALTH CARE—No type of American organization faces greater change than America's health-care organizations. From patients to physicians, from insurers to government, its stakeholders have overloaded the capacity of an outmoded and wasteful feudal system. For health-care leaders, *The Heroic Organization* provides a coherent vision and action plan for riding the rapids of change with confidence and stability.

FOR GOVERNMENT—Public sector leaders face the twin threats of near bankruptcy and loss of public trust. Not since the immediate post-Civil War period has America's governmental financial stability been so precarious or its people so restive. Not only must governmental leaders at local, state, and federal levels reconnect warring stakeholders who pursue the old zero-sum game of "winner take all," they must bring order out of chaos and mobilize support for much needed programs of reform.

FOR PUBLIC SERVICE ORGANIZATIONS—Charity supplies the delicate membrane protecting the nerve fibers of society. In the midst of dramatic wrenching social change, it will fall to America's public-service organizations to prevent the nerves of commitment, good will, and confidence from fraying. Public-service leaders can use the healing power of *Cangleska Wakan* and the seven-step process to meet the needs of an anxious and distressed society, restoring its "nerve" and commitment to a vision of collective progress.

ORGANIZATION OF THE BOOK

The Heroic Organization works on the macro level as a strategic model for reevaluating and redesigning the organization, and on the micro level as a tactical operations manual for creating productive relationships among all organizational stakeholders.

Section I captures the heroic vision of *Cangleska Wakan* and outlines the challenge that makes it so vitally important today. It explains the essential elements of the Sacred Hoop, focusing on the new values and responsibilities each stakeholder group must assume to achieve harmony in the Hoop, and then introduces the *Seven-Step Heroic Process* that translates these new roles into reality. Chapter 1 establishes the need and context for *Cangleska Wakan,* showing how its power provides an ideal model for American achievement in the future. Promoting a philosophy of inclusion rather than of exclusion, *Cangleska Wakan* defines the optimal state of all stakeholder relationships and, thereby, creates a vision of the organization as an entity even greater than the sum of its parts. Chapter 2 introduces the organizational stakeholders, emphasizing healthy interrelationships among all stakeholders in an interdependent process of continuous improvement. Chapter 3 focuses on the *Seven-Step Heroic Process* and the three heroic principles, which define heroic action for every stakeholder in the organization.

Section II applies the seven-step process to each individual stakeholder, showing how an organization can mobilize the full energies of each. Each chapter provides current examples of America's foremost Heroic Organizations, the organizations that represent our best hope and provide us with the best role models for inspiring a new generation of American corporations.

Whether in service or in industry, these corporations offer instructive models because they embody a new way of thinking about how to do business. Intel, which rewon America's lead in the semiconductor industry, manages, in an industry notorious for short tenures at the top, to hold its lead through product and marketing innovation. Rubbermaid has reigned comfortably but never complacently as retailing king for years, holding its position by continuously learning, meeting customer needs, and creating highly specialized marketing tools. Quality of relationships shares importance with quality of products at companies such as Calyx & Corolla, which has cultivated a blooming mail-order niche in the hotly competitive flower business by sealing just-in-time relationships with growers and thrilling customers with quality floral arrangements.

Companies from coast to coast, ranging from Ben & Jerry's Ice Cream in Vermont to Levi Strauss in San Francisco, are setting the pace for heroic organizations across the country. Their case studies serve as role models for success in the new global arena, where every company must meet the standards of "global best." A commitment to *Cangleska Wakan* and the *Seven-Step Heroic Process* makes it possible for any company to meet that challenge and win.

Section III offers a *Heroic Guide to Action,* including a detailed strategy for action and a comprehensive *Mission Effectiveness Assessment,* which measures effectiveness in any organization for each step of the heroic process. You may send your organization's assessment results to The Center for Heroic Leadership, c/o E. C. Murphy, Ltd., at 800-922-5005, a national research center that will provide a diagnostic assessment and comparison with benchmark profiles in a given field. The *Heroic Guide* teaches you how to think holistically about your organization and how to apply this thinking to the critical interrelationships of stakeholders on which success depends: the leadership team, frontline managers, sales and marketing, the frontline workforce, suppliers, shareholders and the board, the community, the environment, government, competitors, and international partners.

By applying the *Seven-Step Heroic Process* to all aspects of your own organization, you can learn to tap the power of *Cangleska Wakan.* The journey begins by establishing a context for heroic action.

PART ONE

THE HEROIC PROCESS – A TIMELESS VISION FOR ORGANIZATIONAL ACHIEVEMENT

— 1 —

CANGLESKA WAKAN
A Context for Action

What happens when people of different ethnic origins, speaking different languages and professing different religions, settle in the same geographical locality and live under the same political sovereignty? Unless a common purpose binds them together, tribal hostilities will consume them and drive them apart . . . . The question Americans confront as a pluralistic society is how to vindicate cherished cultures and traditions without breaking the bonds of cohesion—common ideals, common political institutions, common language, common culture, common fate—that hold the republic together.

ARTHUR M. SCHLESINGER,
The Disuniting of America

In June, 1992, a tramp steamer carrying Chinese refugees ended a grueling 17,000 mile voyage aground a sandbar near New York City. After weathering months cramped in steerage, where they survived mostly on rice and shared a single toilet with nearly 300 people, the terrified refugees were forced to swim ashore in darkness. At least six people died in the wreck and the subsequent struggle to land. Capturing the scene for that evening's news, a photographer snapped an amazing photo: within the huddled circle of bedraggled, bereft refugees, one face stood out. The photo caption read, "Why Is This Man Laughing?"

How on earth could a man who had suffered so much be so happy? Like his companions on the boat, he had arrived in a new land homeless, friendless, and presumably penniless. Worse, he had probably traded the next five or six years of his future just to pay for

3

passage on that overcrowded, unseaworthy vessel, having purchased his "charter ticket" for about $30,000—the going rate for "underground" passage to the United States, typically sponsored by stateside gangs. To repay this debt, he would end up working sixteen-hour days, seven days a week, at a menial job, stopping only to sleep in a barracks-like dormitory where others like him slept in shifts. Yet he laughed, expressing his heartfelt joy that, despite the ordeal he had just endured, and despite the hardships that still lay ahead, he had made it to the U.S.A.

That anonymous man's photo symbolizes America's unique power—a power it has long held over the hearts and minds of both those who live within its borders and those who wish they could. Like millions before him, this man had gladly given up everything he owned for the chance to start over in the fabled land of opportunity. The ethnic communities built by men and women like him—the Little Italys, Chinatowns, Little Havanas—have woven the fabric of modern American society. But while American citizens celebrate their diversity, they equally cherish the values that make them Americans, whether first generation or tenth. America's genius has sprung from its ability to draw strength from and manage this diversity. A population compiled of peoples disconnected by gender, cultural background, race, and religion has remained connected by a shared vision about the land of the free and the home of the brave.

But today, sadly, *e pluribus unum*—"out of many, one," stands more as a challenge than as a motto for our country. In the face of heating racial tensions, splintering agendas among social groups, and the strident cries for individual "rights" backed by fierce litigation, American unity faces a crisis. Today, more than at any other time in history, American leaders face a national challenge to reaffirm America's ability to manage its diversity before the country rips asunder into a battleground of warring "tribes." And the leaders of nations in most corners of the world, from the countries that comprised the former Soviet Union to South Africa and Central America, struggle with the same challenge.

America's bottom-up, decentralized society has become a microcosm and model of the emerging global economy. Its social architecture, in which the economy, culture, and government express, or should express, a shared, voluntarily accepted vision, now informs the whole global environment in which the American system and its organizations must function. American-style pluralism, more than any other force, propels the new world economy.

At the same time, however, America's own pluralistic energies have created such intense demands for rights and privileges that the country stands in danger of losing its cohesion to competing interests or going bankrupt trying to fulfill all the demands. This problem has been aggravated by the recent failure of American leaders in business and government to comprehend and address the risk of disunity. They, especially, have been caught up in the spiraling excesses of pluralism, where the individual drive to succeed, unbalanced by a sense of responsibility to the welfare of the organization or culture, pits stakeholder against stakeholder and group against group in a zero-sum game of winner take all. As a result, our leaders have failed to devote sufficient energies to developing an integrated vision of goals, values, and action that can address the current challenge and reorganize our society in a way that the whole can achieve more than the sum of its parts.

This chapter will establish this sorely needed context for action, urging American business and government leaders to take the first step toward refocusing America's pluralistic energies. Before they can do so, they must examine the special forces creating the challenge, then develop a vision for meeting it. To accomplish this task, leaders at all levels must install a new paradigm for organizational achievement, a paradigm embodied in the ancient Sioux concept of *Cangleska Wakan* (the Sacred Medical Circle), and three guiding principles for translating that paradigm into heroic action. The subsequent chapters in Part One will flesh out an operational blueprint for building a new generation of heroic American organizations based on this paradigm and these principles.

THE CHALLENGE: COMPLEXITY

America's organizations must cut through the noise and confusion of the world's most complex society and build the cohesive stakeholder relationships necessary for survival. America is the most pluralistic society on earth, a kaleidoscope of colors, beliefs, and economic interests all competing for a share of the American dream. As Arthur Schlesinger noted, the complexity has become so great that it strains the bonds that hold the economy and culture together.

Individual stakeholders and the organizations they rely on for work and service have become *disunited* from one another and the overall culture in which they function, with each pursuing "me-first" rather than "me-too" agendas for success.

Such "me-first" agendas do not just spur individual actions, they also drive entire organizations, which pursue self-centered programs without attention to the needs of the whole culture and community in which they operate. For decades many companies have felt little responsibility to the communities and culture in which they've operated. Recently, the consequences have come to haunt most every organization. In two notable cases, the American public took action against the blatant corporate irresponsibility uncovered in the poisoned community of Love Canal in Niagara Falls and in the Exxon *Valdez* oil spill in Alaska, with furious public pressure translating into enormous cleanup costs and huge fines for the companies responsible for the catastrophes. Corporate responsibility goes beyond the community and environment, however. Management, labor, customers, and every other stakeholder in a company contribute to the long-term success of the company, and companies that ignore the impact of their actions invite the sort of crises that rocked Borden, where mismanagement pushed profits into a nose dive and the CEO onto the street, or Sears, whose painful contractions resulted from the company's losing touch with its customers, or the now defunct Eastern Airlines, whose leaders so antagonized labor that the airline eventually self-destructed.

From the neighborhood deli to the regional hospital to the national government and global corporations, America's organizations face the practical problem of respecting and building the key stakeholder relationships, values, and processes essential to their own survival and progress. In spite of the advances in the technology and techniques of communication and service, and possibly because of the additional noise created by them, organizations struggle to find a way to hold things together. If they don't find it, then they will contribute to the failure of the world's greatest laboratory for human achievement.

To meet this challenge, organizations must reunite individuals and their organizations to each other and to the larger democratic community of which they inescapably remain a part. For America to retain its place as a world leader, its organizational leaders in every sector of society must create a vision that addresses the challenge of complexity and can harness America's vast energies behind a common purpose. This starts with American leaders at every level of society recommitting themselves to the heroic principles of our culture and stepping forward and responding to the urgent challenge with a vision of common purpose that taps the unique power of American pluralism.

THE VISION: *CANGLESKA WAKAN*

Ironically, the necessary vision comes not from a contemplation of the present or the future, but from a return to a neglected or forgotten past. Systems theorists remind us that mature and adaptive life forms can always find options for survival in the rich resources of their physical and intellectual history. *Cangleska Wakan,* the Native American concept of the Sacred Medicine Circle, or Hoop, provides just that. A vision of unity arising from complexity, *Cangleska Wakan* shows leaders how to integrate the needs of organizational stakeholders and how to focus everyone's energies to fulfill them. It reduces the complexity to manageable terms, providing a formula for organizational success grounded in the traditions of American pluralism and consistent with the findings of contemporary science. Its principles help us to filter out the "people noise" caused by organizational stakeholders working at cross-purposes with one another, and it offers a practical as well as an inspirational vision of what we can become.

Over a century ago, the Sioux of the Great Plains lived by the tenets of *Cangleska Wakan,* which represented a practical as well as a philosophical model of organization. The Hoop encompassed the relationships, priorities, values, and processes for managing life in a world prone to rapid and often unpredictable changes in the economies, politics, and physical fates of tribal units. The Sioux understood that their existence depended on a practical understanding of the full continuum of relationships in the world, and the Hoop afforded a simple yet powerful tool for keeping those relationships in mind.

Two hundred years ago, the Sioux knew what contemporary Americans are now only beginning to learn, that "what goes around comes around." Today, as American leaders come to grips with the consequences of recent failures and struggle to regain the concepts of reciprocity and integration, they can use the Native American concept of the Hoop as a practical tool for reestablishing balance among all the synergistic relationships in organizational life.

THE PRINCIPLES OF *CANGLESKA WAKAN*

In Sioux culture, the Sacred Hoop encompasses all things, animate and inanimate, that make up the universe. The Hoop is a state of being—an understanding of the universe that connects all things in a mutual destiny. The Hoop explicitly depicts the interrelationships among all elements of life: humans, animals, spirits, air water, earth, and sky. In the Sioux world, no element acts alone; all components act in concert to create harmony or disharmony.

The symbol of the Hoop itself incorporates this principle:

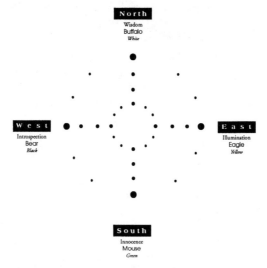

The circle symbolizes the Sioux belief that all things participate in one ordered whole, sharing the same physical and spiritual space. It embraces the idea of inclusion and the potential for everything within the Hoop to grow and change. Each point in the Hoop represents the interrelationships that comprise the universe. Like a compass, the four points signify the directions of the earth, but each point also represents states of mind or understanding—wisdom, innocence, illumination, and introspection—as well as the symbology of colors and animals.

The specific symbols within the Hoop differed from tribe to tribe, but the central principle remained the same: an acknowledgment of the harmony among all elements of the universe. In the Hoop, humans act in concert with nature, not just existing within the universe, but actually contributing to its creation. Each individual element in the Hoop bears responsibility for participating in the creation and balance of the Hoop, and each individual element influences all others. Imagine the circle in constant motion: It is a dynamic, not a static model. Every time a Sioux hunter brought down an antelope to feed his family, he would thank the spirit of the animal for its sacrifice, and in his prayer he would remind his prey that it participated in a circle of life that joined the hunter and the hunted.

In this way, Sioux philosophy maintained an enduring sense of fluidity and change. Living closely with nature for generations brought the Sioux in contact with a cyclical, changing world, where they saw myriad interrelationships every day. The humbling power of the forces around them created a people conscious of their own place in the universe. The Sioux could never have invented a "manifest destiny" as American settlers did, claiming for themselves a God-given right to conquer and dominate all within their reach. Instead, the Sioux saw themselves as woven into the fabric of the world, sharing their needs and purposes with all around them. They respected the world in which they lived to such a degree that, to their ultimate misfortune, they did not ever comprehend the white man's concept of owning land. They *were* the land.

These beliefs stand in stark contrast to the organizational mindset of modern business. Where the Sioux perceive existence as a circle, business people tend to perceive it as a hierarchy of relationships and linear progression, typically envisioning their world in terms of hierarchies and time lines, where events in the past and future bear little relationship to the present and where individuals occupy positions on the rungs of a ladder that, in practice, allow few to excel. In spite of continuing lip service to democratic principles, many organizations retain linear work structures that do not readily translate those ideals into reality. Nothing illustrates this point more than the tangled bureaucracies that characterize our government. One study by E. C. Murphy, Ltd., examining the complexity of government operations at a New York State labor department, found that the four directors of regional statewide services were separated by *seventeen levels of hierarchy* from the frontlines of service to the customer. This kind of pyramid structure actually creates roadblocks of privilege that thwart the full expression of individual potential. These roadblocks disappear, however, if you view the world from the perspective of the Hoop, which replaces standard hierarchical structures with a more connected and dynamic form of organization, one that does not run counter to the democratic principles Americans so ardently espouse.

Sadly, however, business and governmental bureaucracies have become the least democratic institutions in an otherwise increasingly pluralistic and democratic culture. Witness the crisis in public confidence in our governmental leadership. Today, the average citizen doesn't believe that Congress represents and works for the individual, and it's easy to see why. Congressional incumbents spend more time raising funds to perpetuate their own power than they do serving the needs of their constituents. From the failure to create a clear plan to tackle the national debt, or even to define its actual size, to the failure to rectify the influence of lobbyists, Congress has ensconced itself in an Ivory Tower of unaccountability. This led Stanley G. Tate to withdraw his candidacy to head the S & L bailout with the words, "Mr. President, Washington is a vicious city, with all kinds of hidden agendas. It is a city full of rumors, allegations and accusations, without much, if any regard for truthfulness or factuality." Clearly, such a climate divides American leadership from the country's citizens at the precise time it should be connecting with them. Not surprisingly, fewer and fewer people of integrity and purpose feel drawn to government service, leaving critical posts to the self-serving opportunists who maintain the bureaucracy, collusion, and compromise for the benefit of a select few.

The perspective of the Hoop contrasts sharply with standard business and government procedures. Where the Sioux recognized leadership as an act of achieving consensus, government and industrial leaders cling to a traditional view of leadership as a function of rank within the organization. Either deliberately or unwittingly, Western leaders have wielded the coercive power that naturally follows from rank, be it through carrot-and-stick reward systems or through simple dominance. Where the Sioux concept of the Hoop provides a day-to-day operational framework that stresses every individual's contribution to the whole, standard industrial organizational structures have created a world of haves and have nots, where the have nots lack the practical capacity to move up the hierarchy and contribute their full potential. Where the Sioux classified themselves as part of the world—on par with nature and the other stakeholders in the Hoop—managers in American organizations typically see themselves as separate from their community, their environment, and all other stakeholders, be they domestic customers or foreign competitors.

In this global era of rapid changes and increasingly interdependent relationships, the Hoop's perspective makes more sense than the standard organizational philosophies currently governing economic and cultural life in America and other industrialized countries. Today, as the pressure for integration and connection reaches unprecedented levels, the old bulwarks against pluralistic democracy must come down. In spite of all the talk about team learning, governance, stewardship, and continuous improvement, little more than sloganeering has actually occurred, and few organizations have effected any real changes in their fundamental structures. While American organizations have undergone dramatic reengineering, they have typically not undertaken collaborative work redesign. For such an effort to succeed, it must incorporate the concepts of integration, balance, and reciprocity, which take into account the consequences of every stakeholder action.

The principles of the Sioux Hoop provide a practical, comprehensive model for freeing organizational energies and channeling them to build the Heroic Organization. The Heroic Organization recognizes its place in the world, harnesses the abilities of every stakeholder, and uses that energy to obtain the best overall mutual results. The Heroic Organization participates fully and consciously in the world around it, it respects and values every stakeholder's needs, it recognizes the dynamic that exists between every stakeholder and the organization as a whole, from the frontlines to the CEO, from the community to the environment. Heroic leaders lead through consensus, the most democratic and powerful form of leadership, which unites people in purpose and in strength. Heroic leaders accept their fallibility and admit their mistakes, know that every stakeholder lends power to the organization, and that they wield only the power given them by their stakeholders.

TRANSLATING *CANGLESKA WAKAN* FOR THE HEROIC ORGANIZATION

The Heroic Organization seeks to operate along the dynamic, ordered lines so succinctly expressed by *Cangleska Wakan*. The Sioux characterized existence and the process of change within the Hoop with the phrase "walking in a sacred manner," a richer and more comprehensive version of the common expression so often heard in business circles—"walking the talk." The Heroic Organization walks in a sacred manner along the path of potential, reciprocity, and balance.

Translating *Cangleska Wakan* to Organizations

Cangleska Wakan	*Heroic Organization*
Individuals partake from and contribute to the whole: "The Universe" or "The Great Mystery." Each plays an intrinsic role in ongoing creation, and all individuals assume responsibility for the whole and their roles within it.	All stakeholders—from managers to the community—contribute to the same whole: "The Organization." Each plays an intrinsic role in the ongoing creation of that whole, and each accepts responsibility for his or her role and for the whole itself.
The Universe consists of all the entities that contribute to it, from the people to the stars. It is not a solid, tangible reality, but a perception of reality that unifies all that it creates and all that create it.	The organization consists of all of its stakeholders, what they contribute, and what they take. It is not a solid, tangible reality—it exists only on paper and in our minds as a unifying concept that describes the interaction of stakeholders.
The term "sacred" means "filled with intangible power," i.e,. *potential.* The ability of all things in the universe to share in the process of ongoing creation makes all things sacred.	*Potential* provides the key to an organization's power: The potential of each stakeholder to innovate, restructure, create, destroy. The needs and potential of every stakeholder are sacred.
The circular concept of the Hoop requires all "points" that make up	The "chain of command" that serves as the structural basis for most

Cangleska Wakan	Heroic Organization

the circle to possess a significant identity and function, while the Western linear model of hierarchy assigns more significance to some "points" than to others.

organizations functions in a linear fashion, with the CEO at the top and frontline workers at the bottom. In the Heroic Organization, the chain becomes a circle: in it the CEO and frontline worker possess equal power.

In the Hoop, all movement depends on all other movement to create continuous, harmonious, balanced and unified motion. The Hoop accommodates change and encourages movement and growth within it.

The chain of command and the pyramid hierarchy limit or strangle change within an organization. The Heroic Organization encourages stakeholders to evolve, assume new responsibilities, share power and information, and fulfill their potential.

The Hoop concept of time and events specifies that any event results from a multitude of forces—past and present, direct and indirect.

Industrial society's concept of the linear progression of events deemphasizes the many different forces that influence an event and create long-term consequences. Thus, industrial-era organizations typically act on incomplete histories and with narrowly viewed futures. The Heroic Organization continuously evaluates its status in terms of all of its stakeholders, its past achievements, and its future goals.

(continued on next page)

Cangleska Wakan	*Heroic Organization*

In Sioux myths, creatures lend their power to the gods to help create the world. On a secular level, tribal leadership is intrinsically democratic, following the tenets of the Hoop. All individuals contribute to the power of the tribe and win recognition for doing so.

Business and industry have glorified the role of leaders and typically ignored the group effort behind their success. In the Heroic Organization, leaders recognize their own shortcomings. They rely on the efforts of others to create the organizations they lead. They gain their power from their followers.

The Sioux view all elements of the universe as "alive," with the power to grow or change. This *potential* can be influenced and directed according to certain laws, provided you "walk in a sacred manner."

For Heroic Organizations, "walking in a sacred manner" means adhering to a protocol for tapping the potential for growth, change, and *improvement* in all facets of the organization by all stakeholders.

In Sioux religion, "having power" means being able to tap the potential inherent in all created things without being harmed or doing harm. In the secular sense, the tribe holds its power collectively. Chiefs wield no coercive power—they can only lead individuals on a shared path.

"Having power" takes on a new meaning for the Heroic Organization. Power belongs to the stakeholders. Leaders wield power only in the sense that they tap all stakeholders' potential to re-create the organization continuously. Using power unfairly, stealing power, or neglecting stakeholders disrupts the Hoop and will ultimately harm the leader and the organization.

For the Sioux, the nonlinear nature of time means that people must maintain heightened awareness of their environment and observe their world for signals. An individual acts only at the appropriate time— *before* crisis strikes and disrupts the balance of the Hoop.

Production-driven linear scheduling dulls awareness of the world surrounding the organization. Overreliance on schedules rather than on signals narrows the focus and vision of the organization and results in "the boiled-frog syndrome," where the time for action goes unnoticed until it is too late. The Heroic Organization focuses on all its stakeholders' experiences and watches for signals that allow it to anticipate and avert crises before they unbalance the organization.

THE HEROIC ORGANIZATION IN ACTION

Cangleska Wakan inspires a new organizational framework, where the values of shared destiny, communicated through and reinforced by the behavior of every stakeholder in the organization, precede both policy and practice. Each stakeholder shoulders responsibility for his or her own relationship with the organization and its other stakeholders, and each retains the right to act within the limits of that responsibility to achieve his or her individual potential.

Hamot Health Foundation in Erie, Pennsylvania, has embarked on the heroic path of *Cangleska Wakan*, and in doing so has revitalized its ability to serve and thrive within its community. By uniting all of its stakeholders behind one clear purpose, it has transformed itself from a sluggish, fearful organization struggling to make ends meet to a vital, flexible institution ready to take on the challenges of health-care reform.

While Hamot had been providing the Erie community with compassionate medical care for over one hundred years, the combined pressures of a faltering local economy and the national fever to redesign health care began taking a toll on the medical center. The recession of the early Nineties increased Hamot's tally of patients without insurance at the same time that the government was tightening Medicare compensation. Hamot began fighting a losing battle to control its own soaring costs while at the same time trying to meet the needs of a community hard hit by unemployment.

While Hamot's difficulties were apparent, the solutions were not. People in the organization and in the community clearly saw the need for change, but most felt fearful and resistant, afraid that cost cutting might mean more layoffs, and resistant to the unknown responsibilities and structural changes restructuring would bring. Luckily, one of the first major changes undertaken at Hamot was the appointment of a new CEO, John Malone, a leader with a vision to guide Hamot through its crisis.

Malone knew Hamot intimately, having worked there for seventeen years before becoming CEO. However, he wisely chose to learn even more about the company and its problems before he took action, reaching out to stakeholders—doctors, nurses, VPs, employees on all levels—and examining the hospital's situation with them. He made it clear that Hamot needed to change, and he invited everyone to participate in that change, beginning with their ideas on ways Hamot could improve. Malone simply reasoned that the people doing the job know the job best, and therefore know how the job could be done better. He was right.

Hamot's people immersed themselves in a comprehensive assessment of the quality and efficiency of work, using a new technology for organizational diagnosis called Work Imaging™. The assessment produced literally hundreds of ideas on what individual workers could do to save money and time while still improving quality. Once Malone included everyone in shaping the vision to change Hamot, people rose eagerly to the challenge. To start the process, Malone combined the Work Imaging™ information with feedback from the community on Hamot's quality of service to create a full picture of how the hospital operated and the quality of its results. In doing so, he followed a key tenet of *Cangleska Wakan* and the Heroic Organization—knowing yourself.

Malone shared the information, good and bad, with Hamot stakeholders. Armed with that information, they could plot out a strategy to achieve their vision for Hamot's future. At this point in the process, Malone had accomplished two things: he had reduced fear by letting stakeholders see for themselves where the organization stood and how they fit into it, and he had created an alliance among stakeholders, who now shared responsibility for revitalizing Hamot.

Malone reached out to stakeholders again, creating cross-functional teams to address the opportunities for improvement uncovered by the work and quality assessments. These teams drove Hamot's restructuring. Recognizing that only the combined efforts of the teams and the stakeholders they represented could turn Hamot around, Malone continually acknowledged everyone's efforts. While Hamot gained ground, Malone himself did not grab the spotlight—because he knew that doing so would undermine the stakeholders' confidence in the process and lead to debilitating cynicism.

One year after Malone initiated the change program at Hamot, the hospital had eliminated $15 million dollars of waste, nearly 10 percent of its total operating costs, while maintaining and strengthening its reputation as a quality leader. The changes made a tangible, measurable impact everywhere, from the CEO's office to the frontlines, and Malone intended to keep it that way. Pausing to congratulate Hamot's stakeholders on a job well done, Malone inaugurated a second cycle of assessment, aimed at finding out how the new, rejuvenated Hamot Health Foundation could further improve. Hamot, he felt, had only begun to tap its true potential. Like Hamot, the truly heroic organization extends itself to fulfill all of its potential, continuously seeking opportunities for growth and success. The stakeholders at Hamot, from the nurse delivering patient care to the marketing department reaching out to the community, all strive for ongoing, incremental improvements, a habit that typifies authentic heroism and forestalls the advent of another organizational crisis.

BALANCE AVERTS CRISIS

The leaders of the Heroic Organization consciously seek balance by keeping their fingertips on the pulse of stakeholder relationships. Maintaining a constant state of awareness, the Heroic Organization can anticipate and compensate for changes in the business and community environments, thus averting the sorts of crises that have plagued organizations such as IBM, where upstart competition turned the market upside down while Big Blue clung to its original but outdated philosophy of doing business, or Kodak, where years of complacency sent the giant on a downhill slide that the company cannot now easily reverse. Like most American companies, IBM and Kodak waited until crisis erupted before acting and thus incurred tens of thousands of layoffs, numerous restructurings and sell-offs, and two CEOs looking for work.

Recent studies have revealed that most American organizations do not maintain sufficient awareness of changes in their stakeholders' needs. A Gallup poll of executive behavior conducted in 1993 found that 70 percent of all organizational change initiatives occurred as a response to crisis, rather than as a deliberate attempt to innovate. Crisis, not innovation, prompted those 70 percent to improve or restructure themselves. Our comparison of the old hierarchical view of organizations with the heroic vision of the Hoop explains why this has happened. American leaders have too often disconnected themselves from their stakeholders and removed themselves from the frontlines of change. Bound up in their traditional hierarchies, they cannot perceive the changes buffeting the frontlines, let alone respond to them.

Crisis has forced radical restructuring efforts in health care, as in most other industries, from airlines to xerography, and the resultant wholesale staff reductions has meant higher levels of mortality for patients and workers across the corporate landscape. The problem takes on tragic proportions in the turbulent health-care industry, where the costs of late-breaking, desperate change programs may cost lives as well as dollars. A 1993 study by E. C. Murphy, Ltd., found that hospitals that had responded to financial pressure by downsizing across the board as little as 5 percent stood a 400 percent more likely chance that they would experience increased mortality and morbidity rates among Medicare patients. Such organizations failed to redesign the work to eliminate the extraordinary waste that, as reported by health-care workers, typically exceeds 31 percent in most hospitals. Rather than curing the disease, wholesale downsizing instead merely contributed to the waste, creating even greater roadblocks to delivery of quality of service, with patients ultimately paying the price. To reverse that deadly trend, organizations must adopt a methodology that enables them to invent their futures before crisis forces them to do so.

THE THREE-STEP HEROIC PROCESS

Viewing the organization as the sum of its relationships and building on the strengths of those relationships with all stakeholders—leaders, employees, customers, suppliers, competitors, the community, regulatory agencies, the environment, and the global arena—affords organizations the self-awareness they need to act with confidence in a changing world. The tenets of the Hoop suggest three steps any organization can take to tap the full potential of all its stakeholders:

1. Lead Through Strategic Humility

2. Build Heroic Partnerships

3. Walk in a Sacred Manner

Let's look at each of these steps more closely.

BUILD HEROIC
PARTNERSHIPS

The power of the Medicine Circle springs from its concept of partnership and community. The Hoop addresses the most basic and practical questions of organizational life: Who am I, and how do I relate to everyone who influences who I am? For the Sioux, the answers to these questions grew out of the actual experience of life on the Plains as they translated the trial and error lessons of life into definitions of each member's stake in the survival or death of the other. These definitions, and the roles they prescribed for the members of the tribe, connected every stakeholder to every other in terms of tangible expectations and consequences, and they defined a community of common interest that served as the foundation on which a system of values and action could be built.

The absence of this kind of organizational model lies at the heart of America's recent failure to harness the energies of pluralism. Ironically, the absence of a contemporary Medicine Circle of stakeholders has meant that otherwise interesting and creative organizational and leadership techniques have tended to exacerbate rather than resolve the disconnection. Instead of connecting and uniting at a fundamental level, organizations have used a fragmented approach, relying on virtual alliances, team learning, quality improvement, and work reengineering by isolated individuals or groups without paying sufficient attention to the overall impact of these efforts on the whole circle of stakeholders. Not surprisingly, these fragmented efforts have generally produced fragmented results.

The Heroic Organization gains strength from a spiderweb of relationships, where strands of reliance connect each stakeholder to all others. Weaken one strand and you weaken the entire web. Strengthen each strand and you strengthen the whole web. Like the strong strands of the spiderweb, strong bonds among all stakeholders afford the organization flexibility in the face of change, enabling it to capture the results that benefit each and every stakeholder.

General Motors provided a classic case of the consequences of ignoring stakeholder relationships when it threw supplier relationships out the window in the short-term interest of saving money. In his zealous pursuit to cut costs, GM purchasing executive Jose "Inaki"

Lopez alienated suppliers by tearing up contracts, demanding double-digit price cuts, sharing proprietary blueprints with rivals in an effort to strong-arm lower bids, and choosing lower quality suppliers over established suppliers strictly on the basis of price. Lopez's brief reign in purchasing saved money, but at what price? Over two hundred suppliers revolted, forcing GM to spend a lot of time and money placating them. Even now, some major suppliers refuse to invest in technical research for GM, taking their technology to Chrysler or Ford instead. And quality problems exacted a great toll—one ill-fitting ashtray from a new sub-par supplier caused a six-week shutdown of Buick Roadmaster production. At another plant, managers found quality problems in half of a new supplier's parts, which forced them to go begging for help from their old supplier, who had lost the contract to a 5 percent lower bid. The emergency parts, delivered by charter plane, turned GM's 5 percent savings into a 15 percent loss.

GM's ill-advised disconnection from a vital stakeholder in its future illustrates the changes affecting every American company today. Like the Sioux of a century ago, our society faces the threat of a worldwide shift in economic and political forces. And, like the Sioux, we can use the ideals of the Medicine Circle to reexamine our stakeholder relationships and thus better understand the gravity of the challenge we face and better design strategic and tactical plans to meet it. While the era of the free plains has passed, the dignity of the Sioux culture has survived with the strength of *Cangleska Wakan.* Likewise, we can ensure our own survival by developing a deeper understanding of just who can and will influence our lives, how they will do it, and how we can meet their challenges.

WALK IN A SACRED MANNER

To walk in a sacred manner leaders must recognize their place within the Hoop, pursuing change and growth within that context. The Sioux understood the need to "walk in a sacred manner" and develop and follow a formal plan of action if they were to fulfill the vision of the Sacred Medicine Circle. To fulfill the promise of the Hoop, they translated *Cangleska Wakan* into functional steps for everyday living, creating rituals for specific events, such as hunting and healing, that defined the process one should carry out to fulfill the tenets of *Cangleska Wakan* successfully. The resultant protocols for cooperation and assessment supported survival in the harsh and dangerous environment of the plains.

We need similar protocols today. As in the world of the Sioux, their form must follow their function. First, the protocol must reduce complexity to manageable levels by establishing a context for action that defines the immediate challenge and instills a vision for mobilizing people and resources to meet it. Every organization or society must function within a context for action that aligns its resources and activities with the underlying economic, social, and technological forces that create its market and define the needs of its stakeholders.

Second, the protocol must measure organizational success in terms of its benefits to all stakeholders. It must weigh the severity of the challenge in terms of the risk or potential it represents to the organization's vision of success. In the Sioux world, the everyday experience of living close to the natural world dominated people's lives. In modern organizations, the complexity of modern society has often distanced leaders and workers from reality. To get back in touch with reality, an organization must adopt a rigorous strategy for assessing risk and potential and must commit itself to actions that minimize the risks and maximize the potential.

An accurate assessment sets the stage for taking the next step along the heroic path, identifying opportunities, mobilizing support, taking action and evaluating results. Whether the day's events chronicled a victory on the battlefield or success in the hunt, the Sioux examined the impact of these events on their vision of community. All businesspeople must do the same, constantly reviewing far more than the bottom line of this month's P & L. They must go further, assessing the status of every stakeholder relationship. Such an assessment makes it possible to walk in a sacred manner, committing the organization to a process of continuous improvement.

Thermos used this strategy in developing its best-selling new Thermal Electric Grill, introduced in the fall of 1992. The grill revolutionized electric grilling technology and won numerous awards for its sleek designer look, including one from the Industrial Designers Society of America. But the real sizzle occurred at the cash register, where the grill raked in both profits and market share percentage points.

How did Thermos shake up the saturated, sluggish grill market? By reaching out to its stakeholders. Thermos began the Thermal

Grill project in 1990 by pulling together a team of managers from engineering, marketing, manufacturing, and finance. Their assignment: to go into the field and learn about people's cookout needs. The critical decision to focus on the *customer stakeholder* rather than on the product sparked a revolution.

After a month on the road, the team learned several important things about Thermos' potential risks and opportunities. Their customers' lifestyles had changed, and so had their grilling habits. No longer did Dad barbecue in the backyard; Mom did the grilling as often as Dad, and the family lived in a condo or apartment where rules prohibited charcoal grills on the porch. In another trend, suburban homeowners were investing in fancy new outdoor decks, and the typical clunky grill stood out as a rusty eyesore. On the other side of the coin, customers had in the past shunned electric grills because they didn't give real grilled taste. In fact, electric grills represented only 2 percent of the entire grill market.

Thermos pulled together to meet the challenge, hiring a designer firm to design the body of the grill and including them with the original team in every step of the development process. During each phase of the project, from building prototypes to market testing, the team members took turns leading the project as appropriate. Meanwhile, concurrently, engineering worked to develop a whole new technology for electric grilling, combining Thermos's core competency, vacuum technology that keeps food hot or cold, with a technological breakthrough, electric heating rods built into the grilling surface. The resultant electric grill got hot enough to sear food and leave the much-desired characteristic grill marks, just the right combination to get America cooking.

The results bore out in the market, where the Thermal Electric Grill has been one of the hottest selling grills ever. The success of the project has infused Thermos with a new spirit of innovation. Thermos revenues grew 13 percent the year after the grill was introduced, with most growth coming from new products developed hand in hand with stakeholders.

LEAD THROUGH STRATEGIC HUMILITY

Cangleska Wakan defines a protocol for leadership behavior diametrically opposed to most contemporary thinking on the subject of leadership. Americans have tended to laud their leaders as individual heroes single-handedly accomplishing corporate miracles. Like media superstars, corporate heroes often get credit for the whole show, despite the fact that without the work of thousands behind the scenes, the show would never have gone on. Heroic leaders give credit to all the people behind the successes. Those who walk in a sacred manner always recognize and respect the input of those behind the scenes.

To build heroic partnerships with stakeholders and to walk in a sacred manner, heroic leaders must first harmonize their own needs with those of everyone in the organization and the larger community in which it functions. Doing so does not signal weakness or cowardice or capitulation of power. Rather, it reflects an emotionally secure and intellectually powerful act by a person who grasps the immediate challenge and employs the energies of all stakeholders to meet it. To this end, the heroic leader makes a strategic decision to postpone immediate personal gratification in favor of investing in the larger and potentially more rewarding common good.

From the beginning of history, great leaders have understood the value of strategic humility. From Lincoln to Churchill to Sam Walton, great leaders have launched their journeys to success by recognizing and addressing their own weaknesses and mistakes. Who can forget Lincoln's strategic humility in the Gettysburg Address? Lincoln's commitment to finding a solution, not the hollow arrogance of pretending to know the answers, legitimized his leadership and empowered the Union's ultimate victory. Churchill learned the risks of arrogance through his failed military strategies in South Africa and Gallipoli during the First World War. Faced with almost career-ending failure, he turned personal humiliation into an opportunity for learning and eventual triumph. American business icon Sam Walton of Wal-Mart learned the power of strategic humility early in his career, after his initial failure to understand the dynamics of the retail market. Chastened by his early failures, he listened to his wife and employees, who pointed out his ignorance of an emerging market of working women. Once he recognized his ignorance and addressed it, he rewrote retailing history.

Heroic leaders in organizations fulfill the destiny described by the noted mythologist Joseph Campbell, who observed that the true hero quests for knowledge in the service of the larger good. The heroic leader creates a learning culture grounded in strategic humility, diagnosing the needs of stakeholders and finding ways to meet them. This posture provides the key to creating a new generation of "smart," rapid response organizations capable of making the right decisions to put the right people in the right place at the right time for the right reason at the right cost to fulfill stakeholder needs. Leading through strategic humility, heroic leaders become a magnet for power, attracting the energy and commitment of all the stakeholders in the Hoop and uniting them on an organization-wide heroic quest for results.

CONCLUSION

Despite all the talk of equality and democracy in American organizations, too few leaders have been following a paradigm that makes it possible to behave democratically. The vision of *Cangleska Wakan* and the values of freedom, responsibility, and reciprocity it expresses can change that and give any organization direction and a set of principles for developing a practical architecture in synch with the underlying forces of American culture. The goals of balance, integration, awareness, and shared purpose among all stakeholders can transform any organization. As Joseph Campbell observed, the great achievements of mankind have always involved a heroic quest. It's time to renew America's greatness by creating a new generation of organizations led by people who understand the power of strategic humility and the need to build partnerships with stakeholders by walking in a sacred manner. By adopting the values of *Cangleska Wakan* and the protocols for action that naturally stem from those values, organizations can tap all the power that lies dormant within them, and stakeholders can look with confidence to a more abundant future.

— 2 —

STAKEHOLDERS
The Heroic Partners

We must hang together, or surely we will all hang separately.

BENJAMIN FRANKLIN

Cangleska Wakan defines the interconnected and interdependent nature of the stakeholder relationships that make up every organization, be it a society, a government, or a business. The concept recognizes and respects the many stakeholders who act together to create an organization's world, and it applies to any arena in which people interact and share resources, creativity, and a will to survive. Unfortunately, many of today's organizations pay too little attention to all the interrelationships that make up their world. As the world grows steadily more complex, and as technology increasingly fuses the peoples of the world and their problems, success hinges more and more on attending to those interrelationships.

Since the symbol of *Cangleska Wakan* simplifies complexity, it offers a rich metaphor for organizations today. An organization exists as both a microcosm—its internal world—and as part of a macrocosm—its external world. Striking changes in both worlds require a heightened awareness of both individual stakeholders and the ways in which they interact. In the heat of day-to-day operations, however, individual stakeholders can begin ignoring their interconnectedness and, as a result, disconnect themselves from the circle and hamper their own performance. The principles of *Cangleska Wakan* can provide a laserlike tracking beam that cuts through the chaos to reconnect stakeholders to one another and to the vision of shared achievement that defines their individual and collective reasons for existence.

THREE HEROIC PRINCIPLES

The Heroic Organization implements three principles that simplify the complexity of operating in a fast-changing world. These principles enable it to remove itself from the influence of hyped-up, jargon-dominated management theory and deal with the fundamental goal of its work: how to do what it's doing better. The first principle admonishes the organization to "Lead Through Strategic Humility." For the Sioux, strategic humility was a necessity for their survival. Life on the plains, where the forces of nature and the threat of hostile tribes were a constant reminder of personal limitations and the need for self-improvement, taught the valuable lessons of vulnerability and responsibility to the Sioux. They could not afford the comfortable illusion that they could somehow avoid the consequences of their behavior. They understood, in tangible terms, the need to accept full responsibility for their lives and to commit themselves to a philosophy of self-improvement, for if they did not do so they could not survive in a difficult and hostile world.

The Sioux value of humility extended to their theology, where they placed themselves on the lowest level of hierarchy within the universe as they knew it. Humility before the forces evident around them allowed the Sioux to carve some order out of their unpredictable world on a day-to-day basis. For example, though pressed by necessity into a nomadic existence, the Sioux took care to plan their movements to coincide with natural cycles. They arranged to be near the ripening rose berries at harvest time, to be near groves of box elders when the spring sap was running. While they were bound to the dictates of nature, by learning to live within those dictates, they were able to capitalize on them.

The second principle of *Cangleska Wakan*, to "Build Heroic Partnerships," derives from the practical realization that no one can survive alone. Since life on the plains reminded the Sioux daily of the power of cooperation and reciprocity, they shunned the complex bureaucratic work structures and legal mazes that can so easily obscure the reality that "what goes around, comes around." Hard, tangible evidence of the need for cooperation impelled the Sioux to define their relationships clearly in terms of roles and responsibilities for fulfilling shared goals. Whether medicine man or warrior, each person adhered to a code of co-contribution to the tribe's collective welfare and walked in partnership with the other members of the tribe.

The value of partnership is perhaps most vividly demonstrated by the Sioux custom of the "giveaway." The giveaway was an outgrowth of a culture that valued generosity and human relationships and shunned materialism. Status within Sioux tribes was not gained through hoarded personal wealth, but through the wealth that tribe members could afford to give away to others more in need. The ethic of supporting others translated into ceremonial "giveaways," in which Sioux tribe members gave away their possessions when they wished to honor a family member. The ultimate show of respect in this fashion was a bereavement ceremony in which the parents of a dead child, after spending a year accumulating great stores of clothing, horses, utensils and food, would hold a ceremony to give away every one of these possessions, including the clothes on their back. Naked and without shelter, a man and wife thus displayed the Sioux's highest ideal of generosity combined with the utmost tribute for a loved one. In the Sioux world, such generosity did not lead to ruin, as after the ceremony, friends and relatives would provide clothing, food, a tipi, and other essentials for the bereft parents. The social contract of partnership in destiny enabled the Sioux to express their values individually and collectively in this manner.

The third principle, to "Walk in a Sacred Manner," translates the value of self-improvement and the role responsibilities that flow from that goal into a heroic action plan for daily survival. This practical plan defines a step-by-step behavioral process that all stakeholders can adapt to their roles and the fulfillment of their responsibilities. This process provides for everyone a protocol for daily living that guarantees both the rights of the individual stakeholder and their collective obligations to each other. Whether in sharing the spoils of a hunt, or reaching consensus in a tribal council decision, or making an overture of peace with another tribe, the Sioux recognized that the commitment to a clearly understood and mutually supportive protocol for day-to-day commerce among stakeholders provided the ultimate test of their will as a people. Walking in a sacred manner functions today in the Heroic Organization as a formula for achieving heroism in every action.

The three heroic principles give the Hoop its unifying and stabilizing structure. Like the triangular modules of a geodesic dome, the commitment to self-improvement, role cooperation, and a heroic process of action provide strength and resilience, and they pave the way for building heroic stakeholder relationships that can survive the tests of adversity and help to filter out the noise of today's complex and often confusing world.

The Sacred Medicine Circle

Walk in a Sacred Manner

Heroic Action

Self Improvement Cooperation

Lead Through Strategic   **Build Heroic Partnerships**

With this simple model in mind, let's see how they apply to contemporary organizations.

LEAD THROUGH STRATEGIC HUMILITY WITH SELF IMPROVEMENT

Heroic Organizations lead through strategic humility built on a commitment to self-improvement. With strategic humility, the Heroic Organization confronts the arrogance and selfishness that all too often weakens the fabric of organizational life. Shunning the "me first" school of business practices, it also confronts the anxiety and anger that underlies such arrogance, channeling the negative energies that flow from the fear of humiliation into the positive force of humility. In the Heroic Organization, leaders and their fellow members of the Medicine Circle openly acknowledge that they do not know "all the answers." Instead, they embrace uncertainty as an opportunity for growth, recognizing that the key to survival and achievement lies in the willingness to challenge assumptions and improve continuously.

Cannondale, the country's leading maker of upscale bicycles, has ridden to the top of its class on the path of strategic humility and self-improvement. The company has pursued self-improvement from the day it opened its doors. The company was founded on CEO Joe Montgomery's vision of a reinvented bicycle, one that made all existing bicycles archaic in comparison. The nature of the company's business no doubt influences its management style: The mercurial, demanding world of bicycling pressures the company to stay up to the minute in bicycle technology and design to please customers, and an heroic attitude to self-improvement has helped the company keep its edge. Cannondale's meteoric success hasn't changed its commitment to improvement or its awareness of its need to constantly change to stay on top. This commitment translates to strategic humility that extends all the way to the CEO's office. Montgomery still visits the assembly lines two days a week. In an interview with *U.S. News & World Report* ("Cannondale Pedals Its Way to the Top," Jan. 10, 1994), Montgomery shared his realization that when a small business grows large, "you don't get in your car and go to the beach. You come down here and roll up your sleeves and make sure that these people understand that you care as much as you did when you were making half or a third as many bikes."

Strategic humility has enabled Cannondale to differentiate its products and thrill its customers with commitment to service and product excellence. On one visit with a retailer, the company learned that the retailer was unhappy with the amount of time they needed to spend preparing Cannondale cycles for sale. Within hours the company had a proposal to the retailer on items the company could preassemble before shipping the product. Cannondale's demonstrated ongoing commitment to self-improvement makes it an excellent working example of an heroic organization taking action on each of the four principles of self improvement:

1. Become Self-Reliant
2. Honor Those Who Serve by Inviting Them to Participate In Their Own Transformation
3. Create a Reality-Centered Learning Culture
4. Commit to Continuous Improvement

1. Become Self-Reliant

Heroic leaders and organizations such as Cannondale take responsibility for their future by constantly re-creating and redesigning themselves and their organizations from the inside out. Too often, organizations abandon the precept of personal responsibility for solving their problems, turning instead to the outside for the latest management fad or simply waiting for a crisis to precipitate action. By contrast, heroic stakeholders meet change head-on, immersing themselves in the hard work change requires. They relish the opportunity to act, and they accept full accountability for their actions. Heroic stakeholders know that they must take responsibility for designing their own future, because no one else can do it as well as they themselves can. Significant and positive change comes only from accepting personal responsibility and shifting control from external sources to internal ones.

At Cannondale, becoming self-reliant meant throwing away the mold used by other bicycle makers—literally. To keep its reinventive edge, CEO Montgomery decided to eschew the molds that most companies rely on to join frame parts on most bicycles, because any adjustment in the frame's design requires costly retooling to the mold. Instead, Cannondale hand welds its bicycle frames, allowing for instant design changes. This flexibility allows the organization to reinvent its product, and itself, on demand.

2. Honor Those Who Serve by Inviting Them to Participate in Their Own Transformation

Wresting control from the outside involves empowering those on the inside to seize control of their own destiny. Those who serve the customer can ensure their own success only by learning the skills necessary to meet the challenge of change. As we will see, the most successful stories in American organizational reform have been written by organizations that have empowered their people to transform themselves. Rejecting the quick-fix solutions of the latest management fad or the heavy-handed intrusion of government and other external agencies, they have reaffirmed the importance of the medicine circle and have mustered both the energy and resolve to reform from within. In the process, they have demonstrated a willingness to confront the three greatest risks to organizational integrity and self-improvement: avoidance, schizophrenia, and disconnection.

Stakeholders who avoid their responsibility to other stakeholders, particularly those in the frontlines, usually do so because they fear negative outcomes. Battered by crisis and the need for radical change, they often fear the reactions of critics and cynics inside and outside the organization. Any action can result in a negative outcome, but avoidance of a problem *always* results in failure. Such avoidance ushered Kay Whitmore out of his job as CEO of Kodak. Whitmore's tentative restructuring programs were not enough to compensate for the company's free-fall into debt and product obsolescence, forcing the company's board to replace him with a more effective hands-on leader who could reach out to the organization's stakeholders and win their commitment to change.

National studies conducted by E. C. Murphy, Ltd., on the attitudes of frontline workers in business, health care, and public service reveal that over 60 percent of workers in organizations facing radical change, extensive restructuring and even downsizing and over 70 percent of those in organizations facing low to moderate levels of change do want to confront the challenge, even if it ultimately means the elimination or fundamental restructuring of their own jobs. Workers want and need to be involved in discussions that affect their own survival. When leaders fail to include them, they fail to tap into the positive power and influence higher levels of responsibility can induce. Failing to do so quickly erodes leadership credibility and splits off stakeholders into competing camps of self-interest.

Avoidance behavior not only skirts important issues, it creates a threat of its own. When stakeholders cannot participate in a collective survival effort, they tend to act in behalf of their independent survival, which creates a state of organizational schizophrenia where the community of stakeholders becomes a house divided. In turn, these divisions lead to a state of operational disconnection, where one hand not only does not know what the other is doing, but where stakeholders work at cross-purposes and in opposition to one another. Eastern Airlines, Wang Laboratories, and Met Life Insurance Company have all suffered from the effects of avoidance, schizophrenia, and disconnection.

By contrast, heroic leaders connect with all of their stakeholders by inviting them to participate in their own survival, thereby tapping the immense power of positive reinforcement, the most productive of change strategies, which affirms both the right and the responsibility of stakeholders to engineer their own transformation.

Cannondale demonstrated this level of heroism on the international scale when it first introduced its line of mountain bikes in Japan. Warned about the clannish *keiretsu,* and told they would get nowhere without linking with a local company, Cannondale at first approached Mitsubishi with a proposal for a joint venture. Mitsubishi, however, balked at Cannondale's distribution strategy, which, as in the United States, bypassed regional distributors and sold directly to retailers. Cannondale decided to forge its own path, reaching out to retailer stakeholders on its own. The company found that conventional wisdom was wrong: Bike retailers were eager to work with the company one on one. Including these stakeholders in the organization's medicine circle has been profitable for the company in more than one way; besides becoming the most accepted U.S. brand bicycle in Japan, Cannondale is enjoying a healthy profit margin as it competes against bikes laden with extra distribution costs. By turning directly to the retailers and including them as organizational stakeholders, Cannondale successfully redefined the way a U.S. company can do business in Japan.

3. Create a Reality-Centered *Learning* Culture

As the world changes, reality changes with it. Thus, any individual or organization hoping to succeed in the future must change with changing realities. To change successfully, you must develop a reality-centered learning culture driven by a thorough and ongoing assessment of stakeholder relationships. Heroic organizations think of their current knowledge as the tip of an iceberg and that their greatest learning will occur in the future. In contrast to the typical organizational change approach which assumes that stakeholders possess the knowledge necessary to address any challenge that arises, the Heroic Organization recognizes and accepts its own ignorance and that self improvement cannot occur without learning.

Reality-centered stakeholders understand their role in terms of the overall challenge facing their organizations. Their training centers on the need to walk in a sacred manner and focuses on the need to learn and adapt to changing realities. For example, one challenge facing Cannondale is the lower-priced competition from other bicycle makers. Because its bicycles are hand-manufactured, Cannondale's operating expenses are higher than other bicycle makers, resulting in a premium price tag. But CEO Montgomery has made it clear to all stakeholders that the company won't sacrifice design innovation for mass-market pricing. In his thinking, a company can either make a Chevrolet or a Mercedes-Benz, but not both. Cannondale walks in a sacred manner by sticking with its commitment to excellence; the company's reality is its identity as a unique provider of a high-end product.

Thus, when the organizational stakeholders become reality centered, they gain the power to address the most fundamental issues surrounding the organization now and in the future. In turn, they accept total accountability for all their actions. By contrast, stakeholders in nonheroic organizations tend to function in isolation from one another and tend to focus on make-work issues that deliver little direct impact on ultimate achievement.

4. Commit to Continuous Improvement

Members of an heroic organization such as Cannondale view organizational life as an opportunity for continuous growth and development. They see their work as an intrinsically valuable activity, not merely as a means to an end. In the Heroic Organization, people measure their own worth in terms of involvement and creativity, not in terms of the title they hold or the money they make. If working as a member of the team brings the greatest reward of work, then people must commit themselves to grow, evolve, and improve continuously. In the Heroic Organization, work becomes an extension of the self, and work satisfaction accrues from learning and contribution.

The Heroic Organization provides the context in which the purpose and meaning of work resides in work itself. Stakeholders do not join the organization as a means to a quick profitable killing, grabbing "their share" and running. Rather, they strive for commitment to a common pursuit and the resulting satisfaction that comes from connection with and contribution to the organization's overall goals. The ends that their work may produce for them: Salary, benefits, prestige, all accrue naturally as the organization prospers. Everyone in the Heroic Organization gains from continuous improvement as organizational growth propels them and their colleagues on a path of achievement.

COOPERATE FOR SUCCESS

On the plains, the Sioux learned to survive through cooperation. They faced competition for every bite they ate, for every moment of rest. As hunters, they depended on their own skills in an unpredictable world. They could never assume the appearance of their next meal, never know when they must move to find game, when they must fight fires, storms, wild animals, drought, or bloodthirsty rivals. Although they faced one crisis after another, they flourished in their world by adapting to it, sharing the efforts and rewards achieved by cooperating and adapting together in the spirit of *Cangleska Wakan*.

Today, shared achievement requires that same intense sense of interdependence, in which success depends on commitment to cooperation and collaborative self-improvement. This commitment defines the roles of stakeholders much more effectively than the disconnected patterns of role behavior all too prevalent in organizations today. Shared commitment to success produces an integrated architecture of roles in which complementarity, not competitive one-upmanship, dominates and creates a new medicine circle for contemporary organizational strength.

For the most part, the unity that enabled the Sioux to function as a collective with individuals supporting the common good of the group eludes us today. Our nation and our organizations have become more and more fragmented culturally and economically as the priorities of unified success have given way to the onslaught of individual and interest-group excesses. The mania for "me-first" has infected our businesses as well, creating a wellspring of lose-lose scenarios where employees strike companies out of business, where companies wage price wars that deflate not just the competition's but their own profits, or where corporations take more than they give back until they find themselves overextended and unable to manage their acquisitions. However, we can repair the disunity of purpose that has torn our organizations apart by adopting the outlook of the Hoop, and the first step involves the recognition of the power and potential of each of the individual stakeholders in the Hoop.

MAKE ALL STAKEHOLDERS HEROIC PARTNERS

The Hoop defines an organization as a network of relationships and partnerships among all the persons and forces that act in concert inside and outside an organization. Establishing clear roles, and assessing the strengths and weaknesses of each stakeholder enables an organization to "know itself," its world, and its capabilities. Just as a Sioux warriors tested themselves constantly to hone their capabilities—their strength, their stamina, their tolerance for pain—so organizations must constantly sharpen their capabilities in order to minimize the risks and seize the opportunities in a changing market.

Organizations learn about themselves by learning about their relationships with all their stakeholders: customers, leadership, frontline managers, frontline workers, sales and marketing, suppliers, competitors, the board, community, environment, government, and international partners. Each of these stakeholders contributes in a special way to the organization's success, and each poses unique risks and opportunities to the organization. Within the framework of *Cangleska Wakan*, let's explore some new definitions of stakeholder roles and what they offer our organizations.

INITIATE THE ORGANIZATIONAL MEDICINE CIRCLE

Although the organizational medicine circle connects all stakeholders, within the organization itself, five stakeholders construct the essential organizational Hoop: the customers, the frontline workers, the managers, the CEO or leadership team, and the board. Without them, the organization cannot exist. With them the organization obtains reference points parallel the center and the four points of direction of the Sioux Hoop.

The Organizational Medicine Circle

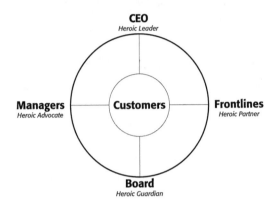

The Sioux associated each directional point in the Hoop with certain other assigned qualities; for example, West also represented Introspection, the animal force of the Bear, and the color Black. East represented Illumination, the Eagle, and Yellow; North was characterized by Wisdom, the Buffalo, and White, and South reflected Innocence, the Mouse, and Green. Likewise, in the Heroic Organization, we associate frontline workers, managers, the CEO, and the Board with certain forces, each yoked to the customer.

The Customer

The organizational Medicine Circle revolves around the customer, the central concern that binds the efforts, the interests, and the aspirations of everyone in the circle. By customer, we do not mean merely the purchasers of goods and services, but every stakeholder, who functions as a customer with respect to all members of the circle. For instance, managers become customers of the CEOs' policies, and CEOs become customers of their Boards' wishes, and *vice versa*. Relationships with customers in this broad sense govern the behavior of each stakeholder with respect to each other stakeholder. The concept of the customer thus aligns all elements in the

Hoop toward a common understanding of the need to work together.

In Sioux culture on the plains, the customer represented the obligation of each member of the tribe to serve and protect every other member. The Plains Indians built a meritocratic culture that honored individual choice and expression of individuality in support of the larger community. Shamans, for example, chose their vocation for personal reasons, but were obligated to fulfill that vocation in support of the tribal community. Likewise, the heroic organizational culture centered on the customer honors individuals and the expression of individuality in support of the entire collection of stakeholders. It instills a balance between individual rights and responsibilities.

Frontline Workers

Frontline workers live and work daily as *heroic partners* with the customer. This constant frontline contact affords them a dual allegiance: first, to serve as the voice of the customer for the organization, and then to speak on behalf of the organization to the customer. The Heroic Organization heeds both allegiances in order to develop responsiveness to customer needs, always respecting both directions of the feedback loop. In too many organizations, personnel on the frontlines lack the power to help their customers and end up channeling problems through an endless spiral of bureaucracy. Here the organization has forgotten one half of the feedback loop. In other organizations the frontlines may possess the power to help customers but find their messages to management falling on deaf ears. Here the organization has forgotten the other half of the feedback loop. In the Heroic Organization, the frontline worker serves as a two-way conduit of information, delivering messages in both directions and adapting his or her work to the needs of both the customer and the organization. While they strive to communicate the benefits of products and services to customers, they also communicate the need to change the organization to provide better benefits to the customer.

The saga of Union Pacific Railroad offers a striking contrast between a frontline-driven Heroic Organization and a bureaucracy-bound, unresponsive one. In 1986, UPRR epitomized backward bureaucracy. Train crews and sales representatives who dealt directly with customers lacked all power to help them. Instead, they passed customer problems through an almost endless decision-making–blame-setting chain, where a sales representative would buck the problem up to the district traffic manager, who would pass it on to the regional traffic manager, who would turn it over to the operations department's general manager, who would nail it on the superintendent's door, who would finally track down the train master to find out what went wrong. Did the train master then, finally, deliver a solution to the customer? No. He sent it back to the superintendent, and on back down the chain. The company maintained a feedback loop, but it merely went through a repetition cycle that never changed a thing.

In 1987, CEO Mike Walsh implemented a major restructuring that reformed UPRR along the lines of the heroic model. His main goals? To link decisions affecting the customer closer to the frontline. To do this he reformed the decision-making process, demanding that all functions work together to meet customers' needs. Today, after an aggressive change program, customer-level teams now resolve most of the customer problems at UPRR. Customers can talk to train crew foremen and get answers. The result? By 1992, volume had risen 18 percent, revenue went up by 25 percent, and failure costs dropped precipitously (saving $750 million in five years). As employees became directly involved in and accountable to the organizational medicine circle of UPRR, they responded to the organization's needs: productivity per employee *nearly doubled* as a direct result of the new focus on frontline customer service.

Managers

In the organizational Medicine Circle, managers function as *heroic advocates* for the customer, a major shift in management perspective from decades past, where managers operated as dictators of company policy. The new role of customer advocate tests most managers' mettle. In the past ten years, decades of inward-looking management have ended in a rude awakening. After thousands of layoffs and corporate restructurings, most organizations employ far fewer middle managers than they did a decade ago, and they assign them far different roles. The Heroic Organization enters this flux with a new agenda: The Medicine Circle redefines management as a frontline hands-on job, with customers the primary focus of their work. This transforms managers from "bodyguards" who separate upper leadership from the frontlines into customer advocates who bring the frontlines to the leaders. As with frontline workers, the Heroic Organization respects both halves of the feedback loop, with managers fulfilling a dual allegiance to communications with customers and communications to leaders that can result in changes that better benefit customers.

Today's managers can accomplish this transformation by redefining their roles as active problem solvers on behalf of the customer. This crucial role, largely abandoned by self-serving upwardly mobile corporate climbers, serves two vital purposes for organizational success: It makes the organization aware of the needs and demands of its customers so that it may change to meet them, and it enables a level of organizational responsiveness that instills customer confidence and loyalty. Managers, as the voice of the customer, lend a guiding hand to decision making at all levels of the organization.

Contrast this approach with the common problem of managers growing distant from the customer and directing their energy into meetings, paperwork, and politics, which do little to benefit the customer. When they do so, managers lose touch with the frontlines. If the manager does not give voice to the customer, customer concerns become mute issues, and customers begin looking elsewhere for benefits. When the upper echelons of any company lose sight of their customer, their market, and their future, they invariably fall on their own swords of arrogance and ignorance.

This nearly happened to UPS when the package carrier ignored the changing needs of its customers, and began losing business. Customers, instead of bowing to UPS's take-it-or-leave-it attitude, began defecting to Federal Express and other carriers ready and willing to provide more flexible service. Before long, UPS realized that it could blame no one but its own culture of arrogance for declining business. No longer could the company get away with a "we know what's best for you" attitude in a world now driven by the dictum "the customer knows best."

To its credit, UPS set out to correct the errors in its ways, wisely reaching out to its customers and learning their true needs. Recognizing that change makes no sense unless it delivers benefits to the frontlines, UPS immediately instituted a comprehensive customer service training program for managers, which altered managers' roles from inward-looking bureaucrats to outward-looking problem solvers for customers. Through this process, managers learned to bring the new service ethic to the frontlines, at the same time feeding information upward in an effort to keep UPS abreast of new developments in the market and the competition. The feedback loop now worked both ways, benefiting not only UPS's customers, but also its CEO.

The CEO

In the organizational Medicine Circle, the CEO plays the *heroic leader*, a title that describes a vastly different role from that in the past. A far cry from the one-man-saves-the-day heroes of popular myth, CEOs in heroic organizations become heroes through service. They do not see themselves as knights in shining armor, swooping in on a white charger to save the day. In fact, the truly heroic leaders do the opposite. Instead of presiding at the top of the organization, they work in its midst, recognizing the value of all stakeholders in their organization's success and seeking harmony among them all.

The heroic CEO leads the organization's partnership with the customer. Mythologist Joseph Campbell defined the hero as a person who sets forth on a quest, perhaps for truth or for a solution to a problem, and after many challenges achieves the goal. Having found fulfillment, the hero returns home to share the fruits of the quest. That return-and-share decision, rather than remaining satisfied with personal accomplishment and aggrandizement, makes a leader truly heroic. In the Heroic Organization, the CEO seeks out customers and brings them into the organizational circle. Like the heroes of old, CEOs embark on a quest on which they must overcome many challenges. In the end, they share the rewards with every stakeholder. Once again, the feedback loop provides two-way communication: The leader speaks to and listens to the customer, constantly changing in a dynamic effort to provide maximum benefits to both the customer and the organization.

Recently, two leaders embarked on an heroic quest to restore competitiveness at Trans World Airlines. When Robin Wilson and Glenn R. Zander took over TWA in 1992, the airline had been plunging in a downward spiral toward bankruptcy, sinking under the debilitating effects of poor service, late flights, and bad management. Zander and Wilson, hand-picked by employees and creditors to take over the organization, started by reaching out to the other organizational stakeholders and asking for their help in saving the airline. The response was swift: In the first month of their tenure, TWA posted the nation's best on-time performance. Labor relations improved when the duo offered to swap a percentage of ownership for $660 million in concessions, and the confidence of creditors grew with a similar equity deal. Employees responded so enthusiastically to the idea of the new TWA that they spent their own money to advertise it. TWA's pilots donated $18,000 to buy billboard ads, and 5,000 union employees chipped in $30,000 to purchase newspaper ads.

Next, Wilson and Zander moved to bring customer stakeholders back into the circle. Customers, disappointed by years of bad service, had lost trust in the company, and as a result the airline had lost its much of its competitive advantage along with its reputation. The co-CEOs, knowing they needed something that would differentiate TWA, decided to target leisure travelers and business executives looking for more comfort on trips. They ordered seats removed from every TWA jet to give passengers 30 percent more leg room, and they spent big to advertise the benefit. Zander and Wilson also targeted travel agents, increasing their commission rates from a paltry 10 percent to a healthy 18 percent, two points above the industry average. As a result, bookings shot up 30 percent in just a few months. While troublesome industry-wide problems still make TWA's future uncertain, industry experts expect Zander and Wilson to make TWA fly. As heroic leaders, they have united stakeholders and reached out to their customers as a central part of their vision, a vision that they serve every day in the best interests of all stakeholders.

The Board

Ideally, the board should serve as both the *heroic guardian* of the customer's interests and as a balancing force with the circle of stakeholders. Whatever their formal title—directors, governors, regents, trustees—and whether they come from within the organization or from outside, the members of the board shoulder responsibility for protecting the organization's superordinate value structure, the overriding values of the Hoop: commitment to the welfare of all stakeholders and dedication to harmony among them.

In their worst form, boards function merely as figureheads who practice "public relations" rather than as key players in the organization's success. Today, however, board members, finding themselves increasingly held responsible for the organization's actions, can no longer duck their responsibility to convey wisdom and commitment to stakeholders. The heroic board can and should govern the organization's personality, its level of commitment to stakeholders, and its success in leadership and strategy. As guardians, the heroic Board serves not just the stockholders, and not just the leadership team, but everyone inside and outside the organization who influences or is influenced by its success. The best board, like the best frontline workers and managers, keeps the feedback loop open, gaining as many insights from stakeholders as it shares with them.

In 1993, K-Mart's board assumed heroic responsibility when it decided to hire an outside consultant to evaluate the pay of Chief Executive Joseph E. Antonini and his management team. The board recognized that salary evaluations by themselves, by persons hired by the CEO, or by the company's human resources department would reflect their subjective relationships with Antonini. To gain an objective evaluation, the board chose a course of action to strictly fulfill their roles as unbiased guardians of K-Mart's corporate culture. Their choice of action highlighted their commitment in two ways: It signaled their willingness to hold the CEO accountable for his salary in terms of his performance, and it emphasized their desire for true impartiality. While the results of the review did not vary greatly from what the board expected, they were able to be confident that they had acted in the stakeholders' best interest. By choosing independence over cronyism, and by acting in the best interests of the organization, the members of K-mart's board followed the heroic path.

COMPLETE THE STAKEHOLDER CIRCLE

To complete the organizational Medicine Circle, you must include all your other stakeholders: sales and marketing, suppliers, competitors, community, environment, government, and international partners. Each of these members contributes in a unique way to the success of the Heroic Organization, which recognizes and values their roles and, in return, demands their participation and investment in the circle.

Sales and Marketing

An organization's sales and marketing team occupies a critical position in the organizational Hoop because sales and marketing both carry the organization's message to the customer and bring messages from the field back to the organization. When they do so skillfully, they build the strong ties with customers that ensure growth.

Like managers, salespeople serve as advocates for the customer, informing customers about products and services and relaying customer needs back to the organization. In a sense, they act as the organization's conscience, reminding the organization about how it should behave with respect to its central concern, the customer. Their role bridges the gap between the outside world and the organization on a basic operating level, providing everyday impetus for all organizational effort. Marketing personnel, on the other hand, provide more generalized outreach, setting the stage for the salespeople and readying the market for their work. While marketing grabs the customer's attention, provides general information, and plants a seed of interest, salespeople nurture that seed to create trust and satisfaction.

The automotive industry's recent push in car leasing illustrates this point nicely. In just ten years—between 1984 and 1994—the number of leased cars has quadrupled, and some auto executives predict that by the end of the decade, half of all cars and trucks on the road will be leased. Leasing has boosted the "sales" of American auto makers in particular, with some experts hailing it as a means of creating greater brand loyalty and smoothing out the industry's famous bust-and-boom sales roller coaster.

This sea change in the way customers buy their transportation resulted from a careful attention to market forces. Today, about 75 percent of car buyers need some sort of financing. With interest on car loans no longer tax deductible, no-deposit low-payment leasing looks increasingly attractive to consumers. American auto makers have responded by aggressively marketing leasing options. In fact, leasing helped Ford's Taurus beat Honda's Accord as America's best-selling car in 1993. Salespeople promote the trend as well, using it to forge strong relationships with customers and cement brand loyalty. With proper care, a short-term lease deal can evolve into a long-term repeat-buy relationship. How does this affect the carmakers? In order to keep the customer satisfied, they must continually offer fresh product, so carmakers work overtime to create improved features, sleeker exteriors, new colors, and flashier dashboards to keep consumers satisfied. Here, marketing and sales have spurred the organizations' continuous improvement, the essence of heroic action.

Suppliers

Within the organizational Medicine Circle, suppliers become true partners, sharing their customers' successes and failures. Although true partnership with suppliers runs counter to ingrained conventions of competition among suppliers, the perspective of the Hoop replaces all that with a model based on trust and integrity, which links companies that can work together to create shared success.

The Chrysler Neon project provides an excellent example of the benefits of supplier partnership. The Neon team depended heavily on suppliers, who furnished 70 percent of the value of the car. With the goal of offering a top-rate car at a rock-bottom price, Chrysler enlisted its suppliers' backing from the beginning. The Neon team laid its costs out on the line and asked its suppliers to help it meet those tough targets. Both parties benefited: The Neon team achieved its goal of a low-cost car, and the suppliers gained a reliable buyer. When the suppliers began working as part of the team, they took full responsibility for their own input. In one instance, a supplier managed to meet the tight cost controls for seats, but when the seats fell short in terms of safety and comfort, ten Chrysler engineers went straight to that supplier's headquarters and after five days of negotiation hammered out performance targets that fulfilled the needs of all involved. By bringing the suppliers into the circle with the team, holding them accountable, and mutually negotiating and setting solid targets, the Chrysler Neon took shape as one of the most revolutionary accomplishments ever to come out of Detroit.

Competitors

The organizational Medicine Circle defines both local and global competitors not as adversaries but as co-creators. This definition may seem facile or even foolhardy in the wake of the downsizings and cutbacks that have swept through American organizations recently in response to the dramatic increase in competition over the last twenty years, but in fact it makes more sense now than ever before. Without deprecating the pain felt by American workers and organizations in the throes of change brought on by competition, we must learn to look at our competitors in a new way, as part of a never-ending cycle of cause and effect. The Heroic Organization recognizes this fact, much as the Sioux recognized that the world consisted of forces that sometimes healed and sometimes harmed, depending on the circumstances. Success, now as then, depends on recognizing both forces and circumstances and reacting to them appropriately. In the business world, benchmarking provides one way to recognize these forces and meet and exceed the competition's standards.

The Chrysler Neon project again provides a striking example of a team including competitors in its perspective. The Neon team based their product's design not only on customer surveys but on competitor benchmarking, making choices based on customer input and competitors' offerings that responded to small-car owners' worries about safety and their habit of using their cars as utility vehicles. That information prompted the Neon team to create the first subcompact with dual airbags, even though doing so meant making up the cost elsewhere, and to meet the tough 1997 federal side-impact standards three years early. Neon also chose fold-down rear seats for greater utility. The team tasted sweet success when, after it had built a Neon prototype, it saw the new Honda Accord, one of the Neon team's primary benchmarks for driveability. While Honda had improved the Accord with more room and contemporary styling, it ended up with a car more difficult to handle and a hefty new price tag. The Neon scored better on all fronts. Through examining the competition, Neon learned where to imitate and where to surpass.

Community

Too few business organizations treat the communities in which they operate as fully participating stakeholders, though the concept of mutual destiny applies here as surely as it does to any other stakeholder relationship. An organization gains resources, workers, education, and social services from the community, while the community gains employment, investment, and services from the organization. Both share the negative consequences of pollution and urbanization and the concomitant rise in crime and health-care problems. Both the organization and the community must work hand in glove to balance these factors, and both must weigh all the benefits and costs of working together. From the organization's point of view, the community represents customers it must satisfy as fully as the purchasers of its products and services. An organization must accept responsibility to help ensure the community's well-being, supporting those services, such as education and recreation, which create a productive climate. Corporate philanthropy means far more than public relations; it contributes directly to the bottom line. Likewise, a community's efforts to improve the climate for business can only improve its own viability.

Alabama's aggressive campaign to entice Mercedes-Benz to build an assembly plant in the state illustrates the heroic concept of pursuing mutual benefits for an organization and a community. Job-hungry Alabama won out over 34 states competing for the first U.S.-based Mercedes-Benz factory by offering an attractive partnership. In return for the $300 million dollar plant and its attendant 1,500 jobs, Alabama promised $200 million in job training and tax breaks, and it even offered to rename a section of the Interstate 20/59 the "Mercedes-Benz Autobahn." In the end, the company saw Alabama as a true partner in its own destiny.

Environment

The Sioux held nothing more sacred than the environment because the land gave them all the prerequisites of life. Unfortunately, many modern organizations have forgotten that their lives depend on a healthy environment. Traditionally, few companies have viewed the environment as an integral part of the organizational circle of stakeholders, and that has often led to negative, often avoidable, results. Today more than ever, as the natural resources of the world continue to shrink under the onslaught of twentieth-century industrial progress, organizations must heed the effects of their activities on the environment, as well as the environment's effect upon them. Increasingly, the case for the environment has become an issue of legislation, delimiting organizations' choice of location, their ability to build and operate new facilities, and their choice of waste management techniques, among other things.

Organizations must understand the environment as a precious and limited resource that deserves a special place within the

Medicine Circle. A given organization's stake in the environment may appear small, but a polluted landscape will inevitably pollute the bottom line, whether in terms of direct profitability or of quality of life for the other members of the circle. On the other side of the equation, heightened concern for the environment offers new opportunities for organizations that can find and market solutions to environmental problems. The perspective of *Cangleska Wakan* takes the long view, preparing organizations to meet the requirements of this fragile relationship.

Imperial Chemical Industries found an opportunity to both serve and profit from its relationship with the environment. Responding to global concern about the level of ozone-depleting chlorofluorocarbons (CFCs) in the atmosphere, ICI launched an aggressive effort to find chemical substitutes for use in refrigeration, air conditioning, and other commercial applications. ICI approached the problem with intelligence and zeal; after identifying a potential substitute compound, HFC 134a, the firm used parallel engineering to develop an environmentally friendly production plant at the same time that it developed the compound, no simple task considering that the chemical plant reactors needed to meet exact specifications for creating the compound. ICI took some calculated risks and ended up with a product in five years, less than half the average time it takes to commercialize a technology in its industry. The competition to market the first CFC substitute grew fierce, but from the beginning of the research process, ICI did not lose sight of its purpose, creating a production process that would yield no wasteful by-products.

Government

The government plays a dual role in the Heroic Organization, that of overseer and of supporter. Government actions sometimes help and sometimes limit business opportunities, but no organization can afford to underestimate the government's role in its success, particularly on the global scale as governments negotiate trade deals such as the North American Free Trade Agreement and the General Agreement on Tariffs and Trade. Ideally, the government works as a collaborator with business, acting as a liaison between business interests and supplying resources for research and development that businesses cannot muster themselves. In return, business organizations work with the government to strengthen the economy, invest in the American workforce, and contribute to national causes.

While the flagrant abuses perpetrated by some contractors serving the government—those that lead to headlines screaming about $800 toilet seats and $200 hammers—provide examples of the worst possible relationship, the Heroic Organization demonstrates the possibilities at the opposite end of the spectrum, eradicating the scheming and arrogance that result in such abuses and working even-handedly with government stakeholders.

For just one example of a mutually beneficial working relationship between government and business organizations consider the newly named ARPA, Advanced Research Projects Agency, formerly DARPA, Defense Advanced Research Projects Agency. ARPA's new name emphasizes its nondefense role in the post cold war era, to advance new technologies that can enhance American competitiveness. With its superior research resources, ARPA can pursue projects that organizations could not afford on their own. One project currently underway, the development of microscopic sensors, was abandoned by Bell Labs because of its costliness. ARPA, convinced of the technology's potential, has dedicated its vast resources to the project, with the ultimate goal of breaking new ground for American businesses.

International Partners

The global village has become a reality, and organizations must increasingly assume a global perspective. That same perspective yields new opportunities for developing international partnerships, which offer terrific opportunities for growth and entrance into foreign markets. However, when companies from two or more nations decide to join forces, they often find themselves treading new ground, which makes trust a paramount concern. Faulty partnerships can damage both parties if they do not first establish a trusting relationship and carefully consider who will commit what resources to what goals and how they will share work, information and profits. The perspective of *Cangleska Wakan* can minimize the risks for both parties because it binds the destinies of both partners.

One company that has capitalized on international partnerships, Satellite Technology Management, Inc., provides private satellite networks for corporations. Founded in 1982, STM quickly lost momentum in the U.S. market as powerful copycat competitors such as GTE Corporation leaped into the market. Within a few years, the company had fallen into such dire straits that the CEO was preparing to retain a bankruptcy attorney. Then a sudden inspiration changed his mind: STM could market its services overseas. The transition proved difficult, and STM spent years laboring to establish alliances with overseas distributors, but, through its dedicated efforts to establish trust and build working relationships, STM finally created seventeen partnerships with international distribution companies in twenty-one countries. The strength of these relationships provide STM's competitive advantage now that the companies that almost forced STM out of business have saturated the U.S. market. Even as big U.S. telecommunications companies turn their eyes toward overseas markets, STM has won the security of market share and reputation, buffers that can help the scrappy entrepreneur stand up to the big boys.

UNITE ALL STAKEHOLDERS IN THE HEROIC PROCESS

Each stakeholder contributes in its own special way to the organizational Medicine Circle. For the Heroic Organization, these contributions go beyond the basic interaction among stakeholders to the nurturing of each stakeholder's well-being. At the same time, stakeholders in the Heroic Organization perceive their roles as proactive rather than as reactive agents within the circle, retaining responsibility for their actions and for actively pursuing the improvement of the organization. Much like an orchestra, which consists of many different instruments together playing a single melody, so the Heroic Organization orchestrates its many stakeholders into a single theme of heroic ideals.

We will explain that theme, the Heroic Process, in the next chapter. The Heroic Process provides a seven step program for translating the ethic of heroism and self-improvement into everyday action. As all stakeholders participate in the Heroic Process in the day-to-day work of the organization, they reinforce the unity and heroic purpose of the organizational medicine circle. Each of the seven steps builds upon the others, not in a linear fashion, but in a circular progression that translates into cyclical improvement.

Stakeholders realize their potential through the Heroic Process, and organizations garner their success through their stakeholders. In the medicine circle, all unite their effort to achieve a shared destiny. We'll discuss each of the stakeholders in more complete detail in Part Two of this book, but first let's examine the Heroic Process and its role in shaping the destiny of the Heroic Organization.

— 3 —
THE SEVEN-STEP
HEROIC PROCESS

North American oil development in the Ecuadorian Amazon has threatened the way of life of the Huaovani, a small, fiercely independent native South American tribe living deep in the jungle. Every day oil companies spill untreated toxic waste into the Huaovani's land and pave the way for continuing colonization and deforestation. As Joe Kane reported in the May 2, 1994, issue of *The New Yorker,* the Sierra Club Legal Defense Fund filed a petition on behalf of the Huaovani with the Inter-American Commission on Human Rights to bring their plight to the attention of both the American oil industry and the U.S. government. To highlight the effort, they brought the leader of the Huaovani to Washington, where he would deliver a letter to President Clinton asking him to visit the Ecuadorian rain forest and explain to his people why the United States was trying to destroy them.

Kane describes a poignant scene where the Huaovani chief, Moi, stood before the gates to the White House, peering in at the manicured lawns and delicately pruned shrubs. Behind him, all along Pennsylvania Avenue, roared the traffic of a thousand cars.

"There are so many cars," he said to Kane. "How long have they been here? A million years?"

"Much less," Kane explained.

"A thousand years?"

"No, eighty, perhaps."

Moi was silent, and after a while he asked, "What will you do in ten more years? In ten years your world will be pure metal. Did your God do this?"

Later, as the two men approached their hotel, Moi passed under a street lamp and pointed to the street. "More people, more cars, more petroleum, more chaos," he said. Then he pointed up at the light. "But *there* are the Huaovani, all alone in the middle of the world."

The great chief of the Sioux nation, Sitting Bull, would have understood Moi's words, for his people had suffered similar devastation of their way of life a hundred years earlier. Both leaders would share the same sadness that in the name of progress and development their foes had forgotten to walk in a sacred manner.

For the Sioux, walking in a sacred manner meant creating protocols for daily living that translated their vision of *Cangleska Wakan* into their every action. Each stakeholder in the Medicine Circle, from war chief to medicine woman, applied the principles of strategic humility and heroic partnership through everyday scripts for living that provided tested blueprints for shared achievement. Each ritual evolved through ongoing trial and error and incorporated the accumulated wisdom of a people who recognized the need for proper behavior when struggling with the challenges to survival on the Great Plains.

For us to survive and prosper in the Great Plains of the new world economy, we too need rituals for translating vision into reality. Unfortunately, modern leadership has generally failed to do so. Whether an individual or an organization, those who seek to make a difference must develop the strength and discipline to act with speed, resolve, and discipline, achieving a new level of conditioning—intellectually, physically, and psychologically—and adopting a plan of action that is at the same time logical and sensitive, resolute and flexible, timeless and timely. True heroes translate their ideals of service into day-to-day action, continuously redesigning and reengineering themselves and their organizations to meet the ever-changing needs of the Medicine Circle. The philosophy of the Medicine Circle makes this a shared challenge, allowing all stakeholders to energize one another within a structure of continuous self-improvement. Ultimately, the heroic Medicine Circle becomes greater than the sum of its parts.

The three heroic principles described in Chapter 2, lead through strategic humility, build heroic partnerships, and walk in a sacred manner, provide a vision for shared achievement and a practical plan for translating the ideals of service into reality. Strategic humility defines the first critical step of organizational *awakening,* a formal recognition of the need to overcome arrogance, without which neither an organization nor its stakeholders can acquire the knowledge necessary to adapt and grow. The second principle, to build heroic partnerships, enables an organization to withstand the threat of adversity and to respond rapidly to the partner's needs. This integrated security network demands a redefinition of organizational stakeholder roles and responsibilities, establishing a social contract of expectations and a job description for every partner. The third and most important of the heroic principles, to walk in a sacred manner, requires both a behavioral blueprint for taking action and the actual commitment to take action.

The future hinges on incorporating these principles into a clear-cut process for organizational transformation. While the task may seem daunting, from the perspective of Sitting Bull or the Huaovani chief, Moi, in essence it embodies but seven steps:

THE SEVEN-STEP HEROIC PROCESS

1. Establish Context
2. Measure Mission Effectiveness
3. Identify Opportunities for Improvement
4. Mobilize Support
5. Take Action
6. Evaluate Results
7. Repeat the Process Continuously

Developed and tested in the frontlines of contemporary life, the Heroic Process provides a practical methodology for translating a modern version of *Cangleska Wakan* into action. Each of the seven steps respects the principles of strategic humility, heroic partnership, and walking in a sacred manner, and each progressively deepens all stakeholders' commitment to the welfare of the Medicine Circle. By following them religiously, organizations reshape their destinies. Recently, two heroic organizations, General Electric Corporation and Hamot Health Foundation, have tapped the power of the Seven-Step Heroic Process, and their stories provide instructive models for those who would do the same.

Walking in a sacred manner has driven both General Electric's and Hamot Health Foundation's efforts to address a new generation of dramatic challenges. For Jack Welch and General Electric, the challenge required a comprehensive realignment and refocusing of GE's resources to become a globally-visionary corporation. For John Malone and the Hamot Health Foundation, the challenge prompted systems-wide organizational restructuring and work redesign to meet the demands of America's economic and social revolution in health care. For both, the transformation began by establishing a new context for action.

CHOOSING HEROISM: THE CASE OF GENERAL ELECTRIC

In the early Eighties, Jack Welch assumed leadership of an American icon. Its name synonymous with one of the greatest inventions of the century, General Electric had accomplished legendary innovations and profits, and not just with its product lines. The company had also pioneered numerous management techniques such as strategic planning and management by objectives. Yet, like so many of America's large corporations, by the early Eighties, GE had grown complacent, resting on the contributions of past generations of stakeholders and failing to assume responsibility for defining a new context for action for the future. Realizing that the company lacked focus and a sense of purpose, at that critical junction Welch set as his first order of business to establish the right context that could serve as an energizing force, one that would allow all stakeholders to understand what they were working for and why.

Step One: Establish Context

Welch understood that stakeholders require a context for action, a reason and purpose for committing their intellectual, spiritual, and physical resources to a collective effort larger than their individual self-interests. Context provides the linchpin in organizational life, connecting stakeholders to one another and the common purpose that gives them reason for bonding and staying together. To establish context, stakeholders must address a challenge and create a vision for meeting it. The challenge encompasses the mission of the organization and a situational assessment of the risks and opportunities it entails. The vision provides a strategic plan for overcoming hurdles to success and includes the organization's goals, its guiding values, and its practical operational plan for taking action. More than anything else, the inability to establish context causes organizational decline. Without context, leaders lack legitimacy and the capacity to mobilize stakeholders to action. Without context, no center, no hub binds together the medicine wheel of cooperation. Its absence creates the threat of *"other esteem,"* the first of seven deadly organizational sins.

"Other esteem" arises when stakeholders search for purpose and identity outside the Medicine Circle. It signals the failure of vision, values, and true partnership, and it occurs when stakeholders either fail to define clearly the purpose for which they've come together or fail to renew the partnership contract to address new challenges. Suffering from *"other esteem,"* stakeholders lack the self-esteem and self-confidence that comes from knowing who they are and what they stand to gain from a collective partnership.

Without a compelling context, stakeholders lose their sense of direction and begin to expend energy and other resources in ways that destabilize the organization as they resist change and cling to the past or ride the wave of others' accomplishments. Lacking context, they frantically search for value in everything but the core mission of the organization, pursuing new ventures that do not coincide with the core business, polishing resumes to secure the "perfect" job, embracing fashionable management techniques, or relinquishing responsibility to outsiders, be they union organizers or consultants. All such other esteem poses the first, and greatest, obstacle to building a heroic organization. Unless you address it head on, it can become a destructive force that inevitably leads to disaffection and irresponsibility, undermining the security of the Medicine Circle and leaving it vulnerable to attack and misuse from both inside and out.

Jack Welch confronted the threat of other esteem head-on when he took over the reins of GE. When he and a concerned group of stakeholders assessed GE's future, they saw impending storms where others saw blue skies. Enjoying a comfortable ride on huge profits from backlogged orders of big ticket items such as steam locomotives, steam turbines, and nuclear power plants, many GE executives found it easy to ignore the fact that new product orders had all but evaporated. As Welch could plainly see, the company's profits depended on aging businesses that were growing slowly or not at all. Of GE's many operating units, only a few held solid market positions, and some of those, such as lighting, had began to erode.

As Welch undertook a situational assessment to define the challenge, he saw a bleak future of declining profits and plummeting market share. To counteract that inevitability, he set about developing a new vision for GE within the context of emphasizing a maximum concentration of resources in the pursuit of unqualified excellence. He set up GE's mission for each of its divisions to become either number one or number two in its market by adhering to a value structure of service and cooperation to all internal and external stakeholders. Although market share doesn't always directly correspond with profits, Welch and his newly energized Medicine Circle of stakeholders wanted only strong businesses in the GE portfolio: Forget "other esteem," stop living off the fat of previous accomplishments, and do whatever it takes to become number one or number two in the market.

Of course, everyone at GE had heard it all before. Earlier CEOs had proposed a lean and focused corporate regimen, but this time the CEO was dead serious about it. The process of establishing context proved arduous and often painful for GE. Stakeholders who did not understand the context resisted efforts to change and impeded progress with passive resistance or by simply ignoring the mandate for change. Many remained stuck in the mind-set that had for decades infected GE, where a system of rigid hierarchy provided security and a reasonably clear path for advancement. In their minds, they had struck a bargain with GE: they had provided their labor, and the company, in return, "took care of them." Now, Welch and a new generation of stakeholders were challenging the legitimacy of that social contract, demanding more than just token work, asking instead that each GE worker recommit to the welfare of the whole organization by examining the substance and purpose of all individual and team effort. They challenged every member of GE's workforce to participate in a comprehensive seven-step process of renewal that began with establishing a new context for action and eventually led to a breakthrough insight into how to measure organizational effectiveness.

Step Two: Measure Mission Effectiveness

Welch and his heroic partners also understood the need to address the second great risk to organizational success, the failure to own and experience reality. Any failure to understand the new realities facing GE would deter the company's mission. Not having measured the effectiveness of the company's mission in light of a changing economy, GE's leadership had failed to update the context within which the corporation had to function as it entered the Eighties. Welch addressed this risk by taking the second step in the Heroic Process by measuring the mission flowing from the vision of being number one or number two. The continuous health of every Medicine Circle requires continuous measurement because only careful measurement can identify all relevant risks and opportunities.

The Heroic Organization even measures the very means of measurement it uses. For centuries, the Sioux had successfully measured the effectiveness of their vision of *Cangleska Wakan* through constant monitoring of natural forces on the Great Plains. They had organized their work structures so they could measure and respond almost instantaneously to changes in the natural flow of seasons, game, and enemies. However, their traditional system of measurement could not cope with the impact of invading settlers, miners, and cavalry, an invasion that constituted a fundamental and far-reaching shift in the economy and ecology of the Great Plains. Unable to adjust their means of measurement, the Sioux and other tribes soon found themselves overwhelmed by the new forces at play in their land. Retaining the disconnected reporting structure of small tribal hunting units that roamed the plains in bands of 100 to 150 braves, wives, children, and elders, the Sioux operated in small autonomous units, suffering or thriving largely in isolation from one another. As a result, they failed to own and experience a new reality. By the time they had assembled the relevant data into a composite picture and heeded the warnings of farsighted chiefs such as Sitting Bull and Crazy Horse, the Sioux had run out of viable options.

Though separated from the Sioux by time, culture, and destiny, GE faced a similar situation in the early Eighties. The company did not own and experience a new reality because it adhered to a traditionally disconnected measurement and reporting structure that made it all but impossible for stakeholders to share resources and information across tribal lines. Recognizing this potentially fatal flaw, Welch initiated a radically new strategy for mission measurement that business circles worldwide have only recently begun to understand. Inspired by the measurement power of GE's world-class medical imaging technology, Welch set out to create a "body scan" of the organization that cut across all borders and leveled all hierarchies.

The measurement problem, as he saw it, stemmed from the company's inability to accurately measure the extent to which it had aligned its far flung resources—human and technological—with the new mission. Put succinctly, Welch wanted to know whether "the right people were in the right place at the right time for the right reason and cost for the mission of the corporation." To find out the answer to this question, a talented team of managers, researchers, and programmers joined forces to develop a brand new tool for systems-wide performance assessment.

The new system evolved around creating a "Work Image" for each GE employee that portrayed the time and money each person spent carrying out his or her day-to-day work. It then combined individual images into larger, cross-functional pictures that resulted in a total Work Image of the organization, its subsidiaries, divisions, and operating units. The Work Images revealed where people really invested their time and energy, and, thus, the financial resources of the company. Welch could now compare these true pictures of work with the company's new mission in an effort to assess the mission's effectiveness. By matching the company's newly espoused priorities with the tangible realities of time and money investment, Welch and his stakeholders could finally measure, and "own," the extent to which their mission had become reality. Not surprisingly, they found an out-of-balance corporation laboring under 30 percent-plus excess weight and torn asunder by competing groups whose priorities conflicted with the needs of the overall corporation.

Welch understood the critical role measurement plays in building credibility and overcoming cynicism and fear. By involving stakeholders in a far-reaching assessment of reality, he translated the vision from an abstraction into a concrete reality of risks and opportunities. The measurement process immersed the corporate stakeholders in reality, replacing anxiety-ridden ambiguity with tangible, unambiguous data harvested from the familiar vineyards in which they labored every day. The process tested traditional assumptions by contrasting the facts of daily work life with both the mission set forth by Welch and the traditional practices that put the organization at risk, and it produced a database for identifying new opportunities the company might seize.

Step Three: Identify Opportunities for Improvement

To tackle the job of restructuring and redesigning the work of one of the world's most complex organizations not only required an accurate assessment of reality but the ability to translate that assessment into a "doable" list of opportunities. The failure to do so and the consequent encouragement of unreasonable expectations is the third great organizational sin. While some may think that heroic behavior involves doing the "undoable," just the opposite holds true. At the heart of heroic leadership lies the ability to transform daunting challenges into doable tasks.

The heroic measurement process should reveal a practical list of opportunities to those who must take action. Welch and his measurement teams established credibility by measuring the most basic and accessible element of corporate life: work. Stakeholders could understand the data because they intimately knew its source. Likewise, they could accept the final analysis, which illustrated mismatches between time and money investments and the corporate mission. By seeing the risks associated with expenditures that did not match the mission of becoming number one or number two, they could focus more intently on opportunities for doing their work more in harmony with the mission. In the end, cross-functional teams produced global diagnoses of the corporation that identified and prioritized opportunities for action. Now, with a data-driven diagnosis in hand, Welch could turn his attention to mobilizing his stakeholders for action.

Step Four: Mobilize Support

The great strength of the Medicine Circle comes about through bonds of reciprocity and cooperation among stakeholders. Heroic leaders deem as their most valuable asset the support of those most affected by the changes they're pursuing. Although Welch began his tenure by earning the sobriquet "Neutron Jack," for an early tendency to "nuke" people first and diagnose later, he quickly came to realize that enlisting the support of others would accomplish more lasting results.

Welch engaged GE's stakeholders in a fierce debate over how a new GE could arise through the creation of a boundaryless organization in which people, ideas, and resources worked together to serve a global vision. As he did so, a new model of thought began to emerge, a model characterized by the now famous admonition to "take control of your destiny or someone else will." Focusing on the opportunities identified through the diagnosis of work, Welch moved to mobilize stakeholders with the clear intention of developing a critical mass of support sufficient to take action. In this way, he began to confront and overcome the fourth deadly organizational sin, the failure to fulfill the basic needs of stakeholders. By sharing the diagnosis and inviting stakeholders to participate, Welch began to fulfill the Medicine Circle's mandate of connecting people to one another in a partnership for mutual success.

Step Five: Take Action

Welch's team stood ready to take action from the beginning. Since they faced an immense challenge to implement their all-encompassing vision, they could not afford to do anything but hit the ground running and continue to move relentlessly forward. To translate their vision of a boundaryless GE into action, they embarked on a continuous process of context redefinition, mission measurement, and opportunity diagnosis. Welch's new generation of GE visionaries created an engine of change through continuous education, employee development, and goal setting. A formal process of action planning and reporting, which enabled leaders and teams from across the whole organization to share lessons and track progress, monitored the entire effort.

Welch called this monitoring process "integrated diversity," which he viewed as an operational framework for forming the concept of boundarylessness into a plan of action. Recognizing the inherent risk of paralysis that dramatic change so often incurs, Welch encouraged and rewarded individual initiatives that fostered the achievement of corporate goals. In this way, he dealt with the fifth great risk to the Medicine Circle of organizational life, the tendency to attempt to do everything at once, which fragments efforts and yields little true accomplishment. GE's new generation of stakeholders were seasoned veterans who understood that a radical agenda of action must, paradoxically, unfold moderately. While Welch insisted on action, he only encouraged and rewarded behavior that pursued collective success, a strategy that exerted a powerful moderating and partnership-building leverage. Through it, GE-ers began to learn how to function as a team. Team action increases the net amount of energy available for implementing change and, at the same time, harnesses it more fully. This, in turn, strengthens the organization's capacity to evaluate results and take advantage of emerging opportunities.

Step Six: Evaluate Results

The sixth deadly organizational sin is the unwillingness or inability to evaluate results and continue to measure risks. Welch's team understood from the outset that the true measure of their commitment would come from their willingness and ability to measure the effectiveness of their own actions. Blaming the ineffectiveness of inherited strategies would be easier—and useless. It took a lot more guts to evaluate one's own shortcomings.

Welch understood the three primary benefits of such measurement. First, the willingness to evaluate results demonstrates resolve and builds credibility by demonstrating strategic humility, as people move beyond their egocentricity to tackle the more important issues related to the common good. Second, it strengthens the heroic partnership by identifying new opportunities for extended team action. For the Heroic Organization, each cycle of measurement functions like a mining expedition searching for opportunities to enfold others in an ever-expanding Medicine Circle of stakeholders committed to achieving a shared vision of success. Finally, each cycle of measurement flushes out destructive elements in the organization, leveraging those who are holding back support or blackmailing the organization through some hidden agenda and forcing them forward to own up to their responsibilities to others.

The commitment to evaluate results propels every heroic journey and signals the maturation of a heroic team from a start-up group of visionaries into a seasoned unit of achievers. No organization can succeed in its mission without the wisdom to measure mission effectiveness from the beginning. GE's team measurement strategy of diagnosing the work enabled the company to measure results with precision and consistency, always comparing apples with apples and holding everyone accountable to the same organizational standards and ideals.

Warren Brueggeman, at the time head of GE's Nuclear Energy business unit, often said, "God gave us two ears and one mouth to warn us that we should spend twice as much time acquiring information as giving it." One of GE's visionary reformers in those early days, he emphasized how deeply the team had committed itself to candid, no-holds-barred assessment: "You can't tolerate lying at any stage of this process," Brueggeman pointed out. "And, the failure to measure your own efforts means you broke your pledge to look at the situation objectively and with an unflinching commitment to the common good." Far from the last word on the subject, that statement reflects the first step forward in an unending cycle of improvement.

Step Seven: Repeat the Process Continuously

The evaluation of results sets the stage for the seventh and most rewarding step of the heroic process, endless repetition. The first cycle of effort builds a high level of tenacity and commitment that creates a powerful momentum for advancing even more rapidly through successive cycles. It's often said that great military victories result from minor victories in the first round of battle that are aggressively followed through in the second round. For example, during World War II's Battle of the Bulge, General George Patton built on the tenacious albeit precarious victory of the American forces at Bastogne to launch a counteroffensive that all but ended the war in Europe. Rushing to the relief of a small Army battalion at risk under the onslaught of overwhelming German forces, Patton contemptuously responded to the Germans' demand to surrender with the now immortal "Nuts!" Then he drove the Third Army up a short 20 mile corridor that had opened up as two German Army groups of over 1.5 million troops each began to regroup. Patton pushed forward, divided the enemy, and initiated what became the final push—the liberation of France and the invasion of Germany itself.

Welch and his team foresaw that victory wouldn't come in the first or even the tenth round of battle, but would emerge over time through a resolute and unflinching commitment to follow through. More than a decade after starting his first GE revolution, Welch has now launched a second. Having demonstrated how to rebalance and rebuild a disconnected colossus into a synergistic rapid response corporate force, doubling revenues from $32 billion to more than $63 billion while restructuring the work force from 380,000 to under 270,000, Welch has now expanded his vision of GE to become a role model for cooperation and reciprocity in the world arena.

From the beginning of their efforts to turn GE around, Welch and his team were driven by a deep concern over the ability of a corporation growing up in a democratic pluralistic tradition to compete in a predator-intensive world economy. Welch's team believed that corporations committed to values of "integrated diversity" would require tremendous discipline and "smarts" if they hoped to compete with multinational corporations from such closed cultures as Japan and South Korea. Without discipline and resolve, the diversity intrinsic to pluralistic organizations can create chaos and tear a team apart. To harness the potentially greater net energy embodied in the pluralistic flow of energy and ideas requires an extremely disciplined and open process of partnership building and strategic humility. Welch and his partners understood that the willingness to measure, learn and take action as a team must translate into a disciplined process so deeply embedded in the culture that all stakeholders would continue to improve.

The following chart graphically summarizes the Seven-Step Heroic Process, not only as GE implemented it but as any organization can use it to create an environment of continuous improvement:

The Logic Flow of the Seven-Step Heroic Process

Step 1: Establish Context

      Action: Define the challenge and vision for meeting it.

      Objective: To unify the Medicine Circle and develop self-confidence and commitment.

      Risk: "Other esteem": searching for purpose and identity outside the Medicine Circle.

      Lesson: Above all, stakeholders must know who they are as a team and why they should work together.

(continued on next page)

Step 2: Measure Mission Effectiveness

      Action: Undertake an organization-wide global assessment: "Are the right people in the right place, at the right time, for the right reason and cost to achieve the mission?"

      Objective: To own and experience reality.

      Risk: Failure to understand the consequences of *not* meeting the challenge.

      Lesson: Overcome fear and resistance to change by immersing stakeholders in information and engaging them in the organization's reality.

Step 3: Identify Opportunities for Improvement

      Action: Use the Work Imaging™ database to identify doable opportunities for action.

      Objective: To develop a data-driven plan of action.

      Risk: Failure to set practical, achievable targets that build strength and confidence.

      Lesson: Stakeholders will understand how to change when they understand the reasons for it.

Step 4: Mobilize Support

      Action: Share the plan.

      Objective: To enfold those who are ready for change.

      Risk: Wasting energy on those who refuse to change.

      Lesson: Focus on building a magnet of positivism for those ready to change.

Step 5: Take Action

      Action: Implement the plan.

      Objective: To honor those who serve by involving them in their own transformation.

      Risk: Attempting to do too much and thus achieving little.

      Lesson: The more radical and far reaching the agenda for action, the more it must be tempered by moderation.

Step 6: Measure Results

> *Action:* Repeat Work Imaging™: Measure success and failure.
>
> *Objective:* To grow and mature from start-up visionaries to seasoned achievers.
>
> *Risk:* Focusing on the present and failing to identify the risks and opportunities ahead.
>
> *Lesson:* By measuring results, leaders strengthen their legitimacy and stakeholders' commitment to the vision.

Step 7: Repeat the Process Continuously

> *Action:* Repeat the Seven-Step Heroic Process.
>
> *Objective:* Build tenacity and create a heroically conditioned organization.
>
> *Risk:* Loss of momentum; unwillingness to sustain the process feeds cynicism and destroys leadership credibility.
>
> *Lesson:* Nothing succeeds like persistence.

Notice how each step emphasizes an action, a concrete objective, inherent risk, and a valuable lesson. Remember, this is a *process*, a series of steps in a constantly repeating cycle of actions. An organization pursuing the Heroic Process never ceases its motion but evolves continuously to reinvent its future. With this schematic view of the Heroic Process in mind, let's look at how a less well-known organization also used it to reinvent itself.

CHOOSING HEROISM: THE CASE OF HAMOT HEALTH FOUNDATION

Heroic leaders and their partners always remember vividly the moment they chose to pursue a heroic path because they make that decision in a stone-cold sober state, recognizing that change must occur and that only *we* can affect that change.

For John Malone, newly-appointed CEO of the Hamot Health Foundation in Erie, Pennsylvania, the arrival of an out-of-control locomotive called health-care reform prompted his decision to choose heroism. For over fifteen years, as chief operating officer of the Foundation's hospital division, Malone had worked as a member of a team that had ridden the wave of health-care expansion and the relatively easy money it generated to create a dominant regional force. However, all of that effort and its payoff came dramatically into question when it became clear that proposed changes in health-care financing would reduce hospital revenues by over 30 percent in less than three years. For Malone and his stakeholder partners on the board, medical staff, and management team, only two choices seemed viable: Take charge of the situation or quit the business.

For all heroic leaders, such decisions involve high stakes and heavy consequences. For Malone and his wife, Linda, the decision to stay meant that they would accept responsibility for restructuring, perhaps even dismembering, a long-standing Medicine Circle of friends. Like Welch, Malone realized that the welfare of the whole organization, even its very survival, would hinge on his willingness to set aside personal bonds of loyalty for the common good. Since health care reform meant a personal decision for him to accept a higher level of responsibility than he had ever anticipated, he determined to address the issue as forthrightly as possible.

Step One : Establish Context

Malone began establishing a new context for action by identifying the challenge threatening the stability and balance of the Medicine Circle. Only he and a few members of the board and executive team grasped the full potential impact of the challenge. Unless he shared this knowledge, and did so quickly, he risked losing the trust and, ultimately, the willingness of stakeholders to accept massive change. The longer he waited, the further his people would withdraw from committing their energies to a new vision of what Hamot might become.

To reach as many stakeholders as possible as quickly as possible, Malone "multi-pathed" his message, convening Town Hall meetings of all employees and physician stakeholders, speaking with a host of local civic and business organizations, and writing op-ed pieces, and holding special briefings for the press to announce that Hamot must slash its total operational budget by over 30 percent during the next three years. While politicians in Washington continued to debate the direction of health-care reform, by the spring of 1993 it was already hitting Hamot hard. As a large regional medical center, Hamot operated as a high-tech and, thus, a high-cost provider of care. Over the years, its dominant position in the marketplace had led to a sense of invincibility and smugness that, in turn, accumulated costs that had little to do with its core mission of patient care. From real estate ventures to the addition of overly expensive technologies and an ever-expanding bureaucracy, Hamot had become a complex and wasteful organization increasingly out of touch with reality. To address that problem, Malone began by defining the challenge in rock-solid terms: From a budget of $162 million, the organization must slim down to under $115 million in three years.

Malone understandably feared that defining the challenge so starkly might cause the majority of Hamot's stakeholders to jump to the conclusion that a draconian period of callous and possibly unethical cost-cutting would ensue, but he and his team knew that they must face the challenge head-on, even if it embodied far more than mere cost-cutting measures. Research conducted by E. C. Murphy, Ltd., and the American Hospital Association had revealed that health care in general was marbled with wasteful fat exceeding $150 billion nationwide: The average health-care worker wasted 31 percent of the work week overcoming administrative paperwork and system roadblocks. That waste arose as the result of a federal structure of work that makes the average hospital's organization over twenty times as complex and potentially disconnected as that of a comparably sized manufacturing business. True to this model, Hamot operated as a vast feudal kingdom of tenuously connected and easily destabilized scientific and service fiefdoms. Simplistic cost-driven downsizing would not attack the underlying problem of such a system, and, more important, could dramatically increase the risks of patient mortality and morbidity up to 400 percent. Malone knew that the challenge of health-care reform would require much more than the mere reduction of head count and costs, it would require the comprehensive restructuring and redesign of work systems at every level of the entire organization. To accomplish this, he knew, he must win the full support of the only people who possessed the knowledge and skill necessary to do it—the very people most affected by cost reduction—the physicians and staff who delivered care.

While politicians, reformers, insurance companies, and consultants claim to know how to restructure health care from the outside-in, any real change can come only from the inside-out. Malone knew he faced the risk that his definition of the challenge would ignite angry, unfocused thinking if it did not mobilize those most affected by the challenge to meet it. Thus, enfolding those with the potential to meet the challenge became his first order of business. With this in mind, he offered a vision of how Hamot could meet the challenge through a comprehensive restructuring and collaborative work redesign process with the overriding objective of preserving the values of quality and patient service. Borrowing from the Hippocratic Oath, he pledged himself and the organization to a path of reform that would "do no harm" to the patient.

In order to display the full range of options for the future to his stakeholders, Malone candidly diagrammed the choices as follows:

Survival—A Choice of Futures

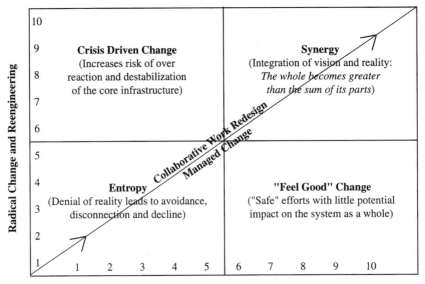

Incremental Improvement

On one axis of change appeared the choice to pursue incremental micro-level change on a piecemeal basis. This approach, in large measure, reflected the last ten years of effort in the health-care industry's Total Quality Management movement. While a great deal of time, money, and effort had gone into the TQM movement, it had not altered the overall structure of health care and may, in fact, have added an additional layer of costs to the system. Nevertheless, the movement had confirmed the importance of quality as a long-term predictor of an organization's ability to stay competitive and profitable. The question: How could Hamot pursue quality while simultaneously cutting costs?

On another axis appeared the option to restructure the system radically through traumatic downsizing and wholesale systems reengineering. Though the term reengineering has come to describe a comprehensive rethinking of how to organize work, it has also become associated with rationalizing top-down, cost-driven downsizing that has little fundamental impact on how an organization carries out its work. In a landmark 1993 study on business restructuring, Gallop reported that over 70 percent of business executives involved in major corporate restructuring and downsizing during the Eighties and the early Nineties admitted that financial crises precipitated a knee-jerk cost-cutting reaction that later conveniently became labeled as work reengineering or even quality improvement. Such organizations ended up smaller but not really different and not really better off as a result of the exercise. In fact, such downsizing typically compacted and intensified the waste that already existed by leaving a smaller number of people to accomplish the same amount of work.

Malone noted that neither of these options adequately addressed the reality that Hamot, and health care in general, faced. Instead, he proposed a vision of customer-focused restructuring through a process of collaborative work redesign. This vision invited every stakeholder in the organization to participate in a comprehensive assessment of the organization's mission performance and to become involved in making it better. As Malone said, "It is not a vision for the meek of heart, but one that honors each stakeholder with the opportunity to participate in his or her own survival."

To guide the implementation of this vision, Malone drew on the heavy investment Hamot had made in continuous quality improvement to develop a core set of values that would guide the process and serve as criteria for identifying opportunities and establishing priorities for action. These values would drive the assessment and establish priorities for restructuring, including work redesign and workforce reduction if necessary:

1. To serve the customer
2. To provide quality
3. To serve those who serve
4. To perform as a team
5. To break down barriers
6. To redesign the work
7. To redesign and improve continuously

The values and their sequence comprised a Socratic logic flow that the board and the executive team debated hotly before unveiling. Malone insisted that the logic make sense to anyone concerned with Hamot's future. While the logic might not increase his popularity, it should at least drive home his credibility and integrity. Thus, he desired a values platform that honored the fundamental reason for Hamot's existence and that compelled all stakeholders, regardless of their "rank," to recognize their responsibility as heroic partners. Malone understood that his integrity as a leader, as demonstrated by his personal commitment to "walking in a sacred manner," offered the key not only to his, but to the organization's survival. Any suspicion of hypocrisy or perception of manipulation would repel stakeholders from one another and from the challenge they faced. The definition and discussion of values must serve as a magnet for attracting stakeholder commitment to the vision. While Malone's definition applies specifically to his organization, a similar logic can apply to most every company, be it a start-up enterprise or a mature multinational conglomerate. Let's explore the logic more thoroughly.

1. TO SERVE THE CUSTOMER. This value affirmed the mission of the organization and the responsibility of each stakeholder to emphasize service above self-interest. An era of entitlement had produced a narcissistic environment in which workers at all levels often acted superior to customers. Malone and his colleagues wanted to replace that arrogance with an understanding that the customer comes first and that nothing matters more than meeting the customer's needs.

2. TO PROVIDE QUALITY. While health-care costs had now replaced quality in the headlines, Malone knew that to renege in this most fundamental of commitments would undermine the most sacred of customer contracts as well as alienate the most dedicated and, therefore, essential members of the Medicine Circle. "Somewhere along the line," Malone noted, "our cynicism overcame our faith and we forgot to recognize the extraordinary importance of physicians and staff whose existence is truly defined by their commitment to service. They're the heroes in this battle. They've never lost sight of what is timeless and central to our mission. If I have to go into battle, I want to stand shoulder-to-shoulder with them; so, I'm not going to give an inch on quality."

3. TO SERVE THOSE WHO SERVE. Since no business in America depends more on its employees for business than a hospital, this value makes eminent sense on both an idealistic and a pragmatic level. To support one standard for customers and another for internal stakeholders creates schizophrenia in organizational life, building a caste system that segregates and, ultimately, disconnects people from one another. Since every employee can and will act as both a salesperson and a customer, this value also makes powerfully good marketing sense.

A Hospital Corporation of American/E. C. Murphy, Ltd., study conducted in 1987 found that the average health-care employee can influence the buying decisions of up to 87 people every 40 to 60 days through immediate contacts with family members and friends, as well as through secondary contacts where family and friends talk to others. At any given time, over 50 percent of the patients in America's community hospitals can trace a referral path to a hospital employee. Wal-Mart executives would give their right arms for such a marketing base. Service to the internal customer, therefore, becomes, a key element in the values logic flow, highlighting the double-edged sword of health-care restructuring, namely, that the people you downsize today can very well become your customers tomorrow.

4. TO PERFORM AS A TEAM. This element of Malone's logic aimed at preserving the integrity of the organization and its position of respect with employees, regardless of their eventual job status. The notion of team goes far beyond a simple sports analogy, which tries to pit *us* against *them*. Here, team performance includes all stakeholders in the Medicine Circle, be they intimately involved in daily service to the customer or people who might not find themselves in need of service now but much later. The best teams are inclusive, not exclusive.

5. TO BREAK DOWN BARRIERS. This value is aimed at reducing territoriality and self-interest, an especially difficult task in health care, which on average boasts the most highly credentialed workforce on the planet. Dr. James Pepicello, former chief of surgery at Hamot, noted, "Health care is a medieval kingdom in which the King of Medicine, the Queen of Nursing, the Count of Hematology, and the Duke of Accounting all engage in a court-like chess game for position." To break down the barriers erected by generations of scientific specialization and huge personal investments in claiming educational and professional territory required a commitment to the sixth and most demanding of all values.

6. TO REDESIGN THE WORK. In redesigning the work, organizational stakeholders must make a total commitment to a new vision of organizational life based on the heroic concepts of integration, reciprocity, and cooperation. Both Malone and Pepicello knew such a commitment would not come easily to independent, entrepreneurial physicians and professionally invested allied health professionals, but they also recognized that Hamot's survival in the new world order of health care demanded nothing less.

To redesign the work, stakeholders must learn to share information about the most basic and important aspect of their organizational life, the way in which any person actually performs work. Malone and his partners knew that this sharing provided the key to mobilizing support and building the committed toughness essential to survival.

7. TO CONTINUE TO REDESIGN AND IMPROVE THE WORK. Malone knew he could not win the battle in the first or even the tenth round, but as with Jack Welch and GE, he would need to muster a tenacious sustained commitment to stay on course until a breakthrough opportunity presented itself. In the Medicine Circle of contemporary life, change is the one and only truly constant for which you must continuously prepare yourself.

Malone used this logic flow to turn his vision of heroic partnership into a practical mission for action that established a framework for implementing the full Seven-Step Heroic Process. By establishing context, Malone defined both the challenge and a vision capable of withstanding and responding to a building storm of anxiety and confusion.

Step Two: Measure Mission Effectiveness

Malone followed up on the Town Hall meetings by putting his plan into action and engaging all 3,000-plus employees, a sample of several thousand patients, the board, the community, and the entire medical staff in a comprehensive Work Imaging™ assessment of the quality and efficiency of Hamot's health care delivery. Work Imaging™, an E. C. Murphy, Ltd., trademarked diagnostic technology based on the same principles used so successfully at General Electric, answered the question, "Are the right people, in the right place, at the right time, for the right reason and cost for quality?" That question became a mantra for reform for the internal consulting teams of managers, physicians, and frontline employees at Hamot who guided the Work Imaging™ process and worked directly with stakeholders to collect work data. Malone described the Work Imaging™ experience as a total organizational performance assessment and challenged his fellow stakeholders to seize the opportunity "to make a good thing of their lives" at Hamot by sharing their best analytical insights on how to perform their work more effectively.

Step Three: Identify Opportunities for Improvement

Hamot's people then benchmarked the data from the Work Imaging™ assessment against a national health-care "best practices" database to identify risks and opportunities for action. They, in turn, evaluated the opportunities against Hamot's vision to determine which opportunities offered the greatest promise. The diagnostic process revealed that the resources of the organization ran significantly at odds with the stated mission. While these results hardly surprised anyone, the fact that they had emerged from an analysis by those who performed the work energized Hamot's people with insights they had not previously anticipated. Malone's confidence in his stakeholder partners proved well-placed when he saw their courage and commitment grow by leaps and bounds.

Ultimately, the benchmark analysis revealed that Hamot needed to remove over 27 percent of the operational costs that were weighing down the organization and preventing it from focusing its energies fully on patient service. Employees estimated that organizational inefficiency exceeded 35 percent of total labor costs and that this directly correlated with patient dissatisfaction and lack of employee empowerment. Physicians, now witnessing one of the greatest professional role revolutions in American history, saw their day-to-day operational existence compromised at every turn by procedural roadblocks that they themselves had helped to create. While much appears in news stories about the role of government and insurance companies in creating paperwork, the Hamot study traced over 70 percent of the problem to the organization itself.

Step Four: Mobilize Support

Working with the internal team of consultants, Malone shared this diagnosis with all stakeholders, including the press, through the same multipath communication method he had used to launch the undertaking. As he shared the data, he noted the areas requiring prompt action. Like a physician leading a team of specialists through the care of a very special patient, Malone walked his stakeholders through the treatment regimen he expected them to follow. For some, it would mean a fundamental life change requiring an exit from the organization. For the vast majority, however, it meant a refocusing and redesigning of their work from the ground up. The latter joined cross-functional work redesign teams with the intent of accelerating change in key areas, addressing such issues as scheduling, the role of management, professional role responsibilities and skills mix, and consolidating and streamlining overlapping departmental functions. In addition, Hamot initiated a comprehensive retraining and outpatient process to assist those suffering a career change.

Step Five: Take Action

Through courage, candor, and a commitment "to walk in a sacred manner," Malone mobilized his stakeholders to take action as a team. By establishing context and openly measuring mission effectiveness, Malone gained eager support from those most ready and willing to assume a higher level of responsibility for their lives. As the process unfolded, new leaders stepped forward who had previously hidden in the underbrush of complexity and waste, expanding the team and enfolding all others ready to change. In the end, a new generation of stakeholders arose, ready and able to carry the mission forward.

Step Six: Evaluate Results

As the change program moved into its second year, results exceeded expectations—Hamot accomplished over $15 million in savings beyond direct cost cuts. And while necessary work force reductions occurred initially, fully two-thirds of the savings came about as a result of team-driven work redesign, which increased the organization's capacity to serve more patients while sustaining, and in most cases improving, the clinical quality of care. The results of a second cycle of Work Imaging™ confirmed these changes while identifying yet another level of opportunities. As Hamot "drills down" through the layers of Work Imaging™ data, it continues uncovering more and more far-reaching opportunities while developing ever-increasing levels of heroic fitness.

Step Seven: Repeat the Process Continuously

Once fully into its second generation, Hamot's process began gaining momentum, focusing first on "redesigning the work, then the people." Because of this ongoing commitment, Hamot feels confident that it can avoid the trauma of massive downsizings and that it can, rather, follow an orderly path of rebalancing in which all stakeholders can reorder and rebalance their lives for the collective benefit of all.

CONCLUSION

For Jack Welch, John Malone, and all their heroic partners, choosing the heroic path represented a commitment to self improvement, partnership, and balance. Each recognized the intrinsic strength of the Medicine Circle as a restorer of balance and wholeness. For both Welch and Malone, the challenge to change became a stimulus for heroic action, which inspired them and their team members to reach inside themselves and find the strength and courage "to make a good thing of their whole lives." In Part Two, we will see how each member of the Medicine Circle can use the Seven-Step Heroic Process to walk in this same sacred manner.

PART TWO

BUILDING
THE MEDICINE CIRCLE
How to Apply the Heroic Process
to Stakeholder Relationships

— 4 —
STAKEHOLDER:
The CEO

More than any other traditional management belief, the idea that the leader of an organization dominates the organization as its supreme authority, creating its mission and manipulating everyone associated with the organization to fulfill that mission, violates the spirit of the Medicine Circle. And no other aspect of the unheroic organization may be harder to discard because it has held sway for so long. Two and a half thousand years ago the Chinese philosopher Sun Tzu wrote a little book called *The Art of War,* which many executives today admire even more than Machiavelli's *The Prince.* While this brilliant treatise on strategy offers insights into achieving victory on ancient battlefields, it also promotes a model of leadership that should make any heroic CEO shudder.

Sun Tzu's *The Art of War* drew the attention of Ho Lu, the king of Wu, who invited the author to test his theory of managing soldiers. The test involved 180 ladies of the palace. Sun Tzu arranged the women into two companies and placed two of the king's favorite concubines at the head of each.

"I presume you know the difference between front and back, right hand and left hand?" he asked the assembled women.

"Yes," they replied.

When, to the sound of drums, Sun Tzu then issued the order, "Right turn!" the women only burst out laughing.

Sun Tzu said patiently, "If words of commands are not clear and distinct, if orders are not clearly understood, the general is to blame. But if his orders are clear and the soldiers nevertheless disobey, then it is the fault of their officers." So saying, he ordered the leaders of the two companies to be beheaded.

Alarmed at this turn of events, the king interceded, saying he felt Sun Tzu had proven his point and that he did not wish to see his favorite concubines beheaded. As the general of the king's forces, Sun Tzu advised the king that he could not accept that command and proceeded to dispatch the two leaders and replace them with the next pair. When next the drum rolled and Sun Tzu issued his orders, the companies executed each with perfect precision.

While this little demonstration won Sun Tzu the job as commander of the king's army (he obviously knew how to control soldiers), and while it may appeal to a CEO who wants to dominate and control an organization, its direct applicability to today's more complex world is limited. For Sun Tzu, top-down orders backed by the real threat of physical punishment could exact compliance in a world of absolute power and limited interdependence. For the CEO of today's pluralistic organizations, such tactics of fear hold the promise of risk, not reward, and violate the very essence of the medicine circle.

Since its creation following the Industrial Revolution, the job of the CEO has received considerably more attention than any other role in organizational life, and most of that attention has centered on age-old ideas that equate leadership with authority, control, and manipulation. From the early 1900s through the late Seventies and Eighties, the definition of the CEO as a commander has dominated the literature of leadership, which outlines the role of the CEO as the center of an organization's power, its supreme authority, its principal destroyer of competition, and its primary author of mission and achievement.

In the heroic context, this definition proves not only false but dangerous. Leadership through fear and manipulation creates a fearful and manipulative culture, one that cannot possibly focus on the well-being of all the organization's stakeholders. The heroic CEO, on the other hand, rules through respect and shared commitment, building a respectful organization that works for the mutual benefit of all its stakeholders.

Recently, E. C. Murphy, Ltd., in cooperation with the American Society for Work Redesign, completed a five-year study examining CEOs' perceptions of their roles. Five distinct models of leadership emerged: the *mythic bystander, feudal autocrat, Hellenic demigod, renaissance manipulator,* and *heroic partner.* The most successful leaders, when asked to graphically depict their view of their organizational world and their role in it, drew variations of the *heroic partnership* model. They intuitively chose the path of the classic hero committed to service for others. For mythologist Joseph Campbell, heroism meant "losing yourself, giving yourself to some higher end." For the heroic CEO, it means rebalancing the organization with a focus on serving the welfare of all with whom the organization comes in contact. The results of this study provide a starting point for examining two heroic CEOs in organizational life today: Andrew Grove of Intel and David Glass of Wal-Mart.

The Mythic Bystander

Some leaders see themselves essentially as nonleaders, equal members with others in the system, endowed with no greater or lesser stature and, accordingly, no greater nor lesser *responsibility* than anyone else. When asked to depict their "leadership world," they usually drew themselves floating alongside other constituencies in an unstructured setting. Their pictures looked like this:

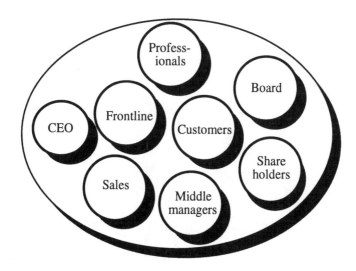

At the heart of the *mythic* world view lies an assumption that the overall structure within which one lives—one's world, one's culture, or one's organization—remains intrinsically ungovernable. The activities within it simply entail interactions among equivalent parts, uncontrolled by any force except natural law. The mythic view may appeal to naive egalitarianism, but it can cripple a CEO. If intervention seems pointless and strategic planning impossible, then one can only react to events and passively play out one's part in them. Behind the mythic view's apparent equality lurks the abdication of personal responsibility and accountability.

The Sixties and Seventies saw much experimentation with mythic management through fads such as the encounter group movement. The limitation of this world view becomes vividly clear through the almost complete elimination of the customer and other outside forces from discussions of organizational well-being. By narcissistically focusing the organization's energy internally, this approach eliminated all other stakeholders from consideration.

The Feudal Autocrat

"Feudal" executives pictured the organization as a vast collection of squabbling constituencies with themselves at the center. Their view corresponds to organizational theorist Gerald Skibbons's "mosaic" model: Organizational members consider themselves virtually autonomous and define organizational life according to their interrelationships with one another rather than within the context of the organization's larger mission, as pictured here:

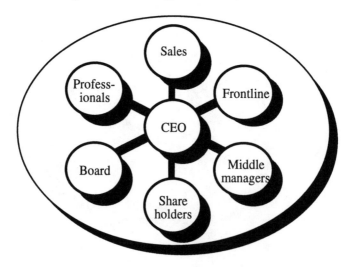

The feudal model conjures up images of the leader as King Arthur surrounded by his knights. Though loyal to Arthur, each knight retains great independence, with only Arthur's leadership joining these detached individuals together. The feudal structure fails because it focuses so intently on the role of the dominant person that it feeds the egocentricity of the leader rather than the mission of the organization. Far from serving as the organization's umbilical cord to the outside world, the feudal CEO becomes the most isolated figure of all. External stakeholders, such as the customer, seldom make it into the drawings this model generates. Deprived of contact with the customer—who, more than any other stakeholder in organizational life, legitimizes authority—the feudal CEO possesses no real platform for leading the organization.

The Hellenic Demigod

Other leaders view themselves more dynamically, picturing the CEO as the dominant force in a way that recalls leadership concepts descended from the ancient Greeks. In their drawings they placed themselves at the "head" of an organizational diagram that seems to echo Aristotle's model of humans as the center of the universe and the measure of all things:

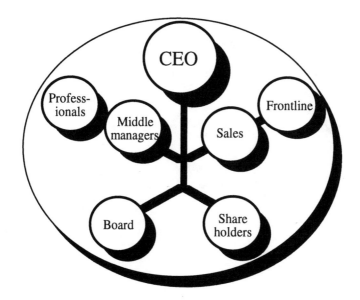

This model carries with it a raw egocentricity based on the conviction that the force of one's individual personality will carry the day. These leaders mold themselves after yesterday's Rockefellers, Carnegies, and Morgans, or after today's Boeskys and the Japanese *keiretsu*. Such leaders make poor delegators, and their reluctance to share power and responsibility often chases away promising young executives. However, the biggest problem with this "rugged individualist" style of leadership arises because the leader cannot possibly be everywhere at once. Ultimately, the organization must pay the price: Important details go unnoticed and strategic balance suffers. Today's world has grown far too complex for any one person, however gifted or charismatic, to energize an entire circle of stakeholders.

The Renaissance Manipulator

Still another role definition springs from a world view dating to the age of Machiavelli. According to this view, the leader stands outside the organization and leads through manipulation:

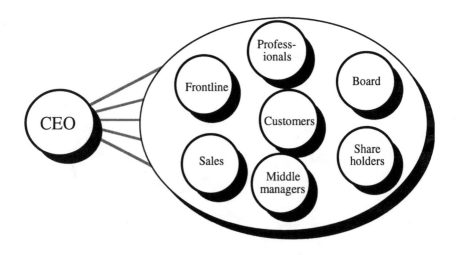

Renaissance leaders and thinkers intoxicated themselves on their newfound power to manipulate through technology and politics. From their approach to leadership would rise the Age of Reason, mercantile nationalism, and the Industrial Revolution, with all the benefits—and drawbacks—they brought with them. The renaissance model shares an obvious shortcoming with the Hellenic model. The leader remains profoundly alone, armed against the complexity of organizational life with only his or her individual resources. But the model contains an even more basic flaw: It simply does not promote the openness and commitment to mutual benefit that a pluralistic culture expects of its leaders. Interestingly, the CEOs who espoused this vision most forcefully usually ran the most troubled organizations. The mythic, Hellenic, and feudal models at least immerse the leader in the organization. The renaissance model, on the other hand, places the CEO permanently outside the organization, defining the CEO's role as detached from, and uncommitted to, all stakeholders.

The Heroic Partner

Heroic leaders define a new model of leadership that adheres to the heroic principles of strategic humility, building partnerships, and walking in a sacred manner. Here, current science and mythology meet.

Leaders who espouse the heroic partnership model view organizational life in ways that support the work of contemporary systems theorists. They recognize the organization's interdependence with the outside world, yet they also recognize the importance of all internal relationships. They seek a dynamic balance between the two, a heroic partnership consistent with the principles of the Medicine Circle. In their drawings, the CEO serves as the agent for focusing the energies of the organization. As does the conductor of a symphony, the heroic CEO directs the cacophony of energy within and without the organization into a focused plan for serving all stakeholders. The CEO does not propel the organization with his or her effort alone; every individual stakeholder supplies his or her own energy to fulfill the organization's mission. When heroic CEOs depict their roles, they produce diagrams like this:

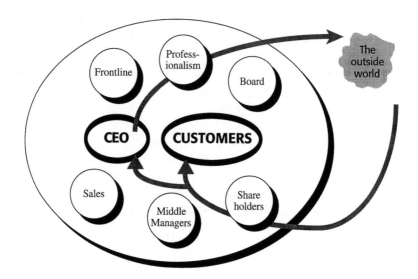

In the organizational Medicine Circle, the CEO acts as the *heroic advocate* for all stakeholders, accepting responsibility for bringing each into the Medicine Circle and for seeing to it that the concerns, needs, and interests of each, especially the customer, become the driving force behind all efforts. In the heroic vision, the customer becomes a principal focus of all energy, establishing a platform of servant leadership where the customer enjoys a position of co-leadership alongside the CEO, at the heart of the organization.

The heroic partnership model differs from the previous models in three respects: First, where the more primitive models paint a static picture of organizational life, the heroic model remains dynamic. It recognizes the importance of process. Second, the heroic model recognizes the world outside the organization. While the renaissance model places the executive outside the organization, it defines the world only as a vantage point from which to manipulate the organization. By contrast, in the heroic partnership model the leader journeys into the world to *find the customer.*

Finally, the heroic partnership model defines leadership as a *duality.* The CEO and the customer share the job of energizing the Heroic Organization, the only arrangement that makes sense in light of a customer-focused mission. In a complex, pluralistic culture such as our own, no one can control an organization solely from within. Real power lies outside—with the customer, who alone determines success or failure in the marketplace. In turn, the customer holds the key to mobilizing energy *within* the organization. Employees are customers, too, and only by recognizing that shared identity can a leader unify the energies of all stakeholders in a binding, motivating commitment. In the Heroic Organization, leadership is not a function of personal achievement but of organizational achievement.

APPLYING THE HEROIC PROCESS TO THE CEO

Heroic CEOs translate customer advocacy into action with the Heroic Process, personally role modeling the behaviors they want all stakeholders to emulate. They define their leadership as a partnership with the customer, in which both their day-to-day power and their strategic vision result from operating within the parameters of service. They are *servant leaders*, asking not "Who will serve me?" but rather "Whom can I serve?" and affirming the values of service by serving those who serve. They apply the Heroic Process to everything they do:

THE HEROIC PROCESS

1. Establish a Context for Action
2. Measure Mission Effectiveness
3. Identify Opportunities for Improvement
4. Mobilize Support
5. Take Action
6. Evaluate Results
7. Repeat the Process Continuously

Two contemporary CEOs have displayed a particularly deep understanding of the heroic leadership model: Andrew Grove of Intel and David Glass of Wal-Mart. Through their applications of the Seven-Step Heroic Process, they reveal their customer focus and their willingness to subordinate themselves to serving their stakeholder's needs.

CASE STUDY: INTEL

In 1986, Andrew Grove, CEO of Intel, faced a daunting task. Although his company had pioneered the Dynamic Random Access Memory (D-RAM) chip and had remained on the cutting edge of memory chip technology in the United States ever since 1968, it now found itself suffering under the onslaught of overseas competition. In the space of two years, Japanese competitors had managed to encroach on Intel's market share of memory chips to the extent that the company lost over $400 million from 1985 to 1986. Profits plunged, and in 1986 Intel bled red ink for the first time in its history. The hemorrhaging company slashed 30 percent of its workforce, closed manufacturing facilities, and cut salaries. Morale sank so low that Grove felt compelled to make personal appearances asking the company's engineers to stay aboard and reassuring them that Intel would survive the slump.

With keen vision, Grove decided that Intel's course should shift from producing memory chips to pursuing a new technology—microprocessors, the chips that run personal computers (PCs). Doing so entailed a terrific risk; at the time, the computer industry was dominated by mainframes and minicomputers, and conventional wisdom dismissed the PC as a fringe market. However, Grove's decision to abandon Intel's core business and risk the company's future on what industry giants, such as IBM, at the time considered a "niche" technology, reflected his ability to foresee the needs of the customer. He seized the opportunity: If Intel was headed down a dead-end street, why not take a different route? The decision took courage, Grove recalled in a later interview. "We were at each other's throats over this." Denial had blinded Intel's managers, but Grove mustered the courage to accept the responsibility of refocusing Intel's strategy, thus breathing new life into a faltering company.

That business decision marked the beginning of a revolution in the computer industry. Intel's founders had always believed that the company would affect great changes in a society where information technology would drive a major revolution. The power of the microprocessor has indeed changed the world; and the creative energy of Intel has contributed greatly to the emergence of the Information Age.

Grove accomplished his revolution by *establishing a context* of focusing on customer needs. Other major computer makers were ignoring the vast majority of potential users because they clung to a limited vision of how people could use computers. Even in his own organization, Grove met some of the same resistance to addressing this new customer base. In 1986, at the beginning of Intel's venture into microprocessors, the company suffered from what Grove later termed "strategic dissonance." At the beginning of Intel's transformation, top management did not adequately articulate and support the company's change in focus from D-RAM to microprocessors. While some of the company's production planners readily shifted capacity over to production of microprocessors, Intel's best development people were still working on D-RAM projects. The schizophrenia resulted in chaos and waste. This situation taught the CEO a valuable lesson, he later related: Major strategic changes demand that management reconcile their words with their actions. Grove has put that lesson to work as the company continues to reinvent itself to meet new challenges.

Intel's skyrocketing growth provided a satisfying *measure of mission effectiveness*. The decision had meant a high-stakes roll of the dice and the investment of millions of dollars to essentially tear the company apart and rebuild it from scratch. Grove's vision proved more than fruitful: Intel's 386 microprocessor chip became the biggest selling product in semiconductor history, and the even higher-powered 486 chip won the race once the company introduced it. In 1992, Intel surpassed Japanese rivals and captured the lead position in the global semiconductor business, an especially satisfying moment for Grove, who had only a few years earlier predicted that the United States stood in danger of becoming a third-rate "techno-colony" in the face of Japan's onslaught in the computer industry. He had even gone so far as to mail a secondhand violin to Richard Darman, the former head of the Office of Management and Budget, with a memo lambasting the Bush administration for "fiddling while Silicon Valley burned." Today, Intel stands as the most profitable company of its size in the world, still growing so fast that it doubles in size roughly every two years.

Nevertheless, Grove continues to *identify opportunities for improvement* in everything Intel does. The company's most recent challenge is the introduction of RISC (Reduced Instruction Set Computing) technology, a microprocessor technology that surpasses even Intel's fastest chip, the Pentium (based on CISC technology—Complex Instruction Set Computing). Motorola and IBM joined forces to create their own powerful new RISC chip, the PowerPC, which threatens Intel's core business. Intel retains a strong advantage, however: Only CISC-style chips support Microsoft Windows, the most popular PC software on the market. Despite this advantage, Grove has set Intel's sights on developing still more advanced chips that can include and surpass the advantages of RISC chips. At the same time, Intel must stay ahead of copycat outfits such as Cyrix and Advanced Micro Devices, which are steadily encroaching on the market for 386 and 486 chips—Intel's bread and butter. To remain competitive, Intel has slashed prices on its 486 chips, and plans aggressive pricing on the Pentium chip. Intel also foils would-be cloners by "self-cloning": Producing variations on its own chips.

Grove's often repeated sentiment, "Only the paranoid survive," has frequently proven only too true in the fiercely competitive computer industry. Since Intel faces enormous challenges to maintain its edge in semiconductor technology, Grove keeps Intel ahead by *mobilizing support*, both intellectual and financial, behind the company's products. The company pours millions of dollars into product development, outspending all other semiconductor manufacturers, domestic and foreign alike. In 1993, Intel invested 2.5 billion dollars—43 percent of 1992 revenues—into R&D and plant improvements. In the cutthroat computer industry, where highly developed intellectual properties quickly become cloned commodities, Intel needs an aggressive stance on innovation to stay ahead. Today, the company works on four or five generations of a product simultaneously, always staying a generation ahead of the competition. In this way, the company's competitors must play catch-up in the dust, while Intel's flagship products blaze the trail to the future.

Intel has never experienced a complacent moment. Once Grove established the vision and *took action*, the company reinvented itself with breathtaking speed. Success came so rapidly, it seemed as if innovation in semiconductor technology had taken on a life of its own. Gordon Moore, Intel's chairman, coined "Moore's Law" to explain the phenomenon: The number of transistors that can be built on the same piece of silicon will double every 18 months. Moore's Law has held true: In 1970, Intel introduced the world's first general-purpose microprocessor, the 4004, which contained 2,300 transistors. Intel's latest release, the Pentium chip, contains over 3 million.

Still, in *evaluating the results* of Intel's success, Grove sees only more opportunity and has positioned the company to become a leader in the consumer-products market. Currently, the company structures its pricing to appeal to the home-computer market because Grove believes that home buyers, not corporations, represent the future market. Corporations can no longer absorb new generations of PCs as quickly as Intel plans to make them. Only consumers and home office users, in their unending quest for novelty and convenience, can provide the demand that Intel needs. The company plans to transform the PC powered by Intel chips into an all-purpose consumer device that will ultimately usurp the TV, telephone, VCR, answering machine, and cable.

The company that built its enormous success on reinventing itself does not shy away from reinventing itself again. It does not matter to Grove that Intel lacks previous experience in the new technologies. The man who came to America with only $20 in his pocket and speaking only rudimentary English has parlayed guts and talent into one of the most successful careers in American business. He succeeded because he loves taking calculated risks. *Repeating continuously* the Heroic Process that has made Intel number one, Grove has recently steered the company into heroic partnerships with Microsoft and Turner Broadcasting to create programmable telephones, Information Highway connecting points, and news and entertainment products. At Intel's labs, engineers are turning out microprocessors at more than double the former rate, raising the stakes in every field in which it chooses to play and steadily advancing to the next level of competition. Whatever direction Intel takes, it will be an heroic path, where unity of purpose and vision combine to guide the company to an ever-expanding customer base.

CHOOSING HEROISM

Andrew Grove chose heroism by reinventing not just a company, but an entire industry according to the principles of customer service. While observers often rank him as one of the toughest CEOs in America, he has always brought this toughness to bear in the interest of the customer. Through his democratization of the computer industry, and his relentless pursuit of customer service, he has truly recognized and fulfilled a customer-oriented mission. On the way, he has consistently put into practice the three principles of heroic behavior. He led through strategic humility by recognizing the threat from competitors and the need for Intel to improve itself continuously. With unflagging courage, he refocused his company on customer needs. He built heroic partnerships with companies such as Microsoft and Turner to create new products that allowed both partner organizations to compete in a new industry. Finally, he walked in a sacred manner by recognizing the need to utilize the decision-making protocol of the Seven Step Heroic Process, from establishing context to continuous improvement.

Another CEO, David Glass of Wal-Mart, recognized in a 1993 *Fortune* survey as America's most admired CEO, also chose heroism. Faced with filling the shoes of perhaps America's most successful CEO, the late Sam Walton, Glass guided the company through a potentially difficult transition without losing Wal-Mart's high level of customer focus. Like Grove, Glass employed the three heroic principles not just to maintain, but to *increase* customer focus.

Lead Through Strategic Humility

When Glass took over the reins at Wal-Mart a few years ago, he saw the need to lead the company forward without uprooting the actions of his predecessor Sam Walton. Walton, an entrepreneurial supernova, had created such a legendary reputation that had Glass tried to override it, he would have encountered nothing but resistance. However, Glass saw no reason to override it; he had to figure out how to use Walton's principles *and* integrate change and progress. Recognizing the genius of his predecessor, he practiced a great deal of strategic humility, as *Fortune* magazine observed during Glass's trip to a newly opened store, where he ran into a customer: "So you're the big man," said the shopper, sizing up Glass. Glass didn't miss a beat. "Nah," he chuckled, "I just front this deal."

Although sales under Glass have grown from $16 billion in 1987 to $55 billion in 1993, he takes great care to award responsibility for the company's success to its associates. Often described as an unprepossessing man, he handles all his organizational duties in a down-to-earth way. When he took over Wal-Mart, he did not to tell employees how *he* was going to run the place, but how *they* were going to run the place by using the basic principles outlined by their beloved Sam Walton. Also realizing that he didn't know all the answers when it came to serving his customers, he decided to spend two to three days a week just visiting stores, where he enlisted the help of customers and frontline employees to refocus each of the Wal-Mart stores on improved customer service.

Build Heroic Partnerships

Glass knows that a service organization cannot survive without those who actually deliver the service. He makes sure that he empowers and heightens the sense of mission for all his frontline associates by allowing them to run each store, even each department, as a small, individually owned company. The managers of each department receive detailed financial statements that show costs and profit margins. Glass reasons that instead of relying on the ghost of one entrepreneur who founded the business, the company must keep 250,000 entrepreneurs out there running their own parts of the business.

Glass holds to the same core value as Walton, employee participation, because he believes that the best ideas come from people on the firing line, and, mirroring that philosophy, he respects and honors them by allowing them both autonomy and continual support. He sees the frontline associates as his best source of information for change. To this end, any associate can call his home phone number. He gets calls at all hours, "even after the bars close." Far from an autocratic boss, Glass behaves as a true partner with his people, breeding trust where a more control-oriented CEO would engender fear.

Walk in a Sacred Manner

David Glass continually walks in a sacred manner by practicing his own form of the Heroic Process. He adopted the still-powerful customer-focused mission of his predecessor, and he spends a great deal of time on the frontlines measuring that mission's effectiveness. By creating heroic partnerships with his associates, he has gotten 250,000 people measuring mission effectiveness daily. Still, he always searches for ways to improve: On a recent visit to a warehouse, when a manager proudly told Glass that the depot was 99 percent in stock, in contrast to the 95 percent industry average, Glass reportedly responded by asking "Why would it only be 99 percent?"

Glass never makes a move without mobilizing support, enlisting customers and associates alike in the quest for ultimate customer service. He goes to great lengths to ensure that both customers and associates join in the continuing process. From his available home phone number to the open door to his office to his frequent visits to the frontlines, he makes himself available for any and all suggestions for improving service.

By leading through strategic humility, building heroic partnerships, and walking in a sacred manner, David Glass, like Andrew Grove, demonstrates the power of heroic leadership in creating and maintaining a customer-focused organization. Through the use of these three principles and the Seven-Step Heroic Process, any CEO can do the same.

— 5 —

STAKEHOLDER:
The Frontline Manager

In his book, *Finding Work without Losing Heart: A Guide for Mid-Career Job Loss* (Bob Adams, 1994), William J. Byron, S.J., former president of Catholic University, now teaching business ethics at Georgetown University noted: "As long ago as 1975, I found myself receiving calls from unemployed executives, usually longtime friends who had unexpectedly lost their jobs. They called me, I soon realized, for three reasons: I was a priest, and confidentiality was important; I was an economist who understood corporate dislocations; I was a university president serving on many boards and could presumably be a helpful 'network' contact."

Father Byron began helping people who, for the first time in American business history, had become targets of corporate downsizing: frontline managers. Accustomed to keeping their jobs when lower-level workers lost theirs, these displaced managers found themselves on the street looking for work after twenty or more years of secure employment. When Father Byron left the presidency of Catholic University in 1992, he spend a year examining the issue more closely, and in 1993, with the support of a Lilley Endowment, he began traveling the country interviewing displaced managers and participating in job-seeker groups around the country.

He recalls the experience, reported in the December 29, 1980, issue of *The Wall Street Journal,* of a senior executive who spent a full year in his New York company's "Hawaiian Room," an outplacement suite: "They joked a lot about it in the executive dining room, and at least once during every annual officers' banquet someone with a few drinks under his belt would imitate a guitar playing 'Aloha' and get a big laugh, but I didn't think any of them seriously believed that they would ever end up in the Hawaiian Room. I certainly didn't." But he did.

In his book, Father Byron details the results of his work with more than 150 out-of-work managers—mid-level on up to chief executive officers, male and female, geographically and industrially diverse. Those who successfully got out of the "Hawaiian Room," he found, relied first and foremost on their psychological, spiritual, and religious resources. "Religion or, as some of those I interviewed preferred to express it, 'spirituality,' was important to about two thirds of the unemployed managers I surveyed."

In the Heroic Organization, the Medicine Circle can supply this "spirituality" for managers, be they Catholic, Protestant, Jew, agnostic, or atheist. While *Cangleska Wakan* certainly enforced the philosophy or "religion" of the Sioux, it can also instill a "secular spirituality" in contemporary organizations.

No other role in the contemporary organization has gone, or is likely to go, through such continual redesign as that of the manager. During the past decade, U.S. businesses and industries have flattened their organizational hierarchies and reduced the number of managers by over 50 percent, from 15 percent of the workforce to less than 8 percent. While the downsizing has corresponded to an increase in American industrial productivity, it has also led to an increase in mid-career job loss and stress on managers who keep their jobs but find their average work week increasing by as much as 30 percent. In the rapidly evolving new economy, organizations more than ever need effective managers who can coordinate, solve problems, teach, and heal the wounds of battle incurred in the frontlines of service.

In the Heroic Organization, frontline managers hold things together and translate strategic organizational vision into operational reality. To them falls the responsibility for ensuring that people actually carry out the organization's customer-driven vision. Upper management may develop an organization's vision, and frontline workers may supply the manpower necessary to carry it out, but, without managers who can move people from vision to action, even the most effective vision will die stillborn.

What does it take to succeed in this role? To answer this question, E. C. Murphy, Ltd., and the American Society for Work Redesign (ASWR) undertook a four-year national study of managers in business, health care, public service, and government, in an effort to identify Benchmark Managers and the characteristics that make them successful. Its ultimate goal: to develop a behavioral "best practices profile" for use in selecting, evaluating, and training managers to succeed in the Nineties and beyond.

The study began in 1989 and is continuing through the Nineties. As of June 1994, it had pinpointed 1,029 out of 18,000 managers as Benchmark Managers. After receiving three confirming recommendations from interviews with superiors, peers, and subordinates, each participated in interviews and Work Imaging™ analyses aimed at identifying the characteristics that made them so effective in the eyes of their associates. The results have begun to establish a new context for defining successful management in the Nineties.

THE CONTEXT:
MANAGING COMPLEXITY

The ASWR study found that middle managers often suffer from role confusion. Responsible to upper management, managers strive to meet targets imposed from above. Yet they also feel responsible to their subordinates, with whom they spend most of their time and from whose ranks they themselves have usually risen. The Benchmark Managers successfully sliced through this confusion by maintaining a singularity of purpose: the customer. As long as managers remain true to a customer driven mission, they can easily justify their actions in response to any challenges they receive from above or below. Managers who continually serve the customer, who look outside, not in, seldom hear accusations of taking sides or selling out.

Role ambiguity isn't the only source of middle-management problems, however; others include organizational schizophrenia and spider webbing. *Organizational schizophrenia* occurs when the vision and the means to attaining the vision do not synchronize. An organization becomes schizophrenic when it pursues objectives inappropriately. Any action or policy that runs contrary to the customer's interest and the organization's long-term mission usually signals organizational schizophrenia. For example, when a large Northeastern hospital responded to criticism for being the most expensive place in town to have a baby by offering area obstetricians a cash bonus for each mother-to-be they admitted, it behaved schizophrenically, sidestepping concerns about price with its cash incentives, a move it quickly abandoned when public outcry blasted the hospital for offering physicians a "bounty."

Spider webbing occurs when managers who remain employed after downsizing find themselves doing more work than before and as a result grow confused about their principal focus and responsibilities. Instead of occupying some box on an organization chart, they more likely feel as though they sit transfixed at the intersection of all the threads in a spider web. This spider-webbing effect blurs lines of authority and undermines the manager's own role, and it contributes greatly to the restiveness of many of today's middle managers. If you absorb the impact of downsizing by taking on extra job responsibilities, you can easily lose your ability to focus on implementing your organization's vision as your work becomes more and more disconnected and fragmented.

Today, more than ever before, role confusion, organizational schizophrenia, and spider webbing threaten to disconnect middle managers from the customer. However, the successful managers in the Benchmark Manager study offer an antidote to these poisons.

Benchmark managers possess *"M-Pathic"* communication skills. Whether speaking to a customer, a subordinate, or a superior, they typically meet the other person more than halfway, tailoring their presentation to the emotional needs and expectations of the listener. "M-pathic" communicators:

- Communicate *empathetically* (i.e., in ways that appeal to diverse constituencies)
- *Multipath* their communications (i.e.; along multiple paths that makes sure the message gets through)
- Use simplifying, problem-solving scripts or *maps* to guide communication (i.e., within a framework people can easily understand)

"People Noise"

Human relationship problems can garble management communications in much the same way that electronic noise corrupts signals on a phone line. Benchmark Managers compensate for this "people noise" by *M-pathing* their communications with empathy, multipathing, and mapping. At the personal level, *M-pathing* means identifying the dominant "relationship style" with which each individual operates, then fine tuning the message in order to reach that individual in the most lucid and authentic way.

The importance of *M-pathing* became clear during the early years of the Benchmark Managers study. Top managers, asked how fine a sieve they used when deciding how to address a person, invariably said they "read" that person very quickly. Initially, they would assign the person to one of four style categories, then build up a more complex personality profile through continued interaction. Over 70 percent of the Benchmark Managers used these four style categories: *Rational, Structured, Intuitive,* and *Personal.*

Relationship Styles

Note the primary characteristics of each style and the fact that the M-Path Relator incorporates all four into the integrated style portrayed by Benchmark Managers.

Benchmark Managers initially relate to and communicate with a person consistent with that person's own style (i.e., how that person usually interacts in everyday organizational situations). Far from assuming that a person *always* displays one relationship style, Benchmark Managers know that every human can relate in different ways at different times. They simply observe behavior and use those observations to make sure their messages come through loud and clear. This approach simplifies the complexity surrounding human relationships and helps eliminate counterproductive "people noise" from management communication.

Benchmark Managers value individuals. Whatever their differences in background and personal style, Benchmark Managers lead through commitment and tend to follow similar behavioral scripts. First, they value *the customer.* Effective managers gain great legitimacy when subordinates believe they consistently act on behalf of the customer. Putting the customer first also helps reduce role confusion. "I don't have to agonize over 'Whom do I work for?' anymore," reported one factory foreman. "I know whom I work for. I'm not management's boy, and I'm not labor's, either. I work for the customer. That gives me someplace to stand where I can stand up to either side and do what needs to be done."

Second, effective managers value *their people as assets.* As a financial services manager noted: "Workers are problem solvers, marketers—they connect us to customers. Ever hear of an ATM [automatic teller machine] or robot delivering commitment?" Benchmark Managers recognize the foremost workforce management challenge of the Nineties: Retaining and motivating a shrinking number of qualified workers and managing an increasingly heterogeneous workforce. In such an environment, hiring and keeping skilled workers, treating and developing them as assets, makes all the difference in the world.

Third, effective managers value *the individual worker.* From both practical and philosophical viewpoints, they know that leadership begins and ends on the individual level. As a food-service manager in the study said: "We don't treat our customers as a quality circle, committee, or task force, so how can I treat my subordinates that way? I want to develop teamwork; it's critical to our success, but I've got to start by showing respect and developing . . . the individual . . . first."

Benchmark Managers employ *"behavioral scripts."* They develop preset routines for responding to common situations.

Consciously or not, when a familiar problem recurs effective managers invoked prepared "sets" of expectations, attitudes, and logic, responding almost on autopilot. They let an "off-the-shelf" script drive their initial reactions while they evaluate the unique situation more closely. That way they can take the initiative, assert influence over the unfolding situation, and set a productive tone even though they lack time to think through every nuance and detail.

Scripted behavior does not imply phoniness. Whenever Benchmark Managers don't feel confident about making a critical decision or firing somebody, they reach into themselves for a script that *simulates* the characteristic they need. When the time comes for action, they find they have what it takes to get through after all. During a threatening crisis or a major change, such role modeling enables them to change before they really feel like changing. As one manager put it, "Feelings will follow."

Another manager, who works with airline flight attendants, reported, "I've always been conscious of a process of 'getting into character' that I go through before I do something stressful. I do deep breathing and imagine that I'm this very assertive person. Then I can clearly think through the points I want to cover."

A purchasing manager offered another view: "Sometimes, when he doesn't know I can see him, my teenage boy goes through this routine in front of the mirror. He adjusts his hair, smoothes down his shirt, and strikes this casual macho pose. He's done it so many times his body can strike that pose automatically. And when that girl he's had his eye on says hello, his heart may rise up in his throat and his blood may hammer so hard he can't hear what she's saying. But he'll strike that pose. See, he doesn't have to *think* about it to *do* it. And that's not really all that different from some of the things I do when some supplier throws me a fast ball. I kind of go on autopilot behind this 'generic wise P.A.' mask while I map a new path."

Partially automating their responses helps effective managers avoid getting snagged on the mechanics of managing. Instead, they concentrate on dealing with people, on solving problems, and on focusing everyone's energies on the customer. The scripts they use also streamline delegating. Most of them follow a Socratic "delegation by questioning" methodology, whereby they gently force frontliners to make their own decisions. In this way, effective managers drive authority as far down into the organization as it can go. Scripts also create the possibility that people who must step into management on short notice can learn the scripts, act them out, and tackle new situations with some framework for action.

The Benchmark Managers in the ASWR study spent most of their time performing just ten key roles, in this order of frequency: Problem Solving, Maintenance, Evaluation, Selection, Conflict, Counseling, Discipline, Exit, Defiance, Termination.

Ten Benchmark Management Roles

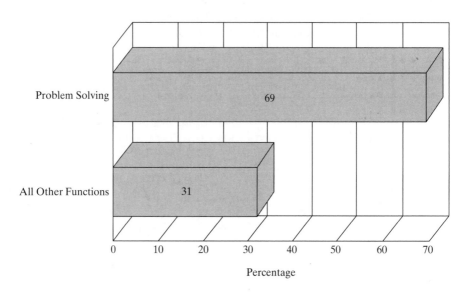

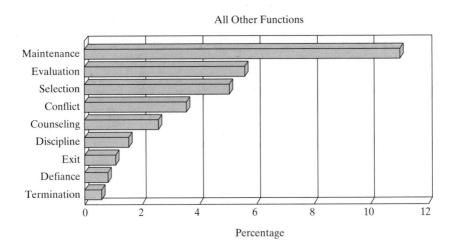

As the top graph shows, a single role—problem solving—consumed more than 72 percent of effective managers' time. The bottom graph displays how they allocated the rest of their time. Top managers tended to concentrate on the positive: Reinforcing and affirming frontliners through problem solving, selection, and constructive evaluation. And they tended to make short work of negative tasks—conflict management, discipline, and termination.

The Benchmark Managers enacted behavioral scripts for each of their roles, with a typical script specifying the psychological tone for a particular transaction, most often, a one-to-one interview. It clarified the manager's goal in the transaction and imposed a structure he or she could follow. Often that structure included a characteristic ratio of listening to talking: Effective managers spent most of their time listening. Only during a termination interview or at the conclusion of an evaluation or discipline interview did they talk more than listen.

Listening and Talking in Key Scripts

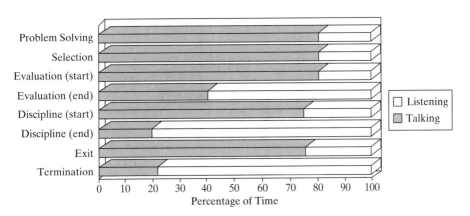

One company that participated in the Benchmark Managers study, J. C. Taylor, Inc., has moved well along the path toward redefining the manager's role, and their efforts parallel the Heroic Process.

THE HEROIC PROCESS

1. Establish a Context for Action
2. Measure Mission Effectiveness
3. Identify Opportunities for Improvement
4. Mobilize Support
5. Take Action
6. Evaluate Results
7. Repeat the Process Continuously

CASE STUDY: J. C. TAYLOR, INC.

J. C. Taylor joined the groundbreaking ASWR project early on. A holding company for businesses ranging from health care to hazardous waste, J. C. Taylor had come to understand only too well the costs of inefficient and unfocused management, and that awareness prompted the company to seek a unifying concept and protocol for harnessing the energies of its managers. Virtually every division at J. C. Taylor had gone through downsizing and restructuring during the Eighties, and as comprehensive Work Imaging™ assessments of the organization revealed, the organization had done little to change the way in which management functioned.

Work images revealed that the average manager at J. C. Taylor was spending less than 25 percent of his or her time supervising, coordinating, and planning in the frontlines of service. Despite the flattening of the corporate office and its subsidiaries, managers spent the bulk of their time and energy on activities that did not support the core mission of the organization, coping instead with coordination and discipline problems, trying to link departments, and providing information up and down the hierarchy. J. C. Taylor teams operated in a disconnected fashion and often repeated work and stumbled over communication blocks. With their hands full working on these problems, managers could not devote themselves to advancing the company's customer-focused vision. Drawn-out meetings and a culture that pushed managers to create long-winded and often unread reports only exacerbated the situation. J. C. Taylor managers felt frustrated over their inability to act, and their morale plunged so low that they could scarcely take the initiative on their own to change the situation. That's when senior leadership stepped up to the plate.

First, they *established a context for action* by declaring that management should, above all, work to provide top-quality customer service. The announcement addressed the question that had been on everyone's mind: Was J. C. Taylor committed to serving customers or just to playing a Monopoly game of buying and selling corporate assets? The reshuffling of the Eighties had heavily undermined confidence and increased levels of anxiety at every level of the workforce, particularly among managers, who had seen 30 to 40 percent of their colleagues disappear. J. C. Taylor's work imaging revealed an all too prevalent problem that crops up when an organization restructures itself the wrong way or for the wrong reason. Too often, while a company eliminates people in order to cut costs, it fails to eliminate the wasteful work that occupies as much as 40 percent of people's time.

At J. C. Taylor, the work images of management revealed that the company had not adequately scripted the management roles before the restructuring. Thus, when it cut management ranks, the remaining 65 percent of the management workforce still carried out 100 percent of the complex and wasteful work that had characterized management work in the past. As the organization downsized and flattened, it only intensified the waste and complexity, compacting it and making it harder and more difficult to reduce. The restructuring had, in the long run, done nothing but increase the tension and stress that managers had always suffered.

To alleviate the problem, top leadership decided to use a formal *measure of mission effectiveness* to address the issue, asking all managers to participate in an assessment of their skills and developmental needs. The assessment utilized the Heroic Manager Developmental Inventory (HMDI), a tool based on the Benchmark Managers study. With it, managers could now measure themselves against highly effective managers and consequently create individual developmental and refocusing programs.

Using the results of this study, every J. C. Taylor manager began to *identify opportunities for improvement* in terms of focusing his or her energies on the customer. This involved, first and foremost, reorganizing work around processes, not tasks. Instead of creating a structure around functions or departments, managers now moved to build the company around core processes, with specific performance goals in mind. Within these processes, management minimized fragmented tasks, eliminated nonvalue-added work, and reduced supervision. They also began to rethink their roles and cast off their old marketing, manufacturing, or finance hats and think more broadly about their responsibilities. Likewise, the corporation examined the results globally, constantly searching for opportunities to improve across the whole organization. Recognizing that if its work satisfies the customer, profits will follow and stock price will rise, the company also decided to link performance objectives to customer satisfaction rather than to profitability and shareholder value. Team evaluation was linked to customer satisfaction; staffers were rewarded not just for individual effort, but for team performance in pursuit of customer satisfaction. The HMDI analysis provided a framework for managerial development the corporation could use to *mobilize support* of the managers, involving them in training sessions that taught them how to adapt the Benchmark Managers' scripts to the specific needs of the company. To identify the potential and developmental needs of candidates who might join the corporation in the future, the company also used the tool as a selection instrument for new managers. Once the company knew the key traits necessary for managers to succeed at J.C. Taylor, it incorporated them into the management performance evaluation system that monitored and tracked management progress.

With all the data in hand, J. C. Taylor could now to *take action* to select, educate, and evaluate managers. The concrete plan for improvement gave all managers new hope for fulfilling the organization's mission, and they used the HMDI analysis to *evaluate results,* monitoring and providing feedback on all management activity. This process helped J. C. Taylor *repeat continuously* the process of improving management, demonstrating their commitment to managers as both individuals and as a stakeholder group.

By putting in place this comprehensive developmental and evaluation process, J. C. Taylor redefined its management in terms that made sense to managers and supported the principles of heroic leadership. By leading through strategic humility, forging heroic partnerships, and walking in a sacred manner, J. C. Taylor continues on its path toward creating a class of Benchmark Managers throughout all of its corporate subsidiaries.

CHOOSING HEROISM

Over 200 businesses besides J. C. Taylor are participating in the ongoing ASWR effort to define the Benchmark Manager. They are demonstrating strategic humility by confronting the need for a new and better way of managing and setting aside preconceived notions. They are meeting the challenges and functional needs of the Nineties from the ground up.

In the process, these heroic organizations are establishing new and more vibrant partnerships that incorporate management's central responsibility to hold the Medicine Circle of stakeholders together. Where the CEO strives to bring the customer into the Medicine Circle, the frontline manager works to translate the vision of customer service into day-to-day operational plans. In this regard, the frontline manager serves as the linchpin in the Medicine Circle of organizational life.

To the manager falls the responsibility to see that all stakeholders gain the practical tools and knowledge necessary to walk in a sacred manner. Every stakeholder depends on the manager to solve problems, select the right people, mend the fabric of emotional health, tap his or her full resources, and, when necessary, take surgically precise action to protect the customer from nonservice-driven behavior. As the study continues and evolves into a soon to be released comprehensive report, these organizations courageously move toward heroic management.

The chemical giant DuPont has also begun redesigning the role of the manager to reflect heroic characteristics, focusing specifically on immersing managers in the frontlines of service and redefining their role as facilitators and problem solvers. This redefinition establishes a new context for management action that follows the precepts of the three heroic principles and has already produced significant results.

Lead Through Strategic Humility

In 1989, DuPont employed a system of payment called "merit pay" or pay for performance. Each year, managers would meet individually with employees to give feedback and discuss performance. The manager would then rate each employee on a scale of 1 to 5, which would form the basis for any raise the employee might receive. However, when leaders in the Human Resources department at DuPont ran across Deming's famous quote—"Remove barriers that rob people of the pride of workmanship. Eliminate the annual rating system"—they began to realize that their system could stand improvement. First, the existing system turned managers into corporate enforcers and distanced them from frontline service. Second, the 1-to-5 rating system had become the sole criterion by which managers gave employees feedback on their performance. Finally, frontline workers tended to modify their behavior in ways they hoped would "fool" managers preparing for the year-end review. Most typically, workers invested energy in "buttering up the manager" rather than in doing their work, and they ended up being graded on their relationship with their manager rather than on the extent to which they took responsibility for serving the customer.

When upper management began to see these problems they realized, through strategic humility, that they needed to involve managers in changing this system. Not surprisingly, the managers eagerly accepted the chance to redesign their roles from enforcers to coordinators and leaders.

Build Heroic Partnerships

DuPont's managers, in turn, went to the employees. Rather than imposing a new system that focused each employee's energy away from serving the manager and toward serving the customer, they formed teams of five to seven people dedicated to the task. Each team's evaluation would now hinge on customer service and not on relationships with a manager. As part of the transformation, each team member became responsible for evaluating each of the others, a move that increased the manager's capacity to lead and assist in team development.

Managers built heroic partnerships by including employees in the customer-driven mission, inviting every employee at DuPont to contribute to developing a list of core values for the organization. Managers then assumed responsibility for applying these principles through teams.

Walk in a Sacred Manner

By redesigning their own and their employees' roles, DuPont's managers created a new protocol for everyday work, walking in a sacred manner and establishing a framework for implementing an evaluation system that measured every individual's contributions to the welfare of the Medicine Circle.

Managers at DuPont now work with upper management and employees to maintain customer service as the company's top priority. Where they had once served as upper management's enforcers and instilled fear in employees, they now translate the organization's customer-focused vision into a practical plan for action. By leading through strategic humility, building heroic partnerships, and walking in a sacred manner, DuPont, like J. C. Taylor, Inc., demonstrates the power of forging an heroic organization.

— 6 —
STAKEHOLDER:
The Board

Sitting Bull, Red Cloud, Crazy Horse, Gall, Four Horns. Most contemporary Americans recognize the names of these Sioux chiefs who engineered one of the most ignoble defeats ever suffered by the armed forces of the United States, the Battle of the Little Big Horn. For George Armstrong Custer that confrontation ended in failure, but for the Sioux, it ended in triumph, as the collective wisdom and experience of the Sioux leaders rallied their people to fight a superior force in a cohesive effort to preserve sacred cultural values. For the Sioux, the Battle of the Little Big Horn represented not just a single confrontation with an enemy, but a necessary and vital step toward reaffirming a whole nation's commitment to a mission of survival.

Every culture respects the collective wisdom of a council of elders, men and women whose achievements have given them the experience and insight to protect, preserve, and extend the guiding values of the culture. In the Sioux culture on the Great Plains, the *naca ominicia*, a select group of older chiefs chosen for their wisdom, courage, and commitment to the vision of *Cangleska Wakan*, fulfilled that function. These elders, literally "those who know all things," guided the momentous decisions of tribal life, confirming or denying the petitions of those who sought the counsel of higher authority and ruling on matters that required an interpretation of the culture's core values. In much the same way, latter-day boards of directors serve their organizations' cultures, protecting them from threats ranging from avaricious raiders to career opportunists, from lethargy and unrest to unreasoned zeal. The most effective boards provide "wisdom services" to operational leaders, guiding the great decisions of corporate life within the framework of their organizations' core values. In the platonic sense, the board serves as the Heroic Organization's *guardian of balance*, sustaining a steadfast focus on the core mission of the organization. The *naca ominicia* personified the principles of platonic guardianship, but today far too many boards of directors have chosen the ill-advised path of Custer, arrogantly riding their custom-built limousines into the face of fiercely resolved global competition.

Too often, contemporary boards lack a clear understanding of their role, and instead of providing balance and stability, they run roughshod over corporate cultural values, unpredictably disrupting the delicate balance of authority and responsibility a culture needs to succeed in a complex competitive world. This most typically occurs when a board fails to define its role within the framework of the organization's underlying mission and the values of all its stakeholders, disconnecting itself from the organization's culture, imposing its authority arbitrarily, micro-managing every situation, and shaking the very foundation of commitment and strategic direction that should bond all stakeholders together in the organizational Medicine Circle.

For an organization to flourish, the board must possess a clear sense of its role and the impact of its actions on every level of organizational life. Peter Drucker defined the board's responsibility this way: "It is the job of the board to (help) think through what business the company is in and what business it should be in." Whether they call themselves directors, governors, regents, or trustees, and whether they come from within the organization or from outside, the members of the board should serve as *the principal protectors of the*

organization's superordinate value structure. They, more than anyone else in the Medicine Circle, can make sure that the organization
remains on a heroic path.

Boards come in all shapes and sizes. Their members may come
from the local community, from all over the country, or from across
the world. A community hospital's board may depend on local business leaders, politicians, and philanthropists, none of whom lives
more than a half-hour's drive away. A Fortune 500 board will more
likely include other companies' top executives, while a small unin-
corporated start-up enterprise may not maintain a formal board at
all; and the board of a not-for-profit organization may consist of
community and national leaders all motivated by a deep concern for
a particular cause. Regardless of the organization's size or the nature
of its mission, however, it probably maintains a stable resource of
advisers on whom the founders rely for strategic counsel.

Every organization relies on some provider of "wisdom services," drawing advice through a formal or informal umbilical cord
that links the organization with the larger culture and society in
which it operates, and regardless of the board's size or composition,
it accepts one clear challenge: to support the vision of the Medicine
Circle and the values of shared success that hold its stakeholders
together. The heroic board supports all the organization's leaders
through its commitment to core values, advocating, nurturing, and
protecting a culture that encourages strategic humility, building
heroic partnerships, and walking in a sacred manner. The task of
meeting this challenge grows more difficult and complex every
year, as today's board members take on such responsibilities as
planning, policy making, evaluation, and, mistakenly, managing.
Their influence has expanded greatly. In a recent poll of 400
Business Week 1000 CEOs, 36 percent said their boards had grown
more assertive in the last five years, and 40 percent felt that their
boards now demanded greater accountability from them ("Business
Week/Harris Executive Poll," *Business Week*, October 23, 1993, pp.
282–9).

At the same time, board members have been experiencing
increased expectations of their own accountability. An E. C. Murphy,
Ltd., study of over 500 American and Canadian board members in
337 business, health-care, and not-for-profit charitable service organizations found that 64 percent had recently experienced greater
and more uncomfortable ambiguity about their roles. Some worried

about personal liability exposure: Board members more and more find themselves being held personally answerable for an organization's mistakes. In several U. S. community hospitals, for example, trustees face personal ridicule and possible financial ruin if pending multimillion-dollar malpractice awards survive appeal. Virtually all board members in the E. C. Murphy study reported that their organizations have dramatically increased personal liability insurance for their directors during the past two years. As a result, some businesses cannot easily fill vacant board seats.

The feelings of ambiguity go far beyond personal liability concerns, however. Dozens of board members shared a more general, unfocused anxiety, saying they felt less satisfied with board membership *in general* than they did a handful of years ago. Many reported an uneasy sense of "accountability for results beyond one's capacity to control." One longtime U. S. community hospital trustee put his misgivings this way: "A few years ago, we knew what our jobs were. We were sometimes advisors, often ambassadors, and almost always fund-raisers. We seldom got involved with the mechanics of giving care. This was health care, after all, not some calculating, percentage-point-shaving kind of business. Looking back, it's amazing how generally successful we were running an institution of this size in such an informal manner. In the 1990s, of course, the regulatory and financial climate has changed dramatically. Being on the board of a hospital today is like being on the board of a defense contractor—the government holds you accountable for an unlimited variety of things. We've gone from very high informality to stifling formality. Today, I am accountable if patients stay in their beds half a day too long, or if we can't deliver quality care to very sick patients for a steadily declining flat reimbursement rate. The problem is that I am liable for too many things that I do not understand."

That sort of complexity has been increasing just as rapidly in arenas outside of health care. One noted industrialist who now sits on the boards of three Fortune 500 companies in the United States and Canada suggested, "In a sense, my unease on the board simply reflects the greater options and the increased risks that the company itself faces in the marketplace. The financial community sends conflicting signals. The analysts still have to feel good about our prospects so that we can access the capital markets and satisfy our shareholders, but with a takeover situation, if we please the analysts too well, we put our autonomy at risk. And, the 'side issues' of a past decade (corporate citizenship, work-place autonomy, the environment, the role of multinationals in geopolitics) are back. In the 1990s, they will be prime concerns, right alongside market position, profitability, and the rest. All in all, the stakes are higher, and the issues more complex than ever before. I do not think I have ever felt less secure of my grasp of the issues."

As with all other stakeholders in the organizational Medicine Circle, the Seven-Step Heroic Process offers a solution to the problems of complexity and ambiguity, because board members can use that process to cut through the complexity and resharpen their focus on their roles as "wisdom providers."

Applying the Heroic Process to the Board

While the aforementioned board members represent the majority, they do not speak for everyone. The E. C. Murphy, Ltd., study found still others who do feel in control of their destinies and in command of the risks. "I serve on three boards," recalled a prominent retired businessman, ". . . a national nonprofit health organization, the symphony, and a high-tech start-up firm connected to the university here. On every one of those boards, there are some members who feel that the effort might not be worth it. But, in my opinion, the reason is that they've lost or never had a clear handle on their role. There is a tendency for board members to believe that they must tackle every issue first hand, and I feel that is a fatally flawed strategy. The key to performing effectively and finding personal satisfaction as a board member is remembering that one's role is to advise and evaluate, not to do."

Heroic board members find a way to stay in touch with the core vision of the organization and work foremost to evaluate vision effectiveness. They approach today's supercharged environment, in which financial, legal, and public-relations pressures can distract corporate focus and stretch the bonds that hold stakeholders together, with unflagging emphasis on core values. While they face a complex and intense challenge, they concentrate on keeping their organizations on an even keel by applying the Seven-Step Heroic Process:

THE HEROIC PROCESS

1. Establish a Context for Action
2. Measure Mission Effectiveness
3. Identify Opportunities for Improvement
4. Mobilize Support
5. Take Action
6. Evaluate Results
7. Repeat the Process Continuously

Let's consider an example of one board that did so successfully.

CASE STUDY:
FAIRMONT GENERAL HOSPITAL

When John Plummer, chairman of the board, and Richard Graham, president of Fairmont General Hospital, accepted the 1993 turnaround hospital-of-the-year award from the American Hospital Association, it signaled to boards of all kinds what the concept of guardianship means and what it can accomplish. During the preceding four years, Plummer, Graham, and their fellow board members had overseen the rebuilding of a Medicine Circle of trust that had been ravaged by the economics of hardship and the politics of cynicism.

The journey to shared achievement began with a recognition that the existence of the hospital, the second largest employer in the community, had reached a crisis point of dire jeopardy. After six months of struggling with one of the longest and most hostile labor strikes in the history of North American health care, casualties on both sides had mounted severely. With no winners in sight, bitterness on both sides had grown so intense that a recent contract settlement represented little more than an armed truce. To make sure Graham got the point, activists shot two holes in the driver's side of his Jeep Cherokee and sent him a note informing him that the next bullets would shatter the window.

As the board members convened to *establish a new context for action*, it became evident that they needed to develop and implement a system for monitoring the overall balance and health of the organization. Only by creating a system for *measuring mission effectiveness* could the organization avert situations such as the one it had just experienced. Such a system would play a vital role in providing early warning of emerging risks and *identifying opportunities for mobilizing support to take decisive action.*

Wisely, the board recognized that such a system must revolve around the organization's core mission of service. Without such a focus, the system could not possibly allow the board members to evaluate the results of their or anyone else's actions. Failure to evaluate results within the context of mission had in the past created a legacy of uninformed and crisis-driven decision making that had only contributed to the labor strife and the resultant economic instability of the organization.

Plummer and Graham also believed that a mission-based evaluation system would help the board stay focused on its proper role in the organization. Without a formal assessment process that represented the interests of all stakeholders in the organization, each member of the board would more easily fall prey to pressures from competing self-interests. The risk of that occurrence had already increased, given the fact that half of the board had been appointed by the City Council, which lacked a well-focused sense of mission and had displayed a volatile history of political expediency in its relations with the hospital. Knowing that only a steady, continuous era of improvement could guarantee the hospital's survival, Graham and Plummer set about designing and implementing a system for measuring the board's and the organization's effectiveness as the first key step in their improvement strategy.

To initiate their strategy, Graham and Plummer led extended board debate and analysis that culminated in a Mission Effectiveness Assessment System (MEAS), a concrete framework that could guide board action in rebuilding the service quality and confidence of the organization to a level that would eventually win national recognition. The debate centered on creating an assessment architecture that would address three core issues: span of time, complexity of the challenge, and performance achieved in light of the challenge.

Crises and opportunities evolve over time. Though either may appear as a sudden event, both trace their origins to the early days of the organization where it first began planning for its future. Thus, to head off crises and to prepare to take advantage of opportunities, the board needed to look at performance both in the past and in the future, as well as in the present. The new assessment system must therefore address the past, present, and future every step of the way.

This decision bore fruit in subsequent years of assessment, as each year the board reviewed the past year's work as a preface to the present. Each time, the board found that its assessment of the past had changed significantly from a year earlier. From the reflective perspective of experience, "present" assessments often appeared distorted and extreme, but as the board carried its assessment process forward, it learned both humility and the need to consider its evaluation of events from both a longer time perspective as well as from a broader view of how the hospital worked and affected the lives of all stakeholders in the Medicine Circle.

This expanded time frame in turn afforded the board a keener awareness of the complexity of the hospital's operations. Too often, board members had simply applied an existing operational template from their prior experiences when assessing Fairmont's operations *without* critically examining differences between their prior experiences and those of the organization to which they were now providing wisdom. Failing to do so can lead to serious misjudgments in assessing both the nature and the importance of key events in a unique organization. While the basic issues of employee empowerment, product and service quality, customer satisfaction, and profit and loss may remain constant in all organizations, the differences created by the technical and ethical complexity of contemporary life requires board members to adopt a more wide-ranging understanding of the unique operational elements in the organizations under their care.

This point became vividly clear in the wake of a major study of operational complexity in business and health care conducted by E. C. Murphy, Ltd., and the Massachusetts Institute of Technology, which revealed that health care operations deal with dramatically more complexity than do most businesses. Due to the complex political environment in which they operate and the specialized nature of their services, hospitals and health-care organizations tend to function in a far more operationally fragmented way than do other businesses or governmental agencies.

For board members at Fairmont, this fact dictated that they exercise extreme care when applying their assumptions regarding operational performance to the realities of a health-care organization. To address this concern, Graham and Plummer led the board through an analysis of operations and the identification of core areas for assessment, including: Direct Customer/Patient Services, Ancillary and Support Services, Technical Quality Assurance, Financial and Information Services, Human Resources/Internal Stakeholder Relations, External Relations, Marketing/Business Development, and Strategic Planning. The board then assessed each of these eight core operational areas within the three time frames of past, present, and future to produce a blueprint for evaluating overall operational performance evaluation.

Board Mission Effectiveness Assessment Form

Directions: Score on a scale from 1 (Low) to 10 (High) to indicate the level of challenge and performance.

Core Operation	*Challenge (C) & Performance (P) by Time Period*					
	Past (prior year)		Present		Future (next year)	
	C	P	C	P	C	P
Direct Customer Services						
Ancillary & Support Services						
Quality Assurance						
Financial & Information Services						
Human Resources/ Internal Relations						
External Relations						
Marketing/Business Development						
Strategic Planning						

The evaluation began with an assessment of the challenge confronting each area, consistent with the first of the seven heroic steps: *establish a context for action*. Too often, boards evaluate organizational performance without first defining the risks or opportunities those actions intend to address. Would a surgeon initiate a surgical procedure without first analyzing the risk to the patient and the opportunity for success? Of course not, but boards and other senior leaders quite routinely fail to evaluate the risks and opportunities inherent in a given challenge before pursuing action or, retrospectively, before judging a particular individual's or group's performance.

To guard against such erroneous assessments, the Fairmont board engaged in a rigorous analysis of the challenges Fairmont faced as it came out of the strike period and progressed through each succeeding year. The challenge assessments for the years ahead reflected the changing nature of the challenge and the degree to which the organization was meeting it. From the intense level "10" survival challenges of clinical quality assurance and the serious economic threats associated with lost revenues during the strike period, the challenge shifted to sustaining customer satisfaction and improving strategic planning during the third year of evaluation.

As the organization emerged from its period of crisis, its concerns evolved by holding onto the gains and moving forward. While courageous performance during the crisis period ensured the organization's survival, assessing the organization's performance potential with respect to emerging challenges drove it both to upgrade the skills of existing staff and to recruit others. The look ahead also pointed to the need for technological improvements and the development of new areas of clinical excellence in such areas as cardiac catherization and radiology.

Using the Mission Effectiveness Assessment System as a vehicle to *evaluate results* and plan for the future, the board maintained its focus on fulfilling its guardianship responsibilities as advocates for the customer and protectors of the organizational Medicine Circle. The board recognized that the complexity of the environment in which it was working required a simple but comprehensive strategy for maintaining focus. The MEAS did just that, creating a framework for reducing potential chaos into a clear, concise, ever-evolving plan of action. As a result, the board, with Plummer's and Graham's guidance, sustained a continuous process of improvement that moved the organization from crisis to achievement. Through *repeating the process continuously*, Fairmont constantly updated its context for action based on tangible opportunities for improvement that offered a high probability of success. The board mobilized the organization to action by creating a magnet of positive expectations for shared achievement which, by 1993, had moved the hospital from national ridicule to national acclaim.

CHOOSING HEROISM

The board of Fairmont General Hospital chose the heroic path when it embraced its responsibility to serve as a guardian. To fulfill this role, it put into practice the three principles of heroic behavior: It led through strategic humility by recognizing its limitations and the need for additional and more accurate information; it confronted the threat of weakened relationships that might cause board members to award unwarranted attention to special political and economic interests by establishing a Mission Effectiveness Assessment System that fulfilled the board's responsibility to build heroic partnerships with the entire Medicine Circle of stakeholders. And, most important, it walked in a sacred manner by recognizing the need to fulfill the decision-making and action-planning protocol of the Seven-Step Heroic Process, proceeding from establishing context to continuous improvement.

Another striking story of a board that chose the heroic path was written by the Department of Chief Administrators of Catholic Education (CASE), led by Frank Savage, executive director, Sr. Anne Leonard, president, and Dr. Jerome Porath, president-elect. Faced with a national crisis of confidence, Savage, Sr. Leonard, and Porath used the three heroic principles to develop a comprehensive plan for renewal.

Lead Through Strategic Humility

As its first priority, the CACE board confronted the fear and ignorance that threatened to blind-side leadership of the world's largest private education system, an organization serving more than 2.5 million students nationwide. Since the dramatic changes in the economic and social fabric of society, coupled with a national crisis of confidence in leadership of the U. S. Catholic Church, added to an already overflowing plate of challenges, the CACE board needed to develop a keener awareness of the threats and opportunities facing the system in order to provide guidance on how to focus resources and mobilize for action.

To address this issue, the board undertook a comprehensive mission-effectiveness assessment involving leaders from across the nation. This first-of-its-kind assessment identified a significant potential gap between leadership's vision for CACE and their ability to fulfill it. While increasing numbers of parents and students were turning to the system for help, especially students from new Asian and Hispanic immigrant groups, loss of confidence in leadership was causing a decline in revenues that had traditionally come from parish and diocesan support. Rather than view this situation with a Marie Antoinette "let them eat cake" attitude, the CACE board admitted the organization's problems with deep humility, saying, in effect, "We came to serve, we have not served well, we will serve better in the future." With that admission, the board could then move on to the second heroic principle.

Build Heroic Partnerships

With the results of the mission effectiveness assessment as a guide, Porath, Sr. Leonard, and Savage developed a plan to strengthen their partnership with parents and students to fill the emerging void. The effort centered on creating the most comprehensive organizational performance-assessment system ever seen in the field of education. To demonstrate the special value of their educational services and to identify opportunities for strengthening them further, CACE has subsequently implemented a comprehensive assessment process that, for the first time, includes *all* stakeholders in a quality-improvement and work-redesign program for education. Building on Porath's groundbreaking work with the 100,000+ students in the Los Angeles Catholic educational system, parents, students, teachers, support staff, administrators, the general public, and educational, governmental, and civic agencies have engaged in a far reaching assessment of how well Catholic Education is fulfilling its mission and contributing as a heroic partner to society. Humility precedes partnership, and partnership precedes walking in a sacred manner, which in turn instills humility and partnership in an unending cycle of improvement.

Walk in a Sacred Manner

Unprecedented in both its scope and openness, the outreach effort has built a foundation for following the Seven-Step Heroic Process. The design and implementation of a comprehensive organizational performance-assessment system established a new context for action driven by an acute awareness of the challenge. In turn, CACE has thoroughly reexamined and reaffirmed the values that define its vision. With this platform, the assessment process has become a vehicle for identifying opportunities to mobilize and reconnect stakeholders to the system.

Through direct involvement in the assessment, parents, students, teachers, and the community all became connected to an agenda for taking action that accurately supports their common goals. By pursuing this agenda, stakeholders learned how to work together on a continuous basis and developed the trust necessary to overcome the financial and social pressures threatening the system's existence.

By practicing strategic humility, building heroic partnerships, and walking in a sacred manner, the board of CACE, like the board of Fairmont General Hospital, has demonstrated the power of heroic behavior in transforming threats to organizational survival into opportunities for renewal and progress. Any board can and must do likewise, using the collective wisdom of its members to serve their organizations as the ultimate guardians of balance.

— 7 —
STAKEHOLDER:
The Frontlines

Customers who order from a "Red Rose" gift catalogue receive a handwritten thank-you note from the person who packed the order. Shoppers who walk into a Wal-Mart anywhere across the country encounter the store's smiling host or hostess. Guests staying at a Marriott Hotel will hear a heartfelt "Good Morning!" from every employee they meet, be it a bellboy or a housekeeper. For the customer, these personalized gestures transform an otherwise anonymous organization into a friendly partner. And, as Disneyland's "no-frown zone" has so successfully emphasized, the face that partner wears makes a big difference. To the customer, frontliners, the people who provide the customer's tactile link with the organization, whether in the form of a prompt Federal Express delivery, a moment of reassurance from a nurse administering a shot, or a greeting from a hotel staffer, are the company. Every frontline action projects the organization's image, but, while many organizational employee training programs stress this fact to frontline employees, all too few organizations recognize that it applies just as well to their own relationships with employees.

Frontline workers, whether health-care professionals, salespeople, factory workers, or store clerks, function in the Medicine Circle as heroic partners with the customer, providing the crucial point of interaction between the organization and those it serves, the point at which the organization literally fulfills its destiny. The frontlines also serve as a conduit of information to the organization, providing the point of contact through which the organization learns about those it serves, and thereby enabling the organization to improve its service. This information loop does not always involve written or vocal communication, but it inhabits every frontline action. It comes in the form of such abstract attributes as quality, timeliness, and helpfulness. The tangible and intangible actions of frontliners send a much more powerful signal than any marketing message could ever hope to deliver. Customers remember their direct experiences with the frontlines long after they have forgotten any marketing promise or television slogan. In this sense, frontliners represent the first and last word in the relationship between any organization and all its stakeholders.

Unfortunately, the traditional organizational hierarchy places frontliners on the "lowest" rungs on the corporate ladder, which automatically defines them as the most expendable stakeholders in the organization. Rather than working to invest these stakeholders in the organizational Medicine Circle with full power, nonheroic organizations continually remind frontliners how easily they can be replaced. Their attitude suggests the old Marine dictum, "If you think you're indispensable, stick your finger in a glass of water, pull it out, and see if you leave a hole." In the traditional scheme of things, though, management views frontliners not as intrinsic components of the organization's success but as merely a faceless pool of human resources. Not surprisingly, such a view discourages frontliners from thinking for themselves and feeling deeply loyal to the operation. Every day, they hear and see a thousand messages of contempt, from the off-limits executive washroom and reserved parking spaces to the myriad executive committees that must review and delay any employee initiative or suggestion. Consider this all-too typical example of the message organizations send the frontlines: In the event of an organizational downsizing, executives wrapped in a cocoon of perquisites and titles rest easy knowing that four thousand other people will join the unemployment lines. Rather than lay off one $500,000-a-year executive (and thus, perhaps, put their own jobs and pay under scrutiny), leaders of the nonheroic organization opt to lay off twenty $25,000-a-year shop floor frontliners. In such an organization, their mere existence justifies the executive's value to the company, while only the impact of their wages on the bottom line defines the value of frontliners.

The Heroic Organization values its frontlines quite differently. In an organizational circle centered on the customer, those who work closest to the customer represent the highest, not the lowest, rung on the corporate ladder. Serving as a two-way information highway between customers and the organization, they wield the power to make or break both the customers' satisfaction with products and services and the organization's ongoing ability to improve that satisfaction. In the Heroic Organization, frontliners function like 911 operators on whose "transmissions" depend the lives of both those in need and those who can fulfill that need.

Today, frontliners offer one of the richest potentials for heroic improvement, simply because they represent such a largely undeveloped resource in so many organizations. Within the Medicine Circle, greater strength results from sharing strength, and given their sheer numbers, frontliners can tap the power of this equation more than any other stakeholder. The Heroic Organization goes beyond recent notions of employee empowerment, which bestows decision-making power at the lowest levels, and strives to make every frontliner a full heroic partner in the organization's endeavors. Full empowerment requires more than lip service to equality; it demands an investment in enabling heroism among frontliners, whether through training, team-driven production, or employee-ownership opportunities.

Although most organizations have been encouraging workforce empowerment lately, recent studies reveal that most management tactics in this area have been manipulative and half-hearted, resulting in relatively few gains in terms of overall organizational success. An *Industry Week* study showed that while three out of four line managers agreed that employee involvement offers the key to organizational competitiveness, only 43 percent believed that their business had effective empowerment efforts ("Is Industry Ready for Adult Relationships?" *Industry Week*, January 21, 1991). Further, fewer than half of all respondents thought that their company "to a great degree" created an environment in which employees enjoy the freedom to speak openly or feel treated with respect, and seven out of ten felt that their organizations' current management styles did not fully encourage employee commitment. Ironically, the study also revealed that top executives, the supposed architects of empowerment, remained out of touch with reality on the frontlines, as they happily described the impact of empowerment on their people while those very people grumbled about empowerment as just another meaningless fad.

In contrast, heroic organizations invested heavily in frontline empowerment and awarded employees the training and tools they needed to perform their jobs heroically. The same *Industry Week* study found that organizations deeply involved in frontliner empowerment invested a lot of time, energy, and money in employee training and that the amount of training directly correlated with the level of frontliner interest and commitment to the organization. These organizations cemented their commitment by incorporating personal empowerment objectives in performance appraisals and by instituting peer review as part of the appraisal process. Organizations deeply committed to empowerment reported a 76 percent improvement in quality, a 73 percent increase in productivity, and a 59 percent rise in profitability. Most telling, however, both managers and frontliners reported a significant increase in personal job satisfaction, with correlating lower rates of absenteeism and turnover.

Alabama World Travel tapped the power of frontliner empowerment only after losing a full-time manager. When the manager left, the agency's employees approached company president Liz Sutton and asked her not to hire another manager, saying they wished to take on the responsibility themselves. This request in itself demonstrated the frontliners' heroic potential because, as a general rule, employee empowerment comes from the top rather than from the bottom of an organization. In most cases, only top managers can change the company's management style and choose to share the power they have previously cloistered. Thus, Alabama World Travel's frontliners showed uncommon commitment when they volunteered to divide up among themselves such management responsibilities as scheduling, visiting corporate accounts, and overseeing travel specialties.

A few months later, positive feedback from customers and lower employee turnover and absenteeism encouraged Sutton to invest further in her employees, sending them to training, conventions, and "cruise-a-thons," hands-on experience previously restricted to management. Employees immediately increased their involvement with the company by holding monthly company-wide meetings focused on one department's specialty where everyone reviewed the progress of the business. AWT flourished in this environment, and today its people possess a deeper understanding of what it takes to make the business successful. That understanding paid off in terms of both loyalty (the company line) and customer service (the bottom line).

As the tale of Alabama World Travel illustrates, when you include frontliners in the organizational Medicine Circle as full heroic partners, they will create a return on the investment in the form of increased commitment and performance. Empowered employees link themselves closely with the organization, a link that translates into concern for the overall welfare of the organization as well as for their role within it. By sharing power and responsibility, heroic organizations improve their ability to serve and, thus, increase their own power in the marketplace.

As organizations continue to flatten their hierarchies and slim themselves down, frontliners' ability to serve customers more fully than ever becomes critical. In the end, maximum productivity comes from every individual frontliner's efforts even more than it does from the work of leadership and management. By enabling frontliners to reach their full potential as contributors to the organization's success, organizations can, in turn, empower themselves to become flexible and responsive in an ever more demanding consumer environment. With the Heroic Process, any organization can tap the hidden power of its workforce, bringing heroism directly to the most important arena of the organization: interaction with the customer.

APPLYING THE HEROIC PROCESS
TO THE FRONTLINES

In the Heroic Organization, the frontliners fulfill a unique role as a two-way transmitter of information between the customer and the organization. Frontliners in the Heroic Organization wield the power to do whatever must be done to meet and exceed customer's needs, but they also wield the power to communicate any need for improvement in the other direction. Empowered frontliners function as the voice and ears of both. Organizations that encourage their frontliners to be deaf and mute handicap the entire organization's ability to perform. The Seven-Step Heroic Process again provides a powerful tool for tapping the full potential of a motivated and committed workforce. By engaging frontline stakeholders in the organizational context of improvement and by enabling them to serve to their fullest ability, organizations increase their own ability to function beyond customer expectations. For example, frontliner empowerment has been so successful at increasing efficiency at North American Tool and Die, profiled next, that competitors have accused the company of selling below cost, when in fact NATD's significant cost edge over its competitors has resulted from frontline-driven improvements in production. Any organization can attain the same results by empowering frontliners to become full partners in the organizational Medicine Circle.

THE HEROIC PROCESS

1. Establish a Context for Action
2. Measure Mission Effectiveness
3. Identify Opportunities for Improvement
4. Mobilize Support
5. Take Action
6. Evaluate Results
7. Repeat the Process Continuously

North American Tool & Die has used these heroic tactics to become one of the most successful and admired organizations in America.

CASE STUDY:
NORTH AMERICAN TOOL & DIE

The transformation of North American Tool & Die (NATD) began after Tom Melohn purchased it and set about creating a new type of company, one free from the politics, bureaucracy, and mistrust he had experienced during his twenty years' stint working in "Big Corporate America." Many observers felt that Melohn had made an unwise choice by selecting the dispirited, struggling NATD for his radical experiment, but not Melohn. His deep-seated faith that people yearn to be valued and to express themselves by committing to an important cause provided the linchpin in his effort to engineer a heroic turnaround for the company. He started with the frontlines, reaching out to all the company's people with a mission of partnership and empowerment.

As soon as he came on board, Melohn began his task by *establishing a context* of absolute honesty in all functions of work. He demonstrated this philosophy immediately by eliminating unaccounted cash payments from the company's vending machine service, payments that totaled thousands of dollars annually. When he shared his decision with employees at a company-wide meeting, he reaffirmed the message: NATD would cherish honesty in all its activities. Melohn next traded in the former owner's company car, a Mercedes, for an Oldsmobile station wagon that could be used for deliveries, and he reversed long-standing policy by paying for his personal gasoline expenses. Finally, to underline the company's scrupulous attention to financial integrity, Melohn hired a "Big Six" accounting firm to conduct the company's year-end audit. While the service cost a bundle for such a small organization, it bought a priceless level of credibility for company leadership.

Honesty affected the frontliners directly and positively from the outset. Shortly after Melohn took the helm, a slump in business forced NATD to cut staff, but unlike many CEOs who hire consultants and then sit back and watch them slash head count, typically without giving warning or weighing other options, Melohn gathered his people together to find ways to ease costs. Totally upfront about NATD's problem, he asked his people for their help. Could anyone take his or her vacation this month? Would people agree to cut back to a 32-hour work week until work picked up again? Reaching out worked: Inclusion in the planning process stunned the frontliners, but once they felt a part of the effort, they quickly supported the cause, responding with creative suggestions on how to achieve the necessary cost cutting. Their ideas ranged from redesigning work for 32-hour schedules to reshuffling staffing for better efficiency to paying for their own coffee. By including the frontliners in the decision, Melohn had driven home his commitment to a context of honesty, at the same time affirming his determination to make a partnership with the frontlines work for the success of all concerned.

Having established the context of honesty, Melohn *measured mission effectiveness* by creating a culture of mutual trust. It didn't come about overnight, and it was severely tested every day, but the choice to trust frontliners soon began to empower people at all levels in the organization. Trust too often eludes those leaders embarking on organizational change programs, because evidence of mistrust crops up everywhere in most organizations, in the form of blocked phone lines, punch-in time clocks, and "need to know" security on information. Trust feels risky to leaders who want to maintain control, and many simply can't let go of the puppet strings without fearing that the organization will fall apart. However, people who feel mistrusted invariably mistrust the organization in return. This cycle of mistrust has bred cynical territorialistic cultures in corporate high-rises all over the country.

The heroic leader knows that only trust can dissolve the strings that lead to unanimated service and rote by-the-book bureaucracy. Like NATD, another heroic organization, Franklin International Institute, Inc., used trust to create a super-motivated workforce focused on superlative customer service. In an interview with *Sales and Marketing Management* ("Customer Service: Evolution and Revolution," May 1991), Franklin's director of customer service described Franklin's philosophy:

> Franklin's customer service representatives are empowered to do 'whatever it takes' to make the customer happy. We believe that service is an art form, and that means we'll often do things that are out of the ordinary. . . . The key is control. For the most part, that involves hiring people who can make good decisions, giving them an extraordinary amount of training, and making sure they have a clear understanding of the company's values and principles.

For NATD and Franklin, control doesn't apply to the work of frontliners; it takes place when recruiters choose frontliners Choosing workers with a high level of integrity automatically controls the "raw material" of personnel, freeing managers from the need to manipulate the strings later. Treating employees as respected equals and allowing them to govern themselves may seem revo-

lutionary to those inculcated in the paternal corporate microman-
agement tradition, but it *works*.

Back at NATD, Melohn willingly risked trusting others in order
to create a new culture. After decades of feeling dehumanized in the
halls of corporate America, he longed to reach out, and he reaffirmed that longing every step of the way. For instance, traditional
company policy deemed overtime at NATD as strictly voluntary, but
when the company needed a graveyard shift to meet high production demands, Melohn asked the head of the new shift to determine
overtime pay. By doing so, Melohn not only validated the value of
employees' contribution to the company, he successfully engaged
them in the decision, and saved money as a result. Amazingly, the
graveyard shift asked for less overtime pay than the company had
been prepared to offer. In the end, employees repaid Melohn's trust
by affirming their own commitment to the well-being of the company, primarily because they knew by the company's actions that the
company trusted them.

Every time Melohn measured mission effectiveness, he maintained a course that many managers would consider risky, but his
trust in his employees paid off time after time. In one instance, he
asked employees to tackle the problem of a job on which the company was losing money. He told them about the problem, gave them
all the relevant cost information about the job, and then he left.
Knowing that the frontliners who worked on the job knew better
than he where and how they could improve production, he gave
those people the tools they needed to solve the problem, then
stepped back and trusted them to come up with a solution. They
did. Sharing trust, which in reality amounts to sharing power,
enabled NATD's frontlines to become full partners in the fate of the
Medicine Circle.

NATD follows no formal system for *identifying opportunities
for improvement*. Instead, everyone in the company looks upon
improvement as an integral part of his or her daily job. No "suggestion box" sits on the factory floor; if someone comes up with an
idea, he or she can act on it. No one needs permission or approval
because NATD trusts its people and invests them with the power to
make good decisions. This freedom has led employees to implement
money- and time-saving ideas, on their own, such as the new
employee who purchased an on-premises oil recycler, an investment
that not only helped the company to behave in an environmentally

responsible fashion, but that paid for itself in saved oil expenses in just one week. Another employee singlehandedly achieved 200 to 500 percent increases in job productivity by automating manufacturing processes—on his own time. Frontliners feel so committed to improving NATD's production that they routinely berate Melohn if they see poor results. Melohn related one such incident in his book, *The New Partnership* (Oliver Wight Publications, 1994, p. 114):

> One Friday afternoon I came by to wish Teresa Bettencourt a good vacation in the week following. Here's how I was greeted: "Tom, aren't we in business to make money? You've got to speed my machine up! We're not making enough profit on this job!"

> Can you believe it? An employee asking—no, *demanding*—that she work harder so that the company can make more profit. . . . She assumed—and properly so—that it was her job to find a better way. And she did, by pointing out the bottleneck in the first place.

Despite its adherence to the entrepreneurial spirit, NATD does not leave its frontliners entirely on their own to solve problems. To support their decisions, Melohn makes sure they receive the tools they need to make the right decisions. For starters, NATD provides full disclosure of all job information, including profits, to all associates. From the beginning of each job, NATD makes sure that all the frontliners who will be working on it understand the requirements for the job. NATD employees collaborate with the customers' engineers to ensure that everyone understands the blueprint, can verify its accuracy, and can continually help the customer accomplish its goals. Then, back at the plant, engineers and toolmakers work together to design the part and determine the appropriate bid.

Melohn can confidently rely on the frontlines to make their own decisions because he *mobilized support* and prepared his people for the challenge. In addition to the environment of trust, NATD mobilizes support through in-house college degree programs for its employees. Frontliners take it upon themselves to share their knowledge as well; employees who attend industry seminars return and hold meetings to teach to others what they have learned. Employees who feel they need more training or upgrading of their skills assume responsibility for hiring a professor, designing a course, and setting up classes. As Melohn reflected:

> Since we couldn't afford new and more efficient capital equipment, we had to compete by "out-thinking" our competitors. And we did—

by human ingenuity. The other immutable fact of life is that you can't possibly do it all yourself. All our employees had to participate in discovering ways to work more effectively—in a new partnership. My job was to provide a climate conducive to creativity. (*The New Partnership,* p. 116)

As a result of this climate, NATD frontliners stand ready to *take action* on an as-needed basis. According to company policy, every employee is a "boss," every employee wields power. Melohn himself describes four elements of power he believes an organization must address: the ability to allocate resources, to make decisions, to gain information, and to have the latitude to act. He knows NATD associates need all four elements of power in order to do their jobs well. As a direct result of allocating power to the frontlines, NATD has drawn a bureaucracy-busting organizational chart with only three levels of management between the frontliners and the CEO. Frontliners take care of the day-to-day operation of the plant, and they meet unexpected challenges head-on. One incident illustrates how the speed and efficiency of an empowered workforce translates into killer competitiveness:

About nine o'clock one evening, Nummi (a major automotive manufacturer) called us in a complete panic. Their day-shift inventory control department had forgotten to order for that evening's delivery from NATD. They'd be out of our parts in three hours and the entire production line would stop—at a cost of $600,000 per hour.

After Tom Parrnelli in Quality Control hung up, he got his coworkers together. The press-room people stopped their scheduled work, set up a new line—all on their own—and manufactured enough automotive parts to tide our customer over. The group in assembly dropped their regular duties and packed up these components. Tom delivered the needed parts in his own camper—just two hours later, at 11:00 p.m., and without any paperwork. Our coworkers were able to turn on a dime to meet Nummi's sudden need. (*The New Partnership,* p. 143–44)

NATD *evaluates results* in terms of both profits and quality. The company has won acclaim for its 99.9 percent defect-free guarantee—on all jobs, always. When wooing one reluctant would-be client, NATD piled industry awards on the buyer's desk until he couldn't see over them. He signed up. The company has been featured on PBS's *In Search of Excellence,* and it invites dozens of organizations each year to visit company headquarters in San Francisco to see how they can emulate NATD's success. That success has produced stunning numbers over the course of twelve years: sales up 28 percent per year, pretax earnings up 2400 percent, productivity up 480 percent, return on investment in the top 10 percent of the Fortune 500. At the same time, employee turnover has fallen to less than 4 percent, absenteeism to less than 1 percent, and customer reject rate to 0.1 percent of "all parts, all year, all customers." But NATD's success offers more than a numerical benchmark and more than a program others might follow. It symbolizes a heartfelt commitment to living the values of honesty, trust, and reciprocity every day. NATD *repeats continuously* that commitment and the actions it drives as it heroically pursues service to the customer and to every employee.

By investing in the hearts and minds of the organization's frontliners, and by linking them in a partnership with the rest of the Medicine Circle, NATD lives its heroic partnership day in and day out. Melohn always gives credit where it is due: to the frontliners who make the crucial competitive difference at North American Tool & Die. Their investment in improving the company—by streamlining their jobs, by personally seeing projects through, by improving their own knowledge and that of their co-workers—provides the key to continuous incremental improvements that compose the lengthy strides NATD makes ahead of the competition.

Choosing Heroism

Empowerment must begin at the top—frontliners cannot assume power themselves. After decades of fostering a work culture that discouraged heroism of any kind on the frontline, organizational leadership must lead frontliners on the path of heroic achievement—and then get out of the way. Once frontliners feel fully empowered and have invested their hearts and minds in the organization, they need the freedom to act. Such a change in philosophy frightens control freaks, but the results can be exhilarating for the organization's future and for everyone taking part in it. A philosophy of true empowerment incorporates the three tenets of heroism: Build heroic partnerships, walk in a sacred manner, and lead through strategic humility.

Build Heroic Partnerships

Building heroic partnerships with the frontlines means going beyond conventional definitions of employee empowerment and linking frontline performance with the organization's performance, both in terms of rewards and accountability. North American Tool & Die built heroic partnerships by concretely linking employees' actions with corporate profits, both in the form of employee stock ownership options that increased with company profits and in the form of special bonus checks for excellent performance. Another heroic organization, Nucor Corporation, has also built heroic partnerships with its frontlines.

Nucor Corporation has found the answers to staying ahead in the tightly competitive steel industry by building heroic partnerships with its frontline stakeholders, partnerships sealed with performance-based rewards. The company has abandoned thick layers of management and instead relies on work teams of 25 to 35 employees who collectively accept responsibility for accomplishing specific work tasks. By giving credit for profits where it is due, the company rewards excellent work with excellent bonuses. Each team starts its task with a standard for production and can win a weekly production bonus if the group exceeds the standards. Nucor's base salaries look low by industry standards, but performance-based bonuses afford workers a far higher earning potential than at most other plants—and they reach that potential time and time again.

Nucor has taken the partnering concept beyond simple monetary incentives, however, engineering a tremendous level of interdependence by encouraging employees to take on bold new challenges. As part of that philosophy, employees work under no official job descriptions, but simply do whatever they have to do to get a job done. Nucor encourages employees to stretch themselves in the pursuit of customer service by removing limits and emphasizing incentives. The interdependence promotes self-policing of workers' actions. If a worker's performance falls below par or he or she needs additional training to perform better, the group will identify the problem and bring it under control.

Heroic empowerment has given Nucor employees the ability to act independently *and* interdependently to make the company fast and flexible. As full partners, Nucor frontliners have fully invested themselves in the company's successes and its failures in a way that honors the tenets of the Medicine Circle.

Lead Through Strategic Humility

When it comes to empowerment, leading through strategic humility means stepping aside and letting the frontliners get involved in leading the company. As Melohn said in his book *The New Partnership,* "profit is generated by fellow employees, not *in spite of* them." Heroic Organizations recognize and live by this simple truth. NATD led through strategic humility by holding to the standard that "everyone is a boss," a view that awarded employees both the power to make their own decisions about how to work and the power to enact those decisions. The results have become legendary in business circles.

Texas Instruments also turned its culture around by leading through strategic humility, after defense cutbacks and tough competition in its other hi-tech markets forced it to reconsider the way it did work. For years TI frontliners had come to work with the attitude, "Put in your forty hours and clear out." The suggestion box collected only dust after the few intrepid souls who had made suggestions watched them waft away in bureaucratic committee smoke. The only ideas that mattered came from the front office. TI "grunts" had learned to keep their mouths shut and to expect little from the company and, eventually, from themselves.

That changed in the Eighties when, humbled by the defense industry crunch, TI's front office admitted that it did not know all the answers. Still, the situation had to become extreme before management tapped the hidden resources of TI's frontline employees. In 1991, the sudden exit of 1,200 executives who opted for an early retirement package designed for only half that many left TI executives with far more direct oversight than they could handle. Almost without a choice, they turned to the people on the factory floor for help.

TI started by creating work teams of frontliners who picked up the slack by scheduling their own jobs, ordering their own supplies, and tracking their own attendance. TI work teams proved more than self-reliant, they became self-motivated to improve the company by cutting waste, improving efficiency, and inventing innovative solutions that top management could never have devised, simply because they did not know that the problems existed. For example, one work team cut the time it took to make a bail ring from 13.8 hours to just 5.5 hours. Now, instead of micromanaging, TI executives know how to "get out of the way," and let the teams flourish.

Walk in a Sacred Manner

Walking in a sacred manner means making a heroic commitment to a protocol of behavior that enables the entire organization to succeed. NATD walked in a sacred manner by adhering to Melohn's simple, yet demanding dictum to adhere to the values of honesty, trust, and partnership—always. Federal Express Corporation, one of the world's most dependable service operations, walks in a sacred manner by following a protocol of employee development and participation that has yielded one of the most reliable workforces in any service industry.

From recruitment to assessment and grievance, Federal Express maintains a fully participative environment. The company's Peer Recruiter Program relies on employees within a discipline to interview candidates applying for positions within that group and to pass their recommendations on to management. The company also employs peer assessment when promoting people. Not only do Federal Express employees voice their opinions when choosing their leaders, they evaluate them during an annual survey, the results of which form a "Leadership Index." If employees don't rate management at least as highly as they rated them the year before, no managers receive a year-end bonus. Employee focus groups also work with managers to develop written plans of action to improve management practices.

The Board of Review offers yet another critical example of Federal Express frontliners' ability to take their destiny into their own hands. The Board, headed by CEO Frederick Smith, reviews employee grievances ranging from disputed performance reviews to termination. The commitment-generating power of the Board of Review and the Guaranteed Fair Treatment Procedure, which also addresses employee concerns, came into play in 1989 when the company took over Tiger International, an air freight carrier.

Recognizing the potential for conflict in absorbing an 85 percent unionized firm, Federal Express, with unions in only a few of its overseas branches, sent teams to Tiger facilities to interview pilots. They brought along a videotape that described what it's like to work for Federal Express and how the Guaranteed Fair Treatment Procedure helps ensure both fair and consistent treatment. Subsequently, both the Tiger and Federal Express pilots voted out the unions.

These formal communication procedures serve an obvious practical function, but they also deliver a more important message: they officially invite frontliners to participate in the company. Federal Express's success hinges on people wanting to go all out for the enterprise, and such a level of involvement can spring only from walking in a sacred manner.

CONCLUSION

Heroically empowering the frontlines represents both one of the most difficult and one of the most vital steps to achieving a vibrantly healthy organizational Medicine Circle. First and foremost, it requires trust, bridging perhaps one of the widest gulfs between management and the frontlines. As the heroic examples of NATD, Nucor, Federal Express, Texas Instruments, and others show, fully including frontliners in the Medicine Circle invigorates an organization beyond its competitive dreams, while at the same time serving the needs and priorities of all stakeholders within the Medicine Circle.

— 8 —

STAKEHOLDER:
Marketing

Door-to-door salespeople, telemarketing computers, junk mail, radio and television commercials, billboards, fax machines, computer bulletin boards, even stadium scoreboards . . . marketing messages blanket our daily experience. While some messages inform and amuse us, those that do not merely add more noise to a cacophony of "try this–buy this–now, for a limited time only, our operators are standing by." Marketing has perhaps become the most tarnished stakeholder in the Medicine Circle, with its greedy, self-serving, manipulative, and intrusive reputation. This not wholly undeserved reputation flows from decades of proliferating mass marketing campaigns that have alienated customers from the organizations that hope to supply them with products and services. However, the public distrust engendered by manipulative marketing techniques erodes quickly when replaced by the alternative of heroic marketing.

THE CONTEXT:
CONNECTING WITH THE CUSTOMER

In the organizational Medicine Circle, marketing connects a company with the customer, establishing a relationship in which customer feedback drives the organization's actions. Heroic marketers function not only as the eyes and ears of the organization, sensing how the organization can better serve customers, but as the organization's conscience, the voice that guides the organization's products and services to market. By paying close attention to the customer's voice, the Heroic Organization continuously improves whatever it sells, be it a paper clip, new desktop-publishing software, window washing, or financial services.

Heroic marketing does not exploit customers; it forms a cooperative relationship with them, defining marketing as a service, not merely as a means of moving product off the shelves. Heroic marketers gather information in an unending quest to give customers exactly what they want. They listen more than they talk as they strive to respect their customers, determine their needs, and create more compelling choices. By attending to the feedback loop, heroic marketing turns the organization into a truly customer-driven enterprise.

Today, information technology allows heroic marketers to reach out to customers individually on an unprecedented scale, drawing them closer to their customers and forging strong, one-on-one relationships with them. Spiegel's successful specialty catalog, *E Style,* offers a striking example of such relationship building. The Chicago-based direct-mail retailer created the catalog, aimed at black women, by using information technology to learn about its customer. The company began by advertising its catalog in *Ebony* and *Essence* magazines and building a mailing list of the women who responded. Then, using its database, Spiegel kept track of these customers' purchasing patterns, using what they bought as a guide for assembling a catalog with a specific appeal to African-American women, such as offering an unusually wide selection of hats. The resulting catalog succeeded resoundingly with sales running 50 percent above the company's original projections.

The Heroic Organization's commitment to the customer suggests a rethinking of the traditional position of marketing in a modern organization. Most organizations center their marketing efforts on products: product teams and product managers create goods and services that they then try to market to potential customers. The new model, on the other hand, focuses marketing efforts on customers. While the language hasn't become common—"customer manager," "customer team"—the practice of focusing on customers and their needs rather than on the product has proven quite successful for the companies that have pioneered it.

GM chose this approach when designing its new luxury car, the Aurora. The company had suffered a bitter disappointment when it learned that its lavishly designed new automobiles lost half of their customer appeal when test consumers learned they weren't driving a Lexus. That customer distrust had arisen due to GM's decades-old habit of ignoring customer input when designing its cars. The new Aurora signals that the company may have learned its lesson: Aurora's development team interviewed 4,200 consumers to find out precisely what they expected from a luxury car, and it conducted focus groups even before engineers drew up the first designs. The team also gathered owners of European luxury cars, including Mercedes-Benz and BMW, for a clinic during which they pinpointed preferred luxury car features. The best features of these cars became Aurora's benchmarks. By letting customers lead the way, GM began redefining itself as a customer-driven organization.

APPLYING THE HEROIC PROCESS TO MARKETING

The heroic marketer lets the customer define the product, and in so doing, sets the course for continuous improvement. As every marketer knows, as products get better, customer expectations grow higher. Only continuous improvement of the product and the processes behind it can keep the organization competing. In this sense, marketing not only brings products to market, it drives continuous improvement by enabling the organization to learn exactly how it must improve. Through the Seven-Step Heroic Process, organizations can constantly and continuously improve their relationships with customers.

The Heroic Process

1. Establish a Context for Action

2. Measure Mission Effectiveness

3. Identify Opportunities for Improvement

4. Mobilize Support

5. Take Action

6. Evaluate Results

7. Repeat the Process Continuously

Rubbermaid, Inc., provides a good example of how one heroic organization has achieved continuous learning and self improvement through marketing.

CASE STUDY: RUBBERMAID, INC.

Sixty years ago, Wooster Rubber Company took a mighty gamble when it decided to diversify from its toy balloon business into manufacturing housewares. The company started small, making rubber dustpans, drain board mats, soap dishes, and sink stoppers, but that first step marked the beginning of a journey that would eventually transform the company, turning the maker of what would come to be known as "the billion dollar dustpan" into a world-class organization.

Today, Rubbermaid, Inc., still makes dustpans and other practical household products. Though now the prosaic dustpan comes in an array of designer colors, it retains the aura of top quality, an aura held securely in place by the Rubbermaid name. As a reminder of its roots, the company keeps its original rubber dustpan protected behind glass at headquarters. That dustpan symbolizes the key to Rubbermaid's success—the ability to make ordinary products extraordinary. A self-termed "marketing machine," Rubbermaid bases its success on its commitment to redesigning itself and its products continuously. It constantly reinvents itself to meet customer needs, concentrating as much on finding new and innovative uses for its existing products as it does on creating new products for new markets.

This commitment has propelled over forty consecutive years of record sales for the company, which skyrocketed a whopping 400 percent in the last decade alone. Rubbermaid's steady success earned it the distinction of being selected as America's most admired company by *Fortune* magazine in 1994.

Rubbermaid strives for excellence in every arena in which it competes, but the company particularly excels at marketing. A few statistics tell the story: Rubbermaid enters a new product category every twelve to eighteen months, obtains 33 percent of sales from products introduced in the past five years, and expects by the year 2000 to be getting 25 percent of total revenues from markets outside the United States. The company turns out new (not just improved) products at the rate of one a day, and nine out of ten of these products meet their commercial targets. While company leadership loudly touts its commitment to dispelling complacency and remaining constantly inventive, you won't find much complacency in the day-to-day workings of the organization. Rubbermaid embraces the philosophy of the Heroic Organization through continuous self-examination and incremental improvement at all levels, all of the time, and it religiously follows the precepts of the Seven-Step Heroic Process.

The *context* of continuous improvement so thoroughly surrounds Rubbermaid, it inspires the company's employee stakeholders every hour of every day. The company values its human resources as its single greatest strength; capable and dedicated employee stakeholders and their shared sense of context make the daily difference in Rubbermaid's success. Everyone at Rubbermaid understands what it takes to stay on top: True commitment to customers and continuous innovation. The company dedicates cross-functional teams made up of employees from marketing, manufacturing, R & D, finance, and other departments to improve specific product lines continually, and the results range from obvious customer aids such as the phone numbers of local waste recyclers printed on Rubbermaid oil-changing pans, to subtle helpful designs such as laundry baskets ergonomically engineered to fit against the waist for easy carrying and the world's only antimicrobial mop bucket. The context: improve everything, no matter how mundane, and do it steadily.

The context of continuous improvement goes right to the top of the organization. At a 1992 trade show, CEO Wolf Schmitt praised his favorite new product: a laundry basket redesigned with a reinforced top lip and handles. To Schmitt, this small detail represented the company's commitment to keep improving itself, its products, its services, and its people, in every nook and cranny of the organization.

Customer service represents another top Rubbermaid priority. The company strives to overcome barriers of size and offer the kind of service you might expect from a local business. For instance, in many home-products categories, consumers recognize no other brand name. This market strength has resulted in some erroneous complaints: When customers buy a poorly made no-name mop that breaks, they can think only of Rubbermaid and consequently send Rubbermaid nasty letters. Amazingly, Rubbermaid replaces those products free and wins better informed and dedicated customers. Former CEO Stanley Gault tried to resolve Rubbermaid's predicament in an interview with *Industry Week*: "Please make certain that every time you buy a plastic product, you look for our name. If we make it, our name is on it. But because you did mean to buy ours and made a mistake, and will not do so in the future, here, have one on us."

Rubbermaid's highly evolved customer focus provides the key to heroic marketing, which entails knowing their customers intimately and honoring their position in the organizational Medicine Circle. Only that knowledge and respect can marshal the tightly focused, personalized marketing today's consumers demand. In 1991, Chevrolet successfully used such customer-focused tactics in marketing its new Caprice, mailing out 175,000 disposable videotapes promoting the product to older drivers who owned five- or six-year-old luxury cars. The company deliberately targeted potential customers who already owned luxury cars but were frugal enough to keep them for five or six years. By targeting older consumers, the company also reached people who remembered Chevy's glory days. These potential customers weren't anonymous names on a mailing list, but people Chevrolet knew it wanted to reach. By knowing and honoring its customers, Chevrolet launched a unique, meaningful, and fruitful campaign.

Marketers keep themselves honest by *measuring mission effectiveness,* learning about the organization by asking stakeholders inside and outside the organization for their input. Rubbermaid works a two-way street: inviting customer input and keeping customers informed. This habit of self-examination began in the early 1980s when Stanley

Gault took the organization's helm. At the outset, he reorganized the company around corporate strengths, in the process shedding unprofitable divisions and centering energy on successful operations. Rubbermaid has since concentrated on its strengths, in the process establishing a culture of constant self-examination. This culture has yielded employees as eager to point out money-saving manufacturing techniques as they are to call up customers and ask how satisfied they feel with their Rubbermaid purchases.

Internally, Rubbermaid keeps in touch with every worker, promoting respect for the interdependency of all of the stakeholders in the organization. Knowing that only strong interdependent connections can enable the company to flourish, the company encourages workers to go beyond the confines of their daily jobs and create new products or accomplish existing tasks more productively. Employees enjoy the autonomy they need to get things done, and they know that management will listen to all their concerns and ideas. Rubbermaid also completes the feedback loop by keeping employees informed about the success of their ideas (one employee's idea to recover scraps that fall from molds has saved the company millions of dollars).

Rubbermaid connects with outside stakeholders by making twenty to twenty-five corporate presentations a year to financial analysts. As a result, the buy recommendations continue, fulfilling the company's stated mission to maximize the value of the company for shareholders. And, the company keeps in touch with customer needs by analyzing cultural trends such as mounting environmental concerns, the growth in home offices, and changing entertainment tastes, invariably coming up with products that meet those needs, such as Litterless Lunchboxes and a new line of bird feeders.

To attract more customers, Rubbermaid works closely with retailer stakeholders to design new marketing programs. Its strong relationships with retailers allow the company to try innovative marketing techniques that retailers might not risk on companies to whom they felt less allegiance. For example, department stores have set up "Everything Rubbermaid" store-within-a-store "boutiques" that create a distinctive space for Rubbermaid products. "Everything Rubbermaid" improves brand-name recognition and increases impulse purchases. Retailers benefit because customers tend to go to housewares sections to find specific items and/or brands, and Rubbermaid has made it very easy for them to set up displays and gain greater profits per square foot. Rubbermaid has further articulated its commitment to retailer stakeholders with its "Invincible Customer Service" (ICS) program, with which employees meet retailers' needs by compressing turnaround time, making faster deliveries, and improving service fill rates.

Identifying opportunities for improvement has become an ingrained attribute of Rubbermaid's corporate culture, but the company does much more than look for trouble spots; it continually strives to identify areas where improvements will contribute most to customer satisfaction. Since Rubbermaid must work tirelessly to differentiate its products from those of its 150 competitors, it keeps samples of competing products in its "War Room" at company headquarters. These rival products serve both as benchmarks and as marketing tools to demonstrate to visiting retailers the superiority of Rubbermaid's own products.

Rubbermaid goes to great lengths improving products that other companies dismiss as too basic to bother reworking. The lowly, uninspiring mailbox, for example, triggered a burst of creativity in one Rubbermaid team, which reinvented the Rubbermaid mailbox with a double-width floor that lets magazines lie flat, an overhang over the door that keeps rain out, and a flag that automatically pops up when mail has arrived. Other product ideas come from customer focus groups. A team reinvented toothbrush holders when a focus group of mothers revealed that they disliked the fact that the average toothbrush holder allowed their family's toothbrushes to touch each other. Consequently, Rubbermaid's new holder positions toothbrushes at oblique angles that keep them from touching. Rubbermaid added a dispenser for holding a shampoo bottle upside down to its shower caddie because consumers expressed a desire to squeeze the last drop from the bottle but a disdain for standing in the shower and shaking out those last drops.

Rubbermaid also knows how to leverage greater sales from its products by recreating a single product to give it multiple identities. For example, it sells the Rubbermaid Action Packer, a sturdy two-tone crate, to automotive stores in an industrial shade of charcoal. In a marine shop, customers will find the same box available in crisp nautical white for storing rope and other boating supplies. Department stores sell the box in pink and green for college students, and in a tan version that matches homeowners' decks. Product managers know that few customers will ever recognize the product's multiple personalities, because they each buy it for a specific need.

Rubbermaid's Continuous Value Improvement Process (CVIP) articulates the company's commitment to *mobilize support* and prepares employees to excel. As part of the CVIP process, all Rubbermaid associates receive a minimum of thirty hours of training so they can better contribute to the quality and productivity of the company and its teams. CVIP training not only connects employees with the Rubbermaid culture of self-improvement, it enables individuals to become productive members of the organization's circle of interactive stakeholders. A second tier of mobilization occurs in Rubbermaid's Management Information Services Department. MIS provides insight for the company's core Housewares Division by transforming raw sales data into accurate, timely, accessible information that allows managers to monitor consumer trends and predict market changes. Timely information translates into timely action.

With good information in hand, Rubbermaid teams *take action* to improve the company by generating new product ideas and enhancements. One team, the Rubbermaid Specialty Products group, goes on daylong reconnaissance mission trips to stores every month to scout out new product opportunities. At the end of the day, the group gathers at a local diner to discuss products they can improve and opportunities they can seize. These cross-functional teams promote cross-fertilization of ideas, a phenomenon that becomes almost frenzied at annual company-wide product meetings, one of which yielded 2,000 new product ideas in *one day.*

Rubbermaid marketers also study cultural trends and apply them to their product divisions. For example, responding to statistics about the most rapidly growing segment of the American population, the elderly, Rubbermaid decided to capitalize on products that met the unique needs of that niche. The result: an increase in the company's line of storage products, a division now growing at a rate of 15 percent annually. The company encouraged other divisions to approach this market as well, increasing the redesigning of products to appeal to elderly people. One division reincarnated the wheelbarrow as the Easy Rider, a lighter vehicle with two front wheels, easier to handle than typical wheelbarrows. That redesigned product succeeded so well, it prompted a spin-off, the Rough Rider, a heavy-duty alternative to ordinary, garden-variety wheelbarrows.

Rubbermaid breaks into new product categories by making its products so much better that customers cannot possibly ignore them. Paying attention to even the smallest details, teams constantly pile on useful and appealing features, often with no market testing beyond the focus groups. This nimbleness both helps forestall competitive copying and puts pressure on teams to get it right the first time. With a new-product success rate of about 90 percent, the strategy has paid off handsomely.

Not all marketers can do it the way Rubbermaid does. Rubbermaid enjoys a base of well-established products, few of which raise the pulse rate in the average consumer. Companies trying to break new ground with new products might adopt a radically different marketing approach, such as the one mounted by game maker Sega of America. Since Sega caters to the MTV generation, its video games must keep pace with the mercurial whims of a teenage market. To stay in touch, Sega conducts intensive one-on-one market research, holding two or three focus groups with teenagers weekly. The company's marketers also keep in close contact with about 150 teenagers with whom they take occasional shopping trips or play a few rounds of *Sonic*. The company parlays what it learns about its customers into new games, which it introduces at the frenetic rate of over sixty a year. By keeping its fingers on the pulse of its buyers, the company manages to meet its customers' ever-changing, ever-rising expectations. Nimbleness pays off for Rubbermaid, thoroughness pays off for Sega.

Evaluating results presents the moment of truth for heroic organizations when they ask, "Did we accomplish what we set out to do? If so, let's not rest on our laurels. If not, let's fix it." Rubbermaid views every product flaw as an opportunity, every market trend as a possibility. Its heroic commitment to continuous improvement is exemplified by its Partnership Teams, internal teams that work with retail "partners." Several practical principles guide these team-retailer partnerships: Clarifying the objective, simplifying the process, seeking true innovation, and establishing a relationship based on trust. Such principles reflect true organizational heroism: Build heroic partnerships, walk in a sacred manner, and lead through strategic humility.

Rubbermaid forges heroic partnerships by partnering with retailer stakeholders, it walks in a sacred manner by developing processes with which to create and enhance those relationships, and it practices strategic humility by choosing a relationship of trust and cooperation rather than one of suspicion and coercion. CEO Wolf Schmitt acknowledges that the level of partnership varies from customer to customer, and that the company cannot afford to ignore the need to improve every relationship. He has described the partnership relationship as a rheostat you can turn up gradually rather than an on-off switch. This philosophy of progress sums up the heroic imperative behind Rubbermaid's marketing success: continuous self-evaluation and incremental improvement in the service of the customer.

CHOOSING HEROISM

Marketing chooses heroism when it becomes the organization's conscience, putting the needs of the customer first, guiding the organization's choices, and providing the impetus for continuous improvement. The path of nonheroism throws useless products at harassed customers, only justifying those customers' cynicism and distrust. Those who choose the heroic path make a commitment to all their customers to honor them with true service that anticipates their needs and exceeds their expectations. Any marketer can embark on that path by applying the three principles of *Cangleska Wakan*.

Build Heroic Partnerships

Organizations can build heroic marketing partnerships with customers in two ways, directly, as Rubbermaid does with its retailer customers, and indirectly, within the organization itself. Rubbermaid dedicates teams to work directly with retailers to meet their unique needs. Whether by creating a unique selling space or by redesigning products in custom colors for one retailer only, Rubbermaid recognizes its ongoing interdependence with its customer and puts that customer's needs first. Think of it as "customer management," whereby your company shapes its product to meet the needs of your customer rather than focusing on creating a product and then seeking a customer for it.

Companies that directly partner with customers include Saturn Corporation, which has adopted a unique personal approach to marketing its vehicles. Using customer testimonies in advertisements and emphasizing personal service, Saturn has managed to live up to its slogan, "A new kind of car, a new kind of company," and it currently enjoys customer relations that rank among the best in its industry. The personal touch extended to inviting 600,000 Saturn owners to a 1994 summer weekend "homecoming" at the plant where GM builds the cars. The event included plant tours, celebrity spokespersons, concerts, and the sort of exposure that stimulates word-of-mouth advertising. Now, after Saturn's success, other car companies are striving to "Saturnize" their operations and create similar deep and lasting relationships with their customers.

Internally, a company can construct heroic marketing partnerships on the organizational level that will benefit the customer. Novell, Inc., the country's leading maker of computer network applications, demonstrated its commitment to heroic partnerships when it engineered a stock-swap merger with WordPerfect Corp., the country's number-one word-processing software firm, and then purchased the Quatro Pro spreadsheet line of Borland International, Inc., uniting the three under one umbrella in order to market them in packaged programs for businesses and consumers. Novell's plan to bundle the programs and sell them as a unit not only creates value for the customer, but it mounts a challenge to industry leaders Microsoft and Lotus Development Corp., which also bundle together their word processing, spreadsheet, and database products.

Walk in a Sacred Manner

Marketers can walk in a sacred manner by fulfilling the commitment to know their customers' needs through a formal, planned process. When they aim to serve the customer, nothing can substitute for the thoroughness of planning. Fly-by-night marketing schemes represent nothing more than hit-or-miss shots in the dark that yield little for customers or the organization. Heroic marketers tackle the complex, demanding task of learning their customers' needs intimately, and by doing so, improve the organization's ability to serve.

Black & Decker set an example of walking in a sacred manner when it launched its new line of Quantum power tools. The company decided to create the line after learning about an emerging market: a growing number of advanced "do-it-yourselfers" who were taking on complex home-improvement jobs, such as building decks.

These potential customers needed more than a low-end $25 electric screwdriver, but they didn't want to invest in pricey professional-quality tools. Black & Decker, which had developed no tools to meet the needs of these nonprofessionals, found itself funneling business to competitors. However, the company knew that starting from its current position, it must do more than simply offer tools that did the same thing as their competitors'; they needed a superior product, and they could create it only by getting to know their customer better than anyone else in the industry did.

To start, the company hired an independent research firm, charging it to locate fifty male homeowners, ages twenty-five to fifty-four, who owned more than six power tools. These fifty men became Black & Decker's marketing laboratory. For four months, Black & Decker marketing executives watched these men in their workshops, asking what they liked or disliked about certain tools, accompanied them on shopping trips to see what they bought and how much they spent, and sometimes even brought an industrial psychologist along to learn yet more about these potential customers' buying decisions. Black & Decker buttressed this in-depth market research with hundreds of interviews with current Black & Decker customers. The research not only shaped the product line in terms of its capabilities, but yielded innovations that differentiated the line from competitors', such as an auto-braking system on power-saw blades that stopped the blades' spinning within two seconds of shut-off, and a sander and circular saw equipped with mini-vacuum bags that inhaled sawdust instead of letting it spill loose.

The resulting Quantum power tool line has exceeded Black & Decker's performance expectations. And, having gone to such lengths to learn about its customer, the company has dedicated itself to staying in touch. Two months after Black & Decker launched the product line, it commenced a three-day phone-a-thon with the goal of reaching 2,500 people to hear their thoughts about Quantum. The company also flew nearly 200 employees from around the world, everyone from assembly-line workers to marketing executives, into the company's Towson, Maryland, headquarters to work the phones. Black & Decker wanted everyone associated with Quantum to hear what the customer had to say firsthand. By walking in a sacred manner, Black & Decker accomplished the most heroic level of marketing: letting the customer lead the organization.

Lead Through Strategic Humility

For the marketing stakeholder, leading through strategic humility means recognizing market forces and accepting accountability for readying the organization to exploit those forces successfully. Organizations that arrogantly resist learning about market forces and choose to turn a blind eye to them risk the fate of stumbling monolith IBM. The IBM debacle shines as a casebook example of arrogance preceding a fall. IBM resisted the major market force that customers preferred relatively inexpensive personal computers, choosing instead to work to protect its lucrative mainframe market. After all, how far would the personal computer go without IBM's backing? As a result, IBM left the market opportunity wide open, and then, when it finally did read forces correctly and got into personal computers, it chose to underplay the significance of PCs by farming out operating systems and microprocessors to then-fledgling Microsoft and Intel.

In contrast, heroic marketers pay close attention to the winds of change in the market. Motorola, for instance, has successfully employed strategic humility to stay ahead in the rapidly evolving world of telecommunications. A renowned leader in quality, the Baldrige-award-winning company has pioneered advances in self-directed work teams, training, and business process reengineering, but has not let its tremendous success invite arrogance. In fact, the company fights complacency by working to keep its employees dissatisfied with the status quo and ready to change whenever needed. This attitude enables the company to renew itself in an industry continually reinventing itself.

You can see proof of Motorola's ability to lead through strategic humility when you examine its choice to promote a new kind of wireless digital communication technology, Motorola Integrated Radio Service (MIRS). This technology combines the features of cellular phones, pagers, and two-way radios into one hand-held instrument. The technology, which uses different frequencies from that of cellular phones, competes dead-on with cellular phone companies, currently Motorola's biggest and best customers. Essentially, then, one Motorola division is working to undermine the prized products and customers of another division, because Motorola believes in creative destruction—obsoleting its own products to stay ahead. The radio service industry will come into being with or without Motorola.

Rather than sit on its hands, the company has set itself up to assume a dominant position in the new industry. By doing so, the company has acknowledged that its cellular technology, advanced as it is, will not provide the last best answer in communication technology. If IBM had been as willing to threaten its own products, it might have avoided its painful decline into obsolescence. After all, a threatened product line doesn't have to lie down and die. At Motorola, the cellular phones division has already begun working on refining technologies that will rival MIRS. Leading through strategic humility, Motorola has created a pattern of continuous improvement and self-renewal by challenging its own dominance.

CONCLUSION

Building heroic partnerships, walking in a sacred manner, and leading through strategic humility can each help connect marketers to their customers. In this regard, marketing, more than any other stakeholder, can help the organization better understand itself and how it can fulfill its overriding purpose: to serve the customer. Heroic marketers defy the stereotypes of greed and manipulation, redefining the concept of marketing as a customer-driven function. By enabling the organization to follow the customers' lead, marketing brings surefootedness to the organization's journey down the path of heroism.

— 9 —

STAKEHOLDER:
The Environment

In a talk to the Portland, Oregon, Angler's Club as part of its twenty-fifth Anniversary celebration, novelist David James Duncan spoke of the importance of contemporary people in industrialized nations adopting the perspective of "native" or "primitive" peoples. By native, David meant "close to the land," and when he used the term "primitive," he employed it in the same sense as the poet Gary Snyder suggests we use it: "The root of the word is 'primary'—the most primitive things, then, are the most basic and essential; things like water, earth, fire, air; things we die instantly without."

To illustrate his point, he cited the example of the Makuna, a Neolithic band of natives living in southeastern Colombia. "The Makuna," he told his audience, "maintain that humans, animals, and all of nature are parts of the same great One—with a capital 'O.' Our ancestors, they say, were magical fish who came ashore along the rivers and turned two-legged. As a result of the songs and actions of these first land beings, everything in the world began to be created: hills and forests, animals and bird people, insect and fish people. And—here's the part I really begin to like—*the creation of the world is never over.*"

How beautifully this captures the spirit of the Sioux concept of the Hoop, with all elements of the environment inextricably bound together and continuously joining forces to create the world in which people live. All people, corporations included, bear responsibility for creating a healthy, life-sustaining world. "According to the Makuna," David concluded, "our oneness with other species . . . is a spiritual responsibility."

ACCEPTING ENVIRONMENTAL ACCOUNTABILITY

The Exxon *Valdez*. Bophal. Three-mile Island. The mere mention of these phrases conjures up images of befouled and dying otters, raging funeral pyres, and human babies born tragically damaged and deformed. The major environmental catastrophes of the past decade created bold headlines that seared into our consciousness and forever linked a huge oil company, a global chemical manufacturer, and the operator of a nuclear power plant with environmental irresponsibility, but every day companies both large and small commit less newsworthy damage, dispersing the by-products of production into the air, water, and earth that sustains all life, overflowing landfills with unnecessary and nondegradable packaging, and depleting finite natural resources, all in the name of commerce.

No stakeholder played a greater role in the Sacred Hoop of Sioux philosophy than the land, and no organizational stakeholder occupies a more important niche in the Heroic Organization's Medicine Circle than the environment from which it draws its resources. No longer can a company ignore its responsibility for protecting the environment, for in a world of polluted rivers, smog-infested cities, and a scarred and infertile landscape, business will choke and die along with the salmon, the eagle, and the fox.

In the process of creating and fulfilling the demands of global consumerism, the world's business organizations have wreaked havoc on the environment with an arrogance that threatens to impoverish and poison communities worldwide. Whether in the form of toxic fumes in the air, depletion of the ozone layer, desertification, radioactive chemicals buried underground, "red tides," or acid rain, companies can no longer consider environmental damage a local problem, wherever it occurs. Every act of environmental irresponsibility, every molecule of toxic waste, every thoughtlessly packaged product affects every organizational stakeholder. As we approach the twenty-first century, an era that could easily conclude with wide-scale environmental devastation, organizations must reevaluate their critical relationship with the world in which they operate and work tirelessly to interact with it in a more enlightened way.

Fully incorporating the environment into the organizational Medicine Circle requires a major shift in perspective for most organizations. Traditionally, organizational leaders mistakenly assumed that they could draw from an unlimited supply of natural resources and that they could not afford to clean up the by-products of production. From this perspective, protecting the environment threatened the bottom line. Today, however, no one can escape the fact that an ethic of continuous growth and consumption that does not heed the impact of that growth on the environment will ultimately ruin the bottom line. Still, all too many business people look at protected wetlands forbidden to developers or waste disposal regulations that subtract from short-term profits as negative rather than as positive conditions. This perspective leads to a definition of environmental protection as an enemy, a barrier an enterprise must overcome or conquer. The exploitative viewpoint has dominated corporate thinking for so long, it has badly disrupted the balance of the Hoop, a fact that not even the most environmentally insensitive executive can any longer ignore.

The perspective of the Hoop begins with a simple truth: Without the environment, no organization would even exist. And it ends with a simple realization: Without a healthy environment, growth and profitability will fade. In years past, a company may have been able to sustain continuous growth without accounting for environmental factors, but as the industrial world has expanded and the demands placed upon the environment have become unsustainable, a company that ignores the environment will end up committing organizational suicide. Ironically, most environmental destruction is needless. Companies do, in fact, possess the means to create a sustainable and harmonious relationship with the environment.

Consider the compelling reasons for including the environment in the organizational Medicine Circle: The world is losing 108 million acres of productive agricultural land and 25 billion tons of topsoil to degradation annually; experts estimate annual worldwide crop losses due to pollution at between 5 and 10 percent and rising;

74 species of plants and animals become extinct each day—1 every 20 minutes; 90,000 hazardous waste sites dot the U.S. landscape alone, and just one of these, a nuclear weapons research facility in Hanford, Washington, stores enough waste to cover all of Manhattan with a radioactive lake 40 feet deep. The situation has gotten so out of control that many scientists speculate that before long environmental degradation will become self-perpetrating—that is, it will self-destruct despite all our efforts to reverse the process.

Given this danger to our planet and ourselves, organizations must begin holding themselves fully accountable for the damage they inflict on the environment. The good old American ethic of "use it up and throw it away" has created a problem of such magnitude that we could actually be throwing our collective future away. While individual activists and environmental organizations such as the Sierra Club and The Nature Conservancy work tirelessly to remind us of the importance of environmental responsibility, little will change until businesses shoulder their full share of the burden. The widely touted Earth Day and the growing popularity of recycling centers in our communities will accomplish nothing if businesses continue to consume resources needlessly, all the while pumping waste into the atmosphere, the water, and the ground. The Hoop offers the only solution: those who have made the mess must clean it up.

As with all corporate strategies, you can adopt one of two postures: act, or be acted upon. Create your own future, or someone else will create it for or impose it on you. The Heroic Organization does not wait for regulators to force environmental action, but, rather, takes the initiative long before public outcry stimulates regulation and legislation. So few companies took the heroic approach to air pollution that in 1992 the Environmental Protection Agency introduced "air pollution credits," a tactic aimed at curbing air pollution within the guidelines set by the Federal Clean Air Act. Under this program, companies that pollute the air with sulfur dioxide, which causes acid rain, must buy credits for each ton of pollution they emit. With fewer credits available at auction each year, companies must take the initiative in limiting the sulfur dioxide their factories expel. Companies can sell their unused credits to other, heavier polluters. By requiring polluters to buy a limited number of permits, the EPA hopes to cut annual sulfur dioxide emissions in half, to about nine million tons, by the year 2000. While these efforts have come under fire as discouraging polluters from choosing alternative pollution control devices, they do stimulate a certain amount of organizational accountability, a trend that will surely grow in the future.

Local communities can also force greater corporate environmental accountability. In a landmark case, the town of Sanger, California, won a $15 million settlement from three chemical companies, Dow Chemical Co., Shell Oil Co., and Occidental Chemical Corp., for DBCP contamination of its drinking-water wells. Although the pesticide DBCP, which causes sterility and cancer, was banned in 1977, it has continued to sift through the sandy soils and into the water table in the San Joaquin Valley. When the problem became known, the town of Sanger demanded that the polluting companies assume responsibility for cleaning up the water supply. For the first time, a community held chemical companies responsible for contamination caused by "normal" farming practices, a legal precedent organizations should take to heart before they find themselves mired in lawsuits.

Protecting the environment has become much more than what some organizational leaders like to disparage as "ecocentrism," as issues of health and safety have attracted the concern of the public at large. As the effects of environmental damage hit the top of the food chain, consumers increasingly voice their outrage over the arrogant attitudes of the companies that have inflicted the damage. Finally, consumers have begun to insist that organizations own the waste they create, reasoning correctly that organizations held accountable for their actions will feel motivated to reduce the amount of waste they produce.

Contrary to the old fear, changing your business practices to reduce or prevent damage to the environment does not thwart growth. In fact, as some companies have learned, learning to control waste can actually improve the bottom line dramatically. 3M, one of the most admired companies in America, turned a commitment to the environment into a $537 million profit. 3M's Pollution Prevention Pays program, started in 1975, created incentives for technical staff to modify product manufacturing methods to prevent hazardous and toxic waste and to reduce costs. Between 1975 and 1990, by pursuing more than 3,000 employee-driven initiatives, 3M reduced its air pollution by 120,000 tons, its waste water by 1 billion gallons, and its solid waste by 410,000 tons. The company has now incorporated environmental concerns into all levels of business planning, including employee performance reviews.

Waste management has been turning profits in other areas as well. In 1994, the Chicago Board of Trade began listing recycled waste on its exchange. Under the CBT system, communities, states, waste haulers, and other trash sellers can enter information about their available recyclables into on-line computers. Potential buyers can then access the database to find out what's for sale. This free-market approach helps alleviate the burden on communities to make recycling cost-efficient, while helping businesses locate the materials they need. It also benefits businesses by regulating the industry, and acting as an oversight agency to guarantee quality and enforce contracts. CBT inspectors evaluate goods for sale, just as they would for the corn, wheat, and other commodities sold on the exchange daily. Eventually, CBT plans to consider trading futures contracts on recyclable materials. CBT's efforts, while certainly profit-motivated, represent a new way of thinking about how organizations handle their waste.

A truly Heroic Organization accepts accountability to *all* of its stakeholders. In the case of the environment, the opposite has usually held true. If organizations actually held themselves accountable for the costs of their actions on the environment and the costs of related health-care and environmental restoration, they would be reflecting the true relationships in the Medicine Circle. As Paul Hawken observed in his book, *The Ecology of Commerce* (Harper Collins: 1993):

> Markets are superb at setting prices, but incapable of recognizing costs. Today we have free markets that cause harm and suffering to both natural and human communities because the market does not reflect the true costs of products and services. . . . Gasoline is cheap in the United States because its price does not reflect the cost of smog, acid rain, and their subsequent effects on health and the environment. Likewise, American food is the cheapest in the world, but the price does not reflect the fact that we have depleted the soil, reducing average topsoil from a depth of twenty-one to six inches over the past hundred years, contaminated our ground water (farmers do not drink from wells in Iowa), and poisoned wildlife through use of pesticides. . . .
>
> [C]oncern about higher costs to consumers ignores the fact that we consumers are already paying the costs in the form of higher health costs, both individually and through higher insurance premiums; in

the form of mitigation costs to cleanup toxic waste sites; in the form of lost economic output; and in the form of environmental degradation, which drives up the cost of resources.

APPLYING THE HEROIC PROCESS
TO THE ENVIRONMENT

Despite some evidence of growing corporate awareness, the environment remains a neglected stakeholder in the minds of most business people. Few offer examples of heroic action in this area, and fewer still acknowledge the uniqueness and fragility of this stakeholder relationship. After so many years of taking, the relationship cries out for giving. The Seven-Step Heroic Process provides a blueprint for successfully integrating the environment into the organizational Medicine Circle.

THE HEROIC PROCESS

1. Establish a Context for Action
2. Measure Mission Effectiveness
3. Identify Opportunities for Improvement
4. Mobilize Support
5. Take Action
6. Evaluate Results
7. Repeat the Process Continuously

One organization that has shown remarkable heroism with respect to the environment is Ben & Jerry's Homemade Ice Cream, and the company did so by applying the seven steps of the Heroic Process.

CASE STUDY:
BEN & JERRY'S

When it comes to giving back to the environment, few organizations can match Ben & Jerry's. Headed by Ben Cohen and Jerry

Greenfield, this off-beat ice cream maker puts its money behind its heart, implementing rather than just paying lip service to its corporate philosophy of "caring capitalism." Beyond Ben & Jerry's generous philanthropic agenda and active support of numerous charities, the company's everyday actions support the values of respect and reciprocity on all levels of business—from contracting with ecologically responsible suppliers to replanting the trees the firm uses to make sticks for its ice cream bars.

Cohen and Greenfield started their ice cream operation in an abandoned Vermont gas station in 1978. Fulfilling their humble hope of remaining in business for one full year, they commemorated the occasion by giving away free ice cream cones. From that gesture onward, the company and its generous business habits began to thrive. Today, the ice cream company does $100 million a year in business, and it still gives away ice cream—tons of it—to charities all over the country. But that sort of charity represents the mere tip of the iceberg. Cohen and Greenfield have incorporated values of corporate responsibility into everything their company does.

Not surprisingly, atop this atypical corporation sits an atypical CEO, Ben Cohen. A product of Sixties counterculture, Cohen flirted with selling his thriving business in 1983 when he felt that his success was turning him into a "businessman," a stereotype that, to him, meant selling out his ideals. However, a friend, company President Fred "Chico" Lager, convinced Cohen that a CEO need not be a product of a company environment, but could, in fact, produce a very different kind of company in his own image. If Cohen didn't like something about the business, he could change it, and in the process could create something good. Cohen decided to translate his ideals into a new kind of organization, one formed on the principles he and his partner upheld in their daily lives. Then and there the two *established the context* by which they would run their company. They expected every employee in the company (only 44 people at the time, but with a growth rate topping 100 percent annually, soon to grow to 500) not only to uphold those values, but to build them into all business decisions.

Early on, Cohen and Greenfield created Ben & Jerry's Statement of Mission, which dedicates the firm "to the creation and demonstration of a new corporate concept of *linked prosperity*." The concept of linked prosperity often creates a unique corporate agenda at Ben & Jerry's. For example, the concept prompted Cohen to share his company's success with the Vermont community in which it operated. When the company needed to expand, it sponsored a Vermont-only public stock offering available only to state residents. By allowing a low minimum investment of only $126, the company made ownership available to almost anyone who wanted a piece of the action. Only later, facing even greater expansion demands, did Ben & Jerry's initiate a traditional public offering.

Ben & Jerry's mission consists of three interrelated parts. Like most companies, Ben & Jerry's pursues a product mission (to make, distribute, and sell the finest-quality ice cream), and an economic mission (to operate the company on a sound financial basis). Unlike most companies, however, Ben & Jerry's also carries out a social mission (to operate the company in a way that actively recognizes the central role that business can play in the structure of society by initiating innovations to improve the quality of life). This aspect of the mission statement prompts the company to purchase raw materials that aid both the environment and the causes the company supports, and it has resulted in ice cream flavors such as "Rain Forest Crunch," which uses nuts from the Amazon rain forest purchased from a company that donates 60 percent of its profits to environmental organizations. "Chocolate Fudge Brownie" ice cream incorporates brownies baked by the Greystone Bakery in Yonkers, New York, a company that uses its profits to house the homeless and train them as bakers. "Wild Maine Blueberry" ice cream results from a contract to buy $330,000 worth of fresh berries from the economically disadvantaged Passamaquoddy Indians in Maine. And "Fresh Georgia Peach" ice cream includes peaches grown by family-owned farms in Georgia. In an interview for the company's profile in *Companies with a Conscience* (Scott and Rothman: Birch Lane Press, 1992), Cohen asserts, "This act—just consciously sourcing our ingredients, even though it might cost us more than somewhere else— ends up bringing about a more positive benefit than probably all of the money that we give away through our foundation."

By choosing vendors who share the company's concern for the environment, Ben & Jerry's chooses accountability. By paying more for their supplies, they absorb the cost of sustaining the environment responsibly. Today, most companies operate in an artificial comfort zone that buffers them from the actual environmental costs of making their products. This, in turn, artificially protects consumers from the impact of their purchasing decisions. Instead of paying at the cash register, consumers pay taxes to support government efforts such as the marginally effective Superfund cleanup law. Far more critically, they also pay in terms of health risks: rising rates of brain, skin, and breast cancer and declining male fertility worldwide. A laissez-faire attitude toward the environment can end up costing more than a fortune; it can cost lives.

Following Ben & Jerry's example, companies can learn how to prosper without accruing the hidden human costs of environmental heedlessness. Internally, you must capture your vision in a mission statement all stakeholders can understand and respect. You can begin by choosing responsible suppliers who reflect your own values or who support some other ethic of accountability you admire. Large corporations, particularly, can make a significant difference by channeling their buying dollars toward ecologically responsible suppliers, creating a domino effect of environmental support as suppliers vie with one another to meet the organization's standards. Every organization bears the responsibility of its choices; Heroic Organizations make those choices count throughout the community of stakeholders.

Ben & Jerry's deeply involves its employees in the organization's choices. The company *measures mission effectiveness* by obtaining employees' input on how to make the company more socially responsible and on how to direct the funds the company sets aside for charitable causes. In 1985, Cohen and Greenfield created the nonprofit Ben & Jerry's foundation to do just that. Initially established through a donation of company stock, the foundation "supports projects which are models for social change; projects infused with a spirit of generosity and hopefulness; projects which enhance people's quality of life; and projects which exhibit creative problem solving." Cohen and Greenfield established the foundation for two reasons: to illuminate their commitment to the environment and the community and to meet their obligations to their new stockholders. In this way, the company honors its fiscal responsibility to its stockholders, while at the same time serving the causes in which the founders believe. Since its inception, the Ben & Jerry's foundation has benefited from an annual donation of 7.5 percent of Ben & Jerry's pretax profits ($528,000 in 1991).

The foundation stands as only one example of Ben & Jerry's philanthropy. Company employees have joined to create the Employee Community Fund, run by volunteer employee committees who distribute funds to nonprofit community and statewide groups in Vermont. The fund draws its revenue from the enormously popular tours of the Ben & Jerry's ice cream plant, which attracts more than 220,000 visitors a year and has become one of the most popular tourist attractions in Vermont.

Ben & Jerry's even knows how to profit from its mistakes, giving factory seconds away free to community organizations in the state, donating them to food banks, or selling them under a special arrangement to Vermont stores whereby a portion of the profits go to local fire and rescue squads, libraries, and other local organizations. These payments totaled over $200,000 in 1991, while that same year ice cream donations exceeded 8,000 gallons. These actions not only profited the community, they added value to Ben & Jerry's reputation asset, an asset as valuable as any tangible piece of factory equipment.

Ben & Jerry's *identifies opportunities for improvement* by assessing the impact of its operation, both socially and fiscally. The company pursues a "two-part bottom line," which includes not only company profits, but how much the company has helped promote environmental and social causes. Not surprisingly, it took some convincing to sell this unconventional tactic to company managers, whose traditional perspective viewed these goals as mutually exclusive. However, by simply adding the variable of "social benefit" to the usual business equation of "price and quality," managers quickly learned that they could make a positive contribution through their management decisions by entwining both goals.

Cohen and Greenfield *prepared for action* by encouraging their employees to don the mantle of social responsibility. The company's social agenda shines throughout the company, beginning at the top with the Director of Social Mission Development, a position that ranks on a par with the CFO. This person does more than fill a corporate philanthropy post, handing out money to charities, but works every day to stimulate everyone's awareness of Ben & Jerry's commitment to social causes. The director reaches out to the company's stakeholders, involving them in the company's agenda of social change and spurring them to join the company's mission with missions of their own. The strong, visible commitment to a social mission has energized Ben & Jerry's employees, who gain fulfillment from the knowledge that they work at a responsible company. Employee enthusiasm for the company's social mission earned Ben

& Jerry's a place in Levering and Moskovitz's *The 100 Best Companies to Work for in America*. As one employee told the authors, "You don't feel like you're just working for a company. I feel like every day I'm working to educate people about different issues, I'm working to save the rain forests."

At Ben & Jerry's, however, employment fuels more than environmental concern. The company's employees enjoy a progressive benefits program including paid maternity and paternity leave, on-site child care, educational assistance, wellness programs, profit sharing, and on-site seminars. They can take home a part of the company in two ways: in stock options and in ice cream rations (up to three pints a day). Fun has become virtually institutionalized at the company: The company-sponsored "Joy Gang," led by Jerry Greenfield, uses its $10,000 annual budget to create employee activities such as Elvis Day, skating in the hallways, miniature car derbies, semi-annual masseuse visits, and to sponsor guest speakers such as Mr. T and sixties counterculture hero Wavy Gravy. Quarterly meetings keep employees up to date on all aspects of the company's interaction with stakeholders. At meetings convened at midnight to accommodate the third shift, other shifts attend wearing pajamas. Meetings often adjourn with strobe lights and dancing. All of this creates a vibrant team spirit.

At Ben & Jerry's, barriers between management and workers have virtually vanished. In keeping with their values, the founders have created an unusual compensation program, whereby no one in the company can make more than seven times the salary of the lowest paid employee. This has set a wage cap hovering around $100,000, which sometimes makes high-level recruiting a challenge. Still, Cohen feels that the benefits outweigh the drawbacks, because when he does hire an executive, he knows that he has recruited a person who shares the company's values. Since executives join Ben & Jerry's for reasons other than money, their motivations translate into deep commitment to the company and its mission.

Cohen and Greenfield set an example for stakeholders by personally *taking action* to forward the company's mission. They dedicate time to creating groups such as the "Green Team," which sponsors charity flea markets, recycling drives, and reforestation projects, and they encourage their employees to think up innovative ways to advance environmental and social causes. Their own actions create an open atmosphere where people eagerly offer new ideas. Once the company tries out any new idea, it carefully *evaluates the results*, as evidenced in the company's annual report sent to stockholders, which includes a social audit along with the traditional financial data. The social audit measures how well the organization has touched the lives of others and made the world a safer, cleaner place. The financial data measures performance in terms of sales, which increased 23 percent in 1989, 32 percent in 1990, and 30 percent in 1991. During the same period, Ben & Jerry's share of the national premium ice cream market grew from 23 to 31 percent.

Ben & Jerry's strives not to waste money and effort on projects that create little return on investment, such as advertising. The company uses no conventional advertising, opting instead to spend money that might buy television time or magazine space advertisements on social causes. The company does advertise for the causes it supports, printing social messages on its pints of ice cream to spread awareness of issues such as the disappearance of the rain forests, but it relies on the more effective promotion it gains from the media in the form of nonpaid magazine, newspaper, and television stories about the company. Why waste hundreds of thousands of dollars on a multiple-page ad in the April issue of *GQ Magazine*, when the noted writer Joe Queenan wrote a glowing profile of the company and its accomplishments in that same issue?

Despite conscious efforts to control the pace of growth, reflecting concern for both product quality and company culture, Ben & Jerry's continues to grow at an astonishing rate. Far from hampering the company's growth, its ongoing commitment to the environment and the community has fueled growth that allows Ben & Jerry's to *repeat continuously* its contributions to the greater good.

CHOOSING HEROISM

By choosing the path of accountability, Ben & Jerry's reinvented the traditional corporate relationship with the environment. The company's every action upholds the three tenets of heroism: build heroic partnerships with stakeholders, walk in a sacred manner, and lead through strategic humility. The organization takes its commitment to heroic partnerships so seriously that it continued to pay its supplying dairy farmers higher prices for milk even after government price supports fell. Ben & Jerry's chose to walk in a sacred manner by creating their nonprofit Ben & Jerry's foundation, which operates separately from the corporation and promotes seemingly conflicting goals: social *and* fiscal responsibility. Finally, the company personifies strategic humility by defining itself in terms of how well it serves the environment and community in which it operates. Any organization can follow these same guidelines.

Build a Heroic Partnership with the Environment

You can start to build a heroic partnership with the environment simply by recognizing the environment as a vital stakeholder in your organization. You don't have to send "green guerrillas" to replant the rain forest to make a difference; acknowledging your company's responsibility for its impact on the environment sets the wheels in motion. When heroic organizations attach accountability to the environment, they connect themselves to every stakeholder whose well-being depends on a healthy environment.

Many organizations choose to sidestep this accountability because of its potential cost. Despite the existence of approximately 90,000 toxic waste sites in the United States, the government's Superfund has tackled only 1,200. If organizations accepted responsibility, wouldn't they be taking on a tremendous financial burden? No. That logic fails for two reasons. First, as the successful lawsuit in Sanger, California, illustrates, the public already wishes to hold organizations accountable for their actions in the environment, and while a company can try to run from public opinion, it can never hide from the consequences of a bad reputation, or litigation. Second, companies can begin by focusing on stopping the *creation* of more waste. Spot cleanups amount to bailing out the Titanic with a teaspoon. Instead of congratulating themselves for finding new ways to dispose of waste, or for polluting only as much as their "pollution credits" legally allow, organizations should be seeking out and implementing ways to decrease the harm they do to the environment by decreasing the waste they create. As 3M has shown, doing so can make an immediate *positive* contribution to the bottom line.

Walk in a Sacred Manner

Walking in a sacred manner means formalizing a protocol that governs how the company will behave in relation to the environment.

Ben & Jerry's officially accomplished this with its mission statement and with the role of the Director of Social Mission Development, but the company most completely realized its mission in the day-to-day evaluation of its actions in the environment. A heroic commitment means much more than words on recycled paper; any company can send out a flurry of mission statements and press releases and never really clean up its act. Such cupidity not only results in continued degradation of the environment, but in erosion of the organization's reputation. Trust, ethical behavior, social and environmental responsibility represent a corporate asset you cannot buy with words alone. You must earn that asset through conscious and meaningful action. Lose that asset, and you'll lose business. Lose enough business, and you'll lose your corporate life.

Perhaps not surprisingly, one of the best examples of walking in a sacred manner comes from a Native American tribe, the Menominee in Wisconsin. Ironically, the tribe demonstrates its heroism in logging, an industry that has long been maligned for its devastation of the environment. The Menominee have practiced a deliberate, sustained-yield logging practice on their 234,000 acres of forest, harvesting 2 billion board-feet of timber over the last 135 years without depleting the forest stock. In terms of total productivity, they outpace the nearby Nicolet National Forest, with more than twice the acreage of commercial forest land, and their stock has steadily increased over each previous measurement of inventory. They accomplish all this while maintaining a diverse, healthy forest that in no way resembles the one-dimensional corn-rows of pines many timber companies plant in the wake of their clear-cuts. Despite the fact that the Menominee must accept lower wages and delay upgrading equipment in order to compete with companies that offer cheaper lumber gained through clear-cutting, the tribe has no intention of changing its methods. As Kenneth Sloan, a forest supervisor in Wisconsin's Department of Natural Resources, explained to author Paul Hawken in his book *The Ecology of Commerce*: "The Menominees would no more separate the forest from its intrinsic ecological and societal value than we would separate one finger on our hand from another."

Other companies also value preserving the forests. Far-sighted corporations such as Wal-Mart and Knoll Group, a large manufacturer of office furniture, have taken an interest in the Menominees' unique product because it offers one of the few truly responsible choices. In fact, both these companies have indicated that they will switch entirely to sustained-yield timber in the next decade, choosing an heroic option that favors the environment over the illusionary cheaper option of lumber cut at a high cost to everyone on the planet.

Lead Through Strategic Humility

All of us have, at some time in our lives, felt humbled by the grandeur of nature's display, be it a crimson sunset, an endless blue ocean, or the miracle of spring greenery forcing its way out of wintered earth. But how many of us extend this reverence into the office or board room? While no one supports wanton destruction of the environment, few individuals feel personally responsible when the organization for which they work does so. The organization affords an illusion of anonymity and a false freedom from accountability, but the Heroic Organization makes it a point to declare its intentions toward all its stakeholders as well as its expectations from those stakeholders. It shatters the illusion that you can run and hide from the consequences of your actions and chooses instead to lead with the true power of strategic humility.

Ben & Jerry's demonstrates strategic humility by choosing to put its concerns about the environment and the community first and by structuring the entire company around the principles of reciprocity and accountability. Other organizations can practice similar strategic humility simply by evaluating the real impact of their actions on the environment. For some companies, such as Natural Cotton Colors, Inc., strategic humility means letting nature lead the way.

Natural Cotton Colors came into being when Sally Fox, a cotton breeder, ran across a strain of naturally brown cotton. Fox's lifelong passion for spinning and weaving inspired her to experiment with the cotton until she created an easy-to-spin variety. After starting out with a few pots of cotton growing on her porch, she embarked on a decade of careful cross-breeding that bore a surprising result: cotton that grew in hues of green, pink, beige, and brown. What started out as a hobby became a fiber phenomenon, with naturally colored cotton now being grown on thousands of acres to supply garment powerhouses such as Levi-Strauss and Esprit. The cotton appeals to clothing manufacturers not only because of its natural, rich colors and its "ecologically sensitive" character, but because it actually works better than bleached, dyed, defoliated cottons. By bowing to nature and exploring its possibilities, Fox discovered its diversity and its creative potential, potential she tapped to create a new business.

CONCLUSION

Organizations that choose to behave in an environmentally responsible fashion do much more than pump out PR and pose in the equivalent of an environmental white hat. Rather, they deem every effort they make on behalf of the environment as not just beneficial but as absolutely necessary. We have reached the point where every organizational action for or against sustainability counts, and counts heavily. The environment links all humans together and with all the other life on the planet. As it stands today, our potential for destruction has far exceeded the human scale, and assessments of the damage have become daunting and perhaps unmeasurable. If we cannot grasp the full impact of our actions, we cannot feel confident in our ability to turn things around, and, more important, we may feel tempted to shrug off our responsibility for turning things around. We must conquer that temptation. How we treat this stakeholder should reflect how we treat ourselves. The future depends on nothing short of total respect and daily actions that prove that respect.

—10—
STAKEHOLDER:
The Community

An ancient Sioux quote eloquently sums up the philosophy behind the Medicine Circle, "With all beings and all things we shall be as relatives." It embodies a simple truth a visitor might expect to see in a spiritual book or emblazoned on a poster, but it appeared in an unlikely place not long ago. Printed in foot-high letters on the side of a delivery truck, the words appealed to all passersby to remember that they belonged to a single family: their community. The truck carried products from The Body Shop, a firm that produces bath and beauty aids from natural materials and maintains a fierce environmental consciousness. The message affirmed that company's ability to connect the most mundane aspects of business into opportunities for promoting education and understanding among all people. Driven by uncommon courage, wisdom, and heart, The Body Shop, profiled later in this chapter, represents the remarkable achievements businesses can make when they link their prosperity with that of the communities on whose well-being they depend.

Combining Fiscal and Social Responsibility

The Medicine Circle represents the Sioux's deeply rooted regard for the community, a concept that extended to include not just their families but all elements that made up their world. In essence, the world view of the Medicine Circle bound a unique culture of hunters, whose economy fostered a sense of independence and made separation from the tribal group fairly easy, for various tribes roamed freely, constantly moving their villages in search of food. This freedom encouraged an individualism that could only have fractured the culture had it not simultaneously respected strong ties of shared interests. The Sioux's political organization exemplified the necessity for developing methods of subordinating the self to a common effort. Successful group living, and the sustenance and protection it provided, demanded a deep regard for the value of preserving the community.

For the Sioux, the community started with respect for the rights of the individual. Sioux culture deigned all tribal members equals; tribes functioned as democracies more egalitarian than our own. Council matters were decided unanimously, rather than by majority, and legal issues were discussed with family and tribe members. Rewards and punishments were never meted out in an authoritarian manner. Maintaining this democratic community demanded responsibility on the part of each of its members. Every individual felt responsible for the welfare of all tribe members, and in reflection of this, the Sioux deemed generosity one of the Four Sacred Virtues by which they organized their society. Unlike the Trumps and other glitterati of our day, who gain social status with the accumulation of wealth, the Sioux gained status with the distribution of wealth. They literally lived by the precept, "If you have more than one of anything, you should give it away." The other three Sacred Virtues—fortitude, wisdom, and childbearing—reveal what the Sioux considered essential to their national well-being. The four virtues also demonstrate what the Sioux considered to be the most dangerous to their culture, the opposing qualities of selfishness, fear, ignorance, and barrenness.

Perhaps no other aspect of people's activities better define the boundaries of self-expression than do the goals they set for themselves. The Sioux honored ideals that bound communities together. The Four Virtues represented a modus operandi for Sioux philosophy, social characteristics not only worthy in themselves, but which molded all other behaviors in ways that sustained the well-being of the tribe. What a contrast to the ideal that represents the sum of self-expression in many modern organizations: profit. As an ideal, profit bends and twists all other intentions to its service, creating an artificial and potentially damaging measure of success. The ideal of profit and its flipside, loss, represents a culture bent on taking and exploiting. The Sioux shunned those characteristics as dangerous to their society, and today, as consumers become more aware and vocal about organizations taking without giving back, they, too, are demanding a new ideal of organizational responsibility, one more in keeping with the tenets of the Medicine Circle.

Manville Corporation has found living in mutual prosperity far more sustainable than the heedless pursuit of profit. Manville once epitomized irresponsible business and was consistently included in Fortune magazine's poll of America's Most Admired Corporations—as an example of what *not* to do. The company ranked at the bottom of the ladder for five consecutive years. Manville earned its black marks during the demolition of the asbestos industry, after studies linked its products with consumer illnesses and deaths. Even though the company had generally met or exceeded government health and safety standards at the time it manufactured asbestos, the company was judged, in retrospect, not to have responsibly weighed all the potential dangers associated with its products. Later, asbestos product-liability claims forced the company to reorganize under Chapter 11, and to turn over approximately 80 percent of its common stock, IOUs of $1.6 billion, almost $1 billion in cash, and 20 percent of its net profits *forever* to a trust to settle these claims.

The company has more than learned its lesson. Today Manville carefully considers the effect its business has on the community before releasing any new products. For example, it has conducted one of the most extensive testing and monitoring campaigns in the industry in order to fully understand the effects of the fiberglass it now manufactures. With nearly fifty years of research and thirty years of human data, the company feels confident that it sells a safe product. It backs up its testing by informing consumers of any potential hazards, going so far as to put cancer warning labels on lumber shipped from its sawmills because studies have identified wood dust as a carcinogen.

The company sticks to its guns even when caution costs it business. When the World Health Organization listed sand as a probable carcinogen, Manville immediately added a cancer warning to its earth products, translating that label into twelve languages to cover all of the company's markets. The company ran into resistance in Japan, where authorities and customers refused to allow bags bearing the word "cancer" into the country. When the Japanese ordered Manville either to take the label off, or to label the bags only in English, the company refused, even though it cost them a potential $20 million in sales to competitors with less strict labeling policies. The story has a happy ending, however. Japanese government officials, impressed with the company's integrity, are opening their doors to Manville products because they feel confident that they are dealing with an honest organization.

Manville's story offers an answer to an important question American organizations should ask themselves: Does it pay to be socially responsible? Manville had suffered financially, both from its carelessness and its caution, yet it obviously feels comfortable choosing the latter course. Many leaders would agree: When Deloitte-Touche Ross surveyed more than 1,000 corporate directors and officers, business school deans, and members of Congress for their views on ethics in American business, 63 percent of respondents said businesses strengthen their competitive position by maintaining high ethical standards. Company performance proves the value of this attitude. When the Ethics Resource Center in Washington, D.C., examined 21 companies with written codes of principles that stressed the value of community well-being, the Center found that if an individual had invested $30,000 in a composite of the Dow Jones in 1960, it would have been worth $134,000 in 1990, but that if the same individual had invested the same $30,000 in community-conscious companies, the stock would be worth over $1 million. Another study, conducted by researchers at Arizona State University, found that a list of the U.S. corporations that have paid dividends for 100 years or more tend to coincide with companies that make ethics a high priority.

Yet, at the same time, American organizations continue struggling to make peace between community consciousness and the bottom line, and too often the bottom line wins out at the community's expense. Corporate America loses up to $300 billion annually in lawsuits, government penalties, and other transgressions. The Deloitte Touche survey also revealed widespread cynicism about Corporate America's ethical prospects: 94 percent of respondents saw widespread ethical problems in the business community. This disparity can find a resolution in the tenets of the Medicine Circle.

In our culture, organizations often separate the pursuit of profit from the pursuit of common good, as if the two ideals represent mutually exclusive goals. "High-minded causes" disdain the pursuit of profit, and profit-driven enterprises become so consumed with their single purpose that they disdain any other motives. Witness the derision of "green" or "cause-related" marketing, where companies tie their product promotions to social and environmental causes as "phony philanthropy." Most consumers see the profit motive behind green marketing—American Express's campaign to make contributions to the Statue of Liberty-Ellis Island foundation not only raised $1.7 million for the foundation but increased new credit card applications by 17 percent. However, in the context of the Medicine Circle, profitability and social responsibility need not be mutually exclusive. The profit motive is a powerful engine a company can harness for virtually any purpose—including a socially responsible one. And, when it works, it sustains the well-being of the whole Medicine Circle.

Most organizations can begin to resolve the issue by simply reframing their motives: How can we derive profits from actions that improve the community rather than harm it? For example, utility companies in New York State set their electricity prices based on power saved rather than on power used, thus coupling profits to reduced demand instead of rising sales. With such "demand side management" utilities subsidize efficiency improvements for customers, then recover the expense through electric charges. By linking profits with social responsibility, they successfully accomplish both goals.

Today's business organizations have become the most powerful force in the world: The decisions they make, their successes and failures, affect more people than do those of governments. In the past, and quite frequently today, businesses have not fostered community responsibilities because they left that responsibility to governments. But as more and more communities demand corporate accountability, it behooves every organization to take the path of "enlightened self-interest." Organizations can effect enormous positive change simply by making responsible decisions, such as Xerox's choice to change its packaging to unbleached cardboard. For a company the size of Xerox, this decision makes a big difference without costing a lot of money: It keeps responsible suppliers in business and strengthens the demand for responsible products. Responsibility can accomplish even more than philanthropy because responsibility reflects a long-term commitment to community welfare, not just a one-shot, short term investment.

The Seven-Step Heroic Process can enable organizations to combine social and fiscal responsibility in a way that strengthens the organization and community simultaneously. Following the tenets of continuous improvement, businesses can forge links of mutual responsibility with their community.

THE HEROIC PROCESS

1. Establish a Context for Action
2. Measure Mission Effectiveness
3. Identify Opportunities for Improvement
4. Mobilize Support
5. Take Action
6. Evaluate Results
7. Repeat the Process Continuously

Anita Roddick of The Body Shop has followed a heroic path of social responsibility more consistently than most corporate leaders, and she has done so while expanding from a single store to over a thousand shops in forty-two countries worldwide in only eighteen years. The path of responsibility and profitability The Body Shop has followed remarkably parallels the Seven Step Heroic Process.

CASE STUDY: THE BODY SHOP

The Body Shop started out as a one-woman show in 1976, when Anita Roddick opened her first cosmetics shop on less than $1,000 and an unshakable faith in her idea, that customers prefer information over meaningless promotions and want to make their own decisions about the products they use. Her philosophy ran against the prevailing wisdom that cosmetic companies sold "hope" and "magic," not mundane moisturizers. Roddick, believing that customers would choose products for their true value, founded her organization on the principles of respect for the customers and sensitivity to the environment. She established a context for the way she would run her business by resolving to adhere to the following ground rules for operation:

- No false promises
- Use only natural ingredients that are easily renewable and not under threat
- Use no products that produce excessive waste or consume excessive energy in production
- Refill and recycle containers
- No animal testing on any products

These basic ground rules instilled a business philosophy that would eventually extend to one of, if not *the* most active social agendas of any business on earth. At the time Roddick based her business simply upon her own values. When Paul Newman started the very successful Newman's Own product line, which makes various prepared foods and donates all pre-tax profits to charity, he said, "There are three rules to running a business. Unfortunately, we don't know any of them." Likewise, Roddick credits her success to her ignorance about how a business "should" be run. To this day other cosmetic companies marvel that her plain packaging, refillable bottles, "mix it yourself" perfumes, and most of all her complete lack of advertising have done so well. After all, she violated every industry rule: She does not sell glamour and mystery, only practical products, and she spells out their sources without ever mentioning a single miracle claim.

Roddick *measured mission effectiveness* by asking customers exactly what they wanted from Body Shop products. Customer feedback in the form of purchases, letters, and in-store evaluations guide Roddick's every move in business. Another kind of feedback—the thousands of annual applications for franchises—affirms the company's appeal. For many, that appeal derives more from the organization's philosophy than from its healthy financial picture. Roddick never considered her millionaire status after The Body Shop went public in 1984 as a measure of mission effectiveness. Her newfound wealth meant nothing to her personally—what she could do with her money excited her. As she wrote in her book, *Body and Soul* (Crown, 1991):

> From that moment, The Body Shop ceased to exist, at least in my eyes, as just another trading business. It became a force for social change. It became a lobby group to campaign on environmental and human rights issues. It became a communicator and educator.

Roddick called her agenda "corporate idealism," and she began pursuing her agenda with an education campaign, Save the Whales. The campaign matched the ideals of The Body Shop because many of its products used jojoba oil, a wax derived from a desert plant that Native Americans had used for centuries to moisturize their skin and hair. Jojoba oil offers almost the same properties as spermaceti, an oil obtained from sperm whales, which the cosmetic industry had once used so heavily in its products, thus providing a major incentive for hunting whales in the first place. Obviously, substituting jojoba for spermaceti could directly help save the whales.

Soon after, Roddick *identified opportunities for improvement* in the company's agenda. Recognizing that the company lacked experience in creating meaningful environmental campaigns, she strengthened The Body Shop's position by partnering with Friends of the Earth, an established environmental organization. With Friends of the Earth, the company created information campaigns on acid rain, recycling, and the threat to the ozone layer. Shortly after, Roddick became involved with the Social Venture Network, a group of businesses, including Ben & Jerry's, Patagonia, and Rhino Records, that allocated profits and/or maintained programs directed toward community causes. Networking with companies with compatible social agendas reaffirmed Roddick's business philosophy and, combined with her Friends of the Earth experience , gave her the confidence to let the company act on its own. In 1986, The Body Shop set up its Environmental Projects Department, which oversees and coordinates campaigning and ensures that the company's products remain environmentally sound.

The organization's efforts sometimes overshadowed its main business—not only in the press, but in its own shops—as some employees lost focus on the organization and got so wrapped up in social mission that their stores became filled with donation boxes, posters, raffles, and the like so that customers could hardly find the products on the shelves. To Roddick's chagrin, some employees even complained about company memos telling them how to sell a new product, because that activity seemed to warp company values. Roddick's vision of community service couldn't continue, of course, if such attitudes ended up putting the company out of business. To forestall this eventuality, Roddick moved to ensure that every employee understood the consequences of an unprofitable business, and she then took firmer control of the company's social mission, narrowing the organization's efforts to just two international campaigns a year, one involving the environment and one involving human rights.

The Body Shop *mobilized support* for its vision from the very beginning. For example, Roddick chose only suppliers that supported her values: All suppliers signed a mandate confirming that none of their ingredients had undergone animal testing in the previous five years. When the company takes a stand on issues, as when it secured five million signatures on a petition against animal testing for cosmetics in Europe, it backs up its position with its own record.

The Body Shop also mobilizes support by mobilizing its own people. The company invests heavily in employee training, focusing on education that develops the values the company holds most dear. The Body Shop Training School in London serves more than 2,000 staff a year, teaching them about human development, urban survival, drug and alcohol abuse, community action, unemployment, and environmental issues. Instead of taking a course on salesmanship, staffers learn about natural ingredients, the origin of each product, and Roddick's adventures in bringing the products to The Body Shop. Her personal travels to find product ideas among the Wodaabe in the Sahara Desert, the Kayapo in the Brazilian rain forest, the Nyinba in Nepal, and many others all provide inspiration and anecdotes for sales personnel. *Talking Shop,* a bi-monthly video magazine produced by the company's own independent video production company and seen by every staff member in every shop, factory, and office worldwide, reinforces this education, and *Body Shop TV,* a weekly news update, keeps store personnel in touch with what's happening in the company. To increase global understanding, the company sponsors job-sharing programs where employees switch places with someone working in a Body Shop in another country for three months.

The Body Shop does more than support social causes that other organizations have already created. The company *takes action* in a thousand ways every day by paying shop employees to work several hours a week in local community projects, ranging from lectures in schools, tree planting, visits to the elderly and patients in hospitals, and organic farming. One shop even sponsored a full-time warden for a wildlife preserve. While the company monitors these projects through the Community Care Department, providing general guidance and support in the form of seed money or training, each shop chooses its own community project.

More impressive, the company takes action on a larger scale. Roddick never forgets the company's main objective of doing good business, but whenever she sees an opportunity to do good business while helping others, she jumps on it. She especially wants to provide opportunity and foster independence for communities in need. The company's choice to locate a soap factory in Easterhouse, Scotland, offers a classic example of the company's philosophy of helping others to help themselves. When Roddick visited Easterhouse at the behest of a community worker from the town who had heard her speak about her business philosophy, she found a community so decimated by unemployment that a European Community report had likened it to the Third World. Seeing hopelessness eating away at the community and widespread poverty, drug abuse, and crime taking a tragic toll, Roddick felt that The Body Shop could create new opportunity by creating new work. Together with her husband, Gordon, she decided to locate The Body Shop's first soap factory in Easterhouse, and, to make their commitment to the community even more solid, they decided to put 25 percent of the profits back into the community in the form of a charitable trust. As Roddick recalled in *Body and Soul,*

> Siting Soapworks in Easterhouse was as much a moral decision as a commercial one, but it was a natural one for us to take since we see business as an integral part of the social fabric of family life. We could have set up the project in a safe suburban industrial park . . . but we chose to employ the unemployable in Easterhouse rather than the already employed. . . . Not one shareholder complained, perhaps because when you take the high moral road it is difficult for anyone to object without sounding like a complete fool.

Easterhouse shines as just one example of The Body Shop creating a local business to benefit a needy community. Still, Roddick balances her philosophy to reach out with practicality; she believes that needy communities, particularly in the Third World, need work, not handouts. Instead of merely exploiting the cheap labor found there, Roddick created a Trade Not Aid policy for The Body Shop, which creates successful, sustainable trade links with Third World communities using traditional skills and materials. Trade Not Aid resulted in The Body Shop carrying handmade Nepalese paper products, which not only provided desperately needed employment, but which helped control a nonnative plant pest that was harming Nepal's natural environment.

Trade Not Aid also successfully created a viable industry for the Kayapo, one of the many threatened tribes in the Brazilian rain forest. When Roddick wanted to develop a plan to create an industry that would not disrupt the Kayapo culture or environment, she hit upon brazil nut oil. The Kayapo were already cultivating brazil nut trees in the rain forest (contrary to popular belief, the trees do not grow there naturally). After explaining her idea and winning local approval, she arranged to provide them with a hand-operated machine to extract the oil from the nuts, which she then purchased for use in Brazil Nut Hair Conditioner. Paying the Kayapo for their work presented a problem, as the culture did not use money. However, the tribal leader, Paulinho Paiakan, who had met with the World Bank, the U.S. Senate, and U.K. Parliament in his efforts to defend his people and stop the destruction of the rain forest, provided a solution. As the Kayapo shared all their responsibilities, so they would share their newfound fortunes; the money they earned would be put to work to help save their culture. One of their first purchases was a small plane to provide communication between Kayapo villages and the outside world and to serve as an air ambulance.

Roddick carefully *evaluates the results* of all these projects, making sure that they achieve the combined goals of running a fiscally sound business and aiding social causes. Not all of The Body Shop's ventures pan out, although the company surpasses the United Nations' success rate in establishing new businesses in the Third World. As the company grows, Roddick *repeats her commitment continuously,* exploring new ways to do business profitably while giving back to the community—on a global scale. Through education and direct involvement, she has created both an example for other businesses and a shift in thinking about how businesses can act to deal with the problems the world faces today. While not every business can emulate The Body Shop, all can learn ways, large and small, to incorporate the company's successful marriage of business and social responsibility.

CHOOSING HEROISM

The Body Shop's business agenda adheres to the three heroic principles: The company builds heroic partnerships with communities to create sustainable businesses, it practices strategic humility by letting communities choose which industry will best meet their needs and cultural values, and it walks in a sacred manner by creating in-house oversight bodies such as the Environmental Projects Department and the Community Care Department. Other businesses can rely on these same principles to guide a socially responsible business philosophy that benefits both the company and the community.

Lead Through Strategic Humility

The Working Assets Funding Service may not have become a household phrase, but that fact does not minimize its tremendous influence on the pursuit of socially responsible business practices. Laura Scher, CEO of WAFS, developed the first donation-linked credit card, an innovation that quickly garnered more than $400,000 for a variety of nonprofit organizations promoting peace, the environment, human rights, and economic justice. Working Assets card holders help determine which organizations will receive the funds. But the WAFS program did more than raise money, it created an idea others could borrow. Thousands of copycats arose in its wake, and a recent count listed more than 3,500 organizations offering donation-linked credit cards.

The company continues to find new ways to help people make contributions to society with their buying decisions, including a long distance phone service that donates 1 percent of charges and a travel service that donates 2 percent of charges to social causes. The company practices strategic humility by including the community as an intrinsic part of its business. Going far beyond a flashy "green campaign," the company earns ever greater credibility, which in turn translates into more business—all of its products have sparked greater demand than the company predicted in its rosiest forecasts, and it continues to yield a healthy return that Wall Street can respect.

Build Heroic Partnerships

In the case of serving the community, heroic partnerships represent a commitment beyond just writing a check and walking away. Companies succeed most with social programs that center on issues familiar to and resolvable by the company and its employees. They build heroic partnerships by investing their knowledge and unique skills. Companies such as Time Warner, which sponsors the Time To Read literacy volunteer program, Home Depot, which works with Habitat for Humanity to build low-income housing, and UPS, which joins forces with the Perishable and Prepared Food Program and which distributed over seven million pounds of food to food banks in just the first year of partnership, all demonstrate the effectiveness of deploying the company's strengths to support community well-being.

Walk in a Sacred Manner

Though organizations that devote their time and money to community-oriented causes generally follow clear-cut policies for running their programs, sometimes an organization must walk in a sacred manner by doing just the opposite, abandoning policies that adversely affect the community. Levi Strauss and Company walked in a sacred manner when it chose to follow a "No Policy" policy for employees with HIV/AIDS. The company treats HIV/AIDS like any other life-threatening illness, and it handles medical coverage, disability leave, and life insurance accordingly. The San Francisco-based company's program ensures that employees with HIV, AIDS, or any other life-threatening disease can live with dignity and respect.

Levi Strauss supports its official stance with education programs for employees called Talk About AIDS, and Talk About AIDS With Your Family. It also sponsors employee assistance programs offering confidential counseling for employees and their families on issues ranging from HIV prevention to rumors about AIDS to grief over the death of a colleague. With its policy, the company hopes to educate employees and alleviate the fear, ignorance, and prejudice surrounding HIV, all the while ensuring that employees grow more capable in coping with AIDS-related issues. The company has implemented its policy so successfully that its educational materials have been translated for use by companies all over the world.

CONCLUSION

The Body Shop, Working Assets, Levi Strauss, Manville, and other heroic organizations have demonstrated that both organizations and communities can benefit from socially responsible business practices. By increasing the strength of the community within which they work, organizations strengthen a crucial link in the Medicine Circle, one that supports the organization with both employees and customers. By choosing business decisions that serve the interest of the community, the Heroic Organization strengthens its own success.

—11—

STAKEHOLDER:
Government

In her book, *The Sacred Hoop*, Paula Gunn Allen relates a Cheyenne tale that beautifully illustrates the philosophy of the Medicine Circle. In the tale, Maheo, the All Spirit, creates part of the world out of the void, making tangible the water, the light, the sky-air, and the peoples of the water:

> "How beautiful their wings are in the light," Maheo said, as the birds wheeled and turned, and became living patterns against the sky.
>
> The loon was the first to drop back to the surface of the lake. "Maheo," he said, looking around, for he knew that Maheo was all about him, "you have made us sky and light to fly in, and you have made us water to swim in. It sounds ungrateful to want something else, yet we still do. When we are tired of swimming and tired of flying, we should like a dry solid place where we could walk and rest. Give us a place to build our nests, please, Maheo."
>
> "So be it," answered Maheo, "but to make such a place I must have your help, all of you. By myself, I have made four things . . . Now I must have help if I am to create more, for my Power will only let me make four things by myself."

To the Cheyenne's way of thinking, even the All Spirit, whose "being was a Universe," wielded limited power, a fact that helped instill respect for the powers of all creatures. The completion of the world required the aid of all. This philosophy of interdependence also applies to the relationships between the components of the organizational Medicine Circle, especially those between business and government. Business and government have often treated each other as adversaries, with government striving to regulate unruly business products and businesses searching for every loophole in regulations and tax laws, but the demands of the new global marketplace argue for replacing the enmity with mutual interest for the sake of American competitiveness. The philosophy of the Medicine Circle offers a workable platform for government and business to manage and enhance their relationship for the benefit of all stakeholders.

Aligning
for a Mutual Destiny

Over the past few years, the government's role in the Medicine Circle has changed considerably. On both the local and federal level, government has become more and more entwined with the private sector, largely as a result of the end of the Cold War. During the Cold War era, the needs of the government of necessity dominated much of our industry, from the production of weapons, planes and ships needed by the armed forces to the pursuit of defense-oriented research. Business profited from this need, albeit under detailed governmental supervision. With the fall of the Iron Curtain, the economy has become more domestically oriented, virtually reversing the respective responsibilities of government and business. More than ever, business now makes the key decisions about employing people, making products, and competing in the global marketplace while government has become more of a supporting player and facilitator.

Global forces contributed hugely to this phenomenon. In a real sense, business' newfound global mobility—of people, capital, and information—has reduced the power of government, while at the same time it has increased both parties' responsibility to the viability of the Medicine Circle. Government policies that overregulate or levy taxes without compensating benefits result in lost business—to competitors overseas, or in the form of domestic companies deciding to relocate operations to friendlier shores. At the same time, the emergence of the global consumer, whose purchasing power gives far greater weight to price and quality than to the origin of products, increasingly drives the rapid rate of economic and technological changes around the globe. Today the government must work to create and protect jobs, or risk losing economic advantage to other parts of the world.

Clearly greater collaboration between government and business offers potential for improving both. The emergence of the global economy has aligned government's and business's interests as never before, and, while the transition from swords to plowshares will continue to wrench our society, the end results look quite promising. Through efforts such as the "technology transfer" program, designed to move taxpayer-funded technologies out of government research labs and into the hands of business, these two traditional adversaries are increasingly finding common ground.

The U.S. government can bring massive power to bear on the private sector. Washington funds about half of all R&D in the United States; one in every six scientists work in federal research laboratories, and 700 government labs spend a combined $25 billion a year. While some foreign competitors, such as Japan, have successfully developed new products and manufacturing technologies with significant assistance from their own governments, American firms have been losing market share in important high-tech industries, including some technologies pioneered in this country. Technology transfer aims to put a stop to this trend by linking the power of government research labs with the interests of private industry.

Before the reversal could occur, however, the government needed to change the way it did business with business. In the past, much of federal research remained classified for security reasons, or it fell into the public domain for anyone to use. Companies often resisted investing in commercializing public-domain innovations without the competitive edge of intellectual property rights. Ironically, foreign companies often snapped up these taxpayer-supported innovations, free of charge, and turned them into advantages against their U.S. rivals. American companies also shied away from doing joint research with federal agencies for fear that their competitors could use the Freedom of Information Act to gain access to any proprietary information that resulted from the research. Only after the government enacted legislation to protect proprietary information and allowed federal labs to grant exclusive licenses for government technology did companies begin to show a keen interest in commercializing federal technology.

The renaming of the Department of Defense's secret Defense Advanced Research Projects Agency, DARPA, to the Advanced Research Projects Agency symbolizes the government's pledge to fulfill its role in the Medicine Circle. ARPA has been directed to prioritize dual-use technologies, projects that can result in both military and commercial applications. In addition, all federally-operated labs are devoting 20 percent of their budgets to commercial and joint-venture research projects with private firms. Critical technologies, including super computers, next-generation manufacturing processes, biotechnology, artificial intelligence, advanced ceramics, robotics, the information superhighway, and the development of an electric car have received special attention. The government has particularly singled out developing technologies that will benefit the economy as a whole, but which may involve too much risk or expense for a single company to undertake on its own. Labs can now work with a company to the point where a theory proves workable and the technology has progressed sufficiently for the company to continue on its own. The program has accomplished two remarkable successes. International Thermal Packaging worked with NASA to develop a self-chilling beverage can. ITP designed the product and NASA supplied the science behind the synthetic polymer used for cooling. And, the Department of Energy joined forces with Industrial Tools to develop the Alpha Nanometre 250, or "Slicer/Dicer," a state-of-the-art industrial cutting machine with an accuracy of 1/150th the width of a human hair that is finding applications in computer disk drives, semiconductors, medical instruments, and the aerospace industry.

On the local level, state and municipal governments have also begun recognizing their critical role in the new economy, and many, like Logan, Utah, are making efforts to help organizations become more competitive. The economic development plan in Logan has created an "incubator" for new businesses, where they can research and develop new products. Partly as a result of the recent recession, when hundreds of large companies slashed payrolls, sometimes devastating communities, other local officials have also refocused on how to contribute to the Medicine Circle of their community by growing local business. Unlike the smokestack-chasing of a decade ago, where officials courted big companies in a winner-take-all game, many local and state programs strive for a stronger, more localized and diversified homegrown business base. In addition to awarding grants for state-of-the-art research and development, most states provide some type of small-company financing, and more than half offer venture capital and new business "incubators" designed to help start-ups. Many local programs do the same.

Predictably, a certain degree of culture clash occurs when government and businesses come together. Lab employees who have worked for the government traditionally pursued theoretical questions, not bottom-line issues. When businesses come with questions about how to make a technology less expensive and more conducive to the bottom line, that may require a major shift in a scientist's thinking. Government contracts that allow lab inventors to collect a share of royalties on their innovation, however, have effectively motivated many scientists to think in business terms. Delays also pose a problem. Government agencies, notorious for their red tape, struggle to streamline processes and make them more businesslike, especially for hi-tech industries.

Interaction between business and government agencies will inevitably expand in the future and the Seven-Step Heroic Process provides a model for guiding that growing relationship through the uncharted waters of collaboration. The Baldrige National Quality Award, a major government effort to balance its contribution to the organizational Medicine Circle, follows the tenets of the Heroic Process.

THE HEROIC PROCESS

1. Establish a Context for Action

2. Measure Mission Effectiveness

3. Identify Opportunities for Improvement

4. Mobilize Support

5. Take Action

6. Evaluate Results

7. Repeat the Process Continuously

CASE STUDY: THE MALCOLM BALDRIGE
NATIONAL QUALITY AWARD

During the Seventies, U.S. companies suffered mounting criticism for their shortsightedness and lack of product and service quality. Foreign competitors capitalized on the United States' quality weaknesses, particularly Japan, whose own transformation into a quality powerhouse had left many U.S. competitors in the dust. As the nation's trade deficit escalated by the billions annually, both businesses and the government became painfully aware of the need for change. The emergence of the global market had created a new consumer, one whose choices hinged more on quality and cost then on nation of origin. For the first time the United States was losing not only its grasp on markets overseas, but on its home turf as well. Consumers voted with their dollars for industry winners, and the United States, which had for so long led the world militarily, was fast losing ground on this new economic battlefield.

In the Eighties, the U.S. government *established a context for action* in the battle for global market share: quality. In order to bring the issue of quality to the forefront, the federal government established the Malcolm Baldrige National Quality Improvement Act of 1987. Thus began the quest for the "gold medal." However, the Baldrige did not just offer a recognition program for its winners, it promoted general quality improvement by supplying guidelines for quality systems that would arm any company with the ability to compete more effectively both domestically and globally.

The National Institute of Standards and Technology enlisted more than 250 experts to create the Baldrige as a blueprint for improvement. The blueprint addresses six criteria, each weighted according to its importance with respect to competitiveness: leadership (15%), planning (15%), human resources utilization (15%), results from quality assurance of products and services (10%), and customer satisfaction (30%). While judges could bestow two awards annually in each of three categories—manufacturers, service companies, and small businesses—some years they awarded fewer honors. They simply found no company worthy in a certain category.

By creating the award, the government clarified quality as a national priority, and thus jarred U.S. business out of its complacency. The Baldrige prize quickly became one of the most coveted in the nation, with hundreds of companies applying for the chance to compete each year. Winners, such as Cadillac, trumpeted their accomplishments in advertisements, and hundreds of major corporations began using the criteria as a basic management manual. The overwhelming response provided a *measure of mission effectiveness*. The Baldrige put structure to decades of unfocused corporate energy. While many companies had adopted the TQM teachings of W. Edwards Deming and Joseph M. Juran, no single definition of TQM existed prior to 1987. The Baldrige did what quality professionals could not do—it got the attention of U.S. business leaders.

The Baldrige criteria set a clear, achievable standard for U.S. companies, even though many adapted the criteria and added amendments to suit their own unique organizations. A 1993 Baldrige winner, Eastman Chemical Company of Kingsport, Tennessee, had used Baldrige criteria for quality improvement since 1987. It pursued the Baldrige in 1988, and, though the company did not win, it did become convinced of the value of Baldrige criteria for managing the company's quality journey. From that time on, the company implemented the Baldrige criteria in an annual assessment of overall quality improvement. Ironically, the first assessment led to negative feedback. After implementing a customer-feedback process to measure customer satisfaction, customer complaints shot up; but where before Eastman would have avoided complaints, with the Baldrige-inspired quality-improvement program in mind, it realized that by listening more closely it could detect opportunities for improvement. Eastman created a feedback loop where none had existed before, and by doing so improved its ability to serve the constituents of its Medicine Circle.

The National Institute of Standards and Technology has continued to *identify opportunities for improvement* in the Baldrige, revising its criteria annually to reflect what Baldrige examiners have learned from the organizations that have applied. When some quality experts criticized the Baldrige for failing to focus on issues such as bureaucracy, financial performance, and speed, the NIST took that criticism under serious consideration. Perhaps the most troubling criticism came from those who thought that the application process could easily become an end unto itself, consuming so much time and money that the effect detracts from the real goal of quality. In the same vein, some critics claimed that a company can simply buy the award by using high-priced consultants and that the award thus favors large companies with resources to hire these consultants. These arguments may contain some truth, but consider the counter arguments, too. High-priced consultants did help IBM and Xerox win Baldrige awards, but they did not help Intel Corporation win its application. And winners such as Globe Metallurgical, Marlow Industries, and Zytec dispel the notion that only big companies can win.

The Baldrige has, however, entered a gray area in the overlap between judging and helping contestants. The demand for consultants with Baldrige expertise has lured Baldrige examiners to the seminar circuit. Each year the NIST sifts through hundreds of applicants volunteering to serve as Baldrige examiners, a job that sometimes includes a modest stipend but normally pays nothing. The true motivation: Any plausible affiliation with the Baldrige can lead to a lucrative new career. To keep everything aboveboard, examiners and judges must divulge all the businesses with which they are affiliated and cannot judge those organizations or their competitors. Examiners can't reveal anything about companies they scrutinize, nor ask for information about others in the competition. While on the job, they cannot accept so much as a souvenir pen. All the same, and despite the fact that no breach of rules has come to light, the NIST continually addresses potential problems with its conflict-of-interest committee. The award itself does ensure some degree of integrity: There are no secrets or short cuts for consultants to sell. A company can win the award only by following a truly comprehensive quality-improvement process.

At its inception, the Baldrige enjoyed a honeymoon during which hundreds applied for the award, but in the past few years, applications have stabilized at about eighty a year. While the award was never designed for mass appeal, but as a proving ground for the best of the best, it has enjoyed widespread impact. The program aimed to *mobilize support* among a wide network of organizations interested in quality improvement, and it has succeeded. While the number of actual Baldrige participants does remain low, U.S. companies have requested tens of thousands of copies of the Baldrige criteria, as well as over 10,000 presentations from Baldrige winners, examiners, and administrators. American business, especially the electronics industry, has clearly accepted the Baldrige criteria as a definitive program for quality improvement.

Taking action on the award has provided a powerful stimulus for U.S. business to improve quality as never before. When the

General Accounting Office surveyed twenty top Baldrige scorers it found that most had improved in such critical areas as market share, sales per employee, return on assets, and the ability to deliver products on time. In the two years after IBM's minicomputer division in Rochester, Minnesota, won the Baldrige, the company doubled its number of new customers and improved market share by 18 percent despite a depressed market; Solectron Corporation grew 9 percent in only three quarters; and GM's Cadillac division, a much-maligned choice when announced, went on to create one of Japan's top five imports of the year—the Cadillac Seville.

The Baldrige award brings with it no guarantees, however. A Baldrige doesn't mean its winner has solved all of its problems, and winning doesn't ensure profits, nor market share, nor growth—nor was it meant to. Some executives mistake the Baldrige as a cure-all, ignoring the fact that it should instill discipline and serve as both an ideal and a spur for improvement. In keeping with that purpose, the NIST *evaluates the results* of the Baldrige process by requiring winners to share their successful strategies with other organizations in the form of seminars, speeches, and site visits. In this way, the nation's companies can share best practices, strengthening the competitiveness of every organization involved. The Baldrige thus represents a way for American business and the government to walk in a sacred manner and strengthen the entire Medicine Circle.

Eastman Chemical used the Baldrige award to enhance its homegrown quality-improvement program, which itself reflected the Seven-Step Heroic Process. The program began with a review and assessment of customer relationships, including suppliers; it identified opportunities for improvement; it initiated projects to make those improvements; and it reported the results back to the customer. Some of the quality strategies the company shares with other Baldrige-hopefuls include its MEPS program (Make Eastman the Preferred Supplier). MEPS encompasses an ongoing cumulative series of team projects seeking to improve processes that link the company to its customers. Anyone in the company can initiate MEPS projects, which often arise out of a specific problem with a customer or group of customers. Projects range from improving response time to customers' technical questions, to planning new office locations, to helping customers with specific problems.

Eastman does especially well when it comes to measuring customer satisfaction. The company uses a variety of ways, including call reports and nonsales contacts with customers, to obtain input on customer needs and satisfaction, but it works hardest on improving its complaint process and its customer satisfaction survey. The company maintains a twenty-four hour toll free number for complaints, promising to resolve or respond to any complaint within thirty days. Its customer satisfaction survey includes twenty-five performance factors, such as on-time and correct delivery, product quality, pricing, and sharing market information. Every eighteen months, the company invites customers to rate both Eastman and their best "other supplier" on a scale of 1 to 10 for each performance factor. In this way, the company measures not only its own performance, but how well it stacks up against the competition. The sales department accepts responsibility to get back to the customer and discuss survey results, focusing specifically on where the customer's ratings differ significantly from the median of all customers or where the customer has rated Eastman significantly higher or lower than a competitor. At the same time, a sales representative can make a customer aware of current improvement efforts. After all, as Sam Walton once said, "An improvement's not an improvement until your customer knows about it."

The Baldrige award embodies a commitment to *repeat continuously* the improvement process. The award itself continuously undergoes reevaluation to ensure that the application truly reflects quality processes and that feedback meets organizations' needs. Most important, the Baldrige represents a first step in mutual collaboration between business and government toward a common goal of national competitiveness. On the international front, the Baldrige has helped to brighten the foreign businessperson's view of U.S. quality in general. The award has gained so many admirers overseas that the European Community, Sweden, and Mexico have all created quality awards modeled on the Baldrige's assessment system and its overall goals. In concept and execution, the Baldrige supports the concept of the Medicine Circle and mutual destiny.

CHOOSING HEROISM

The three heroic principles provide guidelines for action that unite the interests of both business and government. Government agencies and businesses can practice strategic humility by learning from one another's strengths. Industrial Tools and the Department Of Energy learned this lesson during creation of the "Slicer/Dicer." Likewise, the National Test Facility in Colorado Springs, a division of the Ballistic Missile Defense Organization, has fought defense budget cuts by broadening its customer base to include commercial industries. Government agencies and businesses can also build heroic partnerships to make businesses and the country more competitive. Symatech, the computer consortium, and the U.S. Display Consortium linked together behind the country's technological needs. Finally, as government and business learn to walk in a sacred manner, as they have done in creating and pursuing the Baldrige award, they set the stage for more successful working relationships in the future.

The collaboration between business and community government in the city of Rochester, New York, demonstrates the power of the three heroic principles. Rochester has long been a leading center for optics-based industry, and for decades, Kodak, Xerox, and Bausch & Lomb provided the three pillars on which the community relied for its well-being. In the Eighties, however, that relationship encountered a major challenge: Competition from overseas was eroding Rochester's market, even within its own city limits. The science of light and vision was evolving far more rapidly than the manufacturing technologies in the city's businesses. The problem became glaringly apparent when Kodak benchmarked outside vendors in a search for a supplier-partner and found that suppliers in Rochester, and throughout the United States, fell far short of world class. In fact, certain foreign producers outclassed Kodak itself.

The revelation, and Kodak's subsequent acquisition of a Taiwanese lens maker, shook the community to its roots. When a 1987 study by the Joint Logistics Commanders established that only 2 percent of the optical components used in the United States came from domestic manufacturers, domestic optics manufacturers responded with fear and sought protection, forming the American Precision Optics Manufacturers Association, which pressed the Department of Defense for protectionist legislation that would limit procurement of a wide range of precision optics to domestic sources for five years. The DOD rejected the plan, and instead pledged to support the development of new optics manufacturing technology in the commercial sector. Officials and business people in Rochester recognized that they didn't need artificial protection as much as they needed to improve themselves.

Lead Through Strategic Humility

The improvement strategy in Rochester began with the decision to lead through strategic humility and recognize that the community needed to change. At the heart of the competitiveness problem for optics companies in Rochester lay the fact that labor-intensive production techniques and technology, which had remained virtually unchanged since before World War II, were identical the world over, meaning that U.S.-based manufacturers could scarcely compete with the lower cost structures of foreign companies. Thus, in order to compete, the Rochester companies needed to improve their level of competence.

A major part of the problem also stemmed from the education crisis that afflicted Rochester as much as so many other communities in the United States. Optics companies could not find workers with enough education for even basic manufacturing work. To make matters worse, the community that had offered the first optical technician program and the first bachelor's and Ph.D. degrees in optical technology in the United States was suffering a sharp decline in students. As the community began to see that technological leadership required a skilled and knowledgeable workforce, it began at the bottom, with school reform. A task force consisting of local interest groups authored a report called "A Call to Action," which challenged the business community to become involved in the effort to revitalize Rochester's schools. The business community supported the effort wholeheartedly. Kodak, for example, announced a plan to place 2,400 employees into schools to work directly with local teachers on science and math education. Wegman's, a leading supermarket chain, pioneered a scholarship program for disadvantaged students. Together, business and educators began working to make the community more competitive.

Build Heroic Partnerships

The second step to becoming more competitive involved offering a more competitive product. Once more, businesses and the community rallied together to find a solution. It all started when local businesses reached out to build heroic partnerships with government leaders. Kodak took the lead by shifting its strategic focus from marketing photographic materials to manufacturing sophisticated optoelectronic equipment. From this commitment emerged the OPTICAM project, a technological breakthrough for optics manufacturing. The OPTICAM machine automates many processes traditionally done by hand, such as calibrating and measuring the curvature of lenses during production. High Technology of Rochester, a government group set up to foster new companies and technological development in the community, added its support at the inception of the project. Together with the Chamber of Commerce, HTR raised $4 million for the undertaking, and the University of Rochester pledged $6 million to construct a new Center for Optics Manufacturing to house the OPTICAM.

Still, since the project required substantially more financing, the project leaders decided to approach the federal government. Before doing so, they solidified their position even further by building heroic partnerships with their main rivals, the University of Arizona and the University of Central Florida, the only other schools that could rival Rochester's OPTICAM effort. By presenting a united front dedicated to increasing U.S. competitiveness in optics technology, the OPTICAM leaders secured a federal grant to complete the project.

Walk in a Sacred Manner

The success of the OPTICAM project stimulated and reinforced the community's commitment to working together. The need to establish a community core competency in optics has led businesses such as Kodak and Xerox to collaborate with other companies on a wide range of optics and imaging projects. Scientists from Kodak and Xerox have established relationships with the University of Rochester and the Rochester Institute of Technology to collaborate on electronic imaging problems such as pattern recognition and image compression. APOMA, the group that originally sought the protectionist measures, has prospered, growing to include over sixty corporations.

As the walls between competitive companies give way to cooperation and collaboration, business and government agencies are learning to walk in a sacred manner for the health of the Medicine Circle. Cooperation takes the form of quality process exchange programs similar to those shared by Baldrige winners, or even direct help in getting businesses running, as when Xerox and Kodak allowed start-up Hampshire Instruments to study and learn from their copier assembly facilities, and even lent the fledgling company some workers. Meanwhile, High Technology of Rochester has established a business incubator and venture capital fund to attract and nurture small high-tech companies. In its first year of operation, HTR helped over one hundred spin-off companies get started from local businesses and universities.

CONCLUSION

Rochester, today the third largest producer of optics technology and products in the world, has demonstrated the strength a community gains when business and government put their resources together. Projects on the national level only reinforce the power of adopting the perspective of *Cangleska Wakan*. By recognizing their shared interests, business and government can strengthen each other to keep America competitive in the new global economy.

—12—
STAKEHOLDER:
Suppliers

As the Sioux and all peoples living close to the land knew, nature provides the best model for human behavior. Business people in our high-tech society like to use sports and military metaphors to describe relationships with suppliers—playing hardball, using guerrilla tactics to whip them into shape—but the lowly *Rhizobium* bacteria provides a metaphor more consistent with the spirit of the Medicine Circle. All organisms need large amounts of nitrogen to form amino acids and other dynamic molecules that create protoplasm, the very substance of life. In many parts of the world beans provide a major source of nutrients for people, and bean crops depend on a cooperative arrangement with the *Rhizobium*, which inhabit the roots of the plants and create numerous nodules packed with bacteria. The bacteria pump nitrogen into the soil through a process called nitrogen fixation. Without this mutually beneficial relationship, bean plants and the people who rely on them for their very lives would perish. It's a classic case of customer-company-supplier interdependence.

Employing this natural model, many of America's most competitive organizations have begun tapping the power of supplier partnerships, which offer tremendous opportunities for organizations to cut costs and increase efficiency and productivity. However, in a competitive world where combat rather than cooperation rules so much business behavior, supplier partnerships test organizational standards of trust because they demand a willingness to share prosperity. As in any trust relationship, company-supplier partnerships entail a level of risk causing both sides to become naturally cautious. If a company pursues supplier partnerships as a manipulative ploy designed simply to promote self-interest, exploiting information and strong-arming suppliers into cutting profit margins, its suppliers will eventually rebel. By the same token, if a supplier uses its partnership as a sole supplier to gouge prices, its customers will look elsewhere for their nutrients. Clearly, such adversarial attitudes build the sort of distrust that characterizes the nonheroic organization.

COMPETITIVE PARTNERING

Since true partnerships depend on trust, the Heroic Organization seeks out trustworthy partners, using the perspective of the Medicine Circle to heal the wounds of mistrust and bridge the gap between two parties who depend on each other for their livelihoods. Heroic partnership breathes life into both the company and its suppliers. Just as the success of any given product improves the health of both organizations, the success of the relationship that creates the product keeps both organizations competitively fit. In such an heroic partnership, neither organization takes advantage of the other, because both recognize that every stakeholder must remain strong in order for mutual benefits to accrue. An unprofitable supplier stakeholder forced to cut spending on research and development ultimately becomes a weak link in the Medicine Circle, as does a company forced to lose business because of high costs.

The concept of company-supplier partnerships inevitably draws comparisons to Japanese *keiretsu*, which operate as "families" of networked organizations. Heroic competitive partnerships borrow the best aspects of the *keiretsu* without adopting the downside of exclusive relationships: Obligation that stifles competitiveness. As Japanese business success has amply demonstrated, *keiretsu* represents a powerhouse of potential with its commitment to mutual destiny. Those involved in a *keiretsu* share cost-cutting and quality improvement initiatives, innovations, and, of course, profits. Unfortunately, such relationships can grow too comfortable, and they invite abuse. The debacle of Japan's new airport near Osaka, which has run years behind schedule and hundreds of millions of dollars over cost, exemplifies the price of comfortable noncompetitive relationships. Lack of competition gives suppliers little incentive to innovate or to cut costs. By contrast, heroic competitive partnering allows organizations the benefits of a shared purpose, without the pitfalls of complacency.

As in the symbolic relationship between two organisms as different as a bacterium and a bean plant, competitive partnering promotes cooperation without destroying individuality. It entwines interdependence with competition. In the Heroic Organization, partnership means more than a guaranteed purchase order because it instills equally high levels of responsibility and empowerment. Willing to take on the same responsibilities as the company in such areas as quality improvement and cost-cutting, supplier partners become co-creators. Suppliers to Motorola learn specific organizational TQM techniques at "Motorola University"; Ford requires its suppliers to improve continuously by competing for its Q1 quality award; and suppliers to Scott Paper participate in activity-based costing, a process that allows Scott to help determine the costs of its supplies.

Successful supplier partnering, based on trust and directed by mutual commitment, does not function as a closed process, nor does it imply exclusivity. Competitive partnering in the Medicine Circle reflects an ongoing commitment to remain just that—competitive. Heroic Organizations banish complacency from supplier partnerships by encouraging appropriate competition. While customer-supplier partnerships can and do evolve into long-term commitments, they come with no ironclad guarantees. Competitive products depend on competitive suppliers.

Motorola handles the issue of competitive partnering by grading its long-term supplier partners. Every two years Motorola teams tour suppliers' plants, judging how well they stack up against their competitors in terms of quality and timeliness. Motorola also rates suppliers on a monthly index that combines cost and quality, comparing the scores, anonymously, with other suppliers and showing how much of Motorola's business each supplier gets. Motorola doesn't set out to punish poorly performing suppliers, but to identify opportunities for improvement and ensure that the company obtains the best supplies available. Through this process, most suppliers end up saving substantial amounts of money on cost-cutting opportunities identified by Motorola teams. And the relationship isn't all one-way; Motorola has established a fifteen-member council of suppliers to rate Motorola's own practices and offer suggestions for improvement.

Mutual trust, opportunity, and responsibility imbue the most successful competitive partnerships. Detroit's Big Three discovered the power of competitive partnering by devising strategies to compete against Japan's powerful *keiretsu*. The solutions that Ford, Chrysler, and General Motors put to work in building cars like the Mondeo, Neon and Saturn parallel the continuous learning of the Seven-Step Heroic Process.

THE HEROIC PROCESS

1. Establish a Context for Action

2. Measure Mission Effectiveness

3. Identify Opportunities for Improvement

4. Mobilize Support

5. Take Action

6. Evaluate Results

7. Repeat the Process Continuously

CASE STUDY: FORD, CHRYSLER, AND GENERAL MOTORS

After being pounded by the Japanese throughout the Eighties, Detroit's Big Three knew that they would have to change their ways drastically to survive, and their success has exceeded their best hopes and expectations. American automakers, having won a reputation as lazy, wasteful, and obsolete, fought back with the power of cooperation and the principles of the Heroic Organization. The effort got results: A U.S. automobile, the Ford Taurus, climbed back into the number-one slot of best-selling car in the States for two years in a row; Saturn, one of GM's most successful product launches in decades, gained the widespread admiration of buyers; and the Mondeo, the first American-made "world car," is prepared to take on Japanese companies around the globe.

The turnaround has caused a good deal of pain, of course: Thousands of layoffs and scores of plant closings paid a hard price for decades of complacency. In the end, however, the companies once ridiculed for their fumbling have become models of self-improvement, and they could never have done it without changing their relationships with suppliers.

The new relationships centered on partnership. After years of complacency, the U.S. automakers finally began borrowing lessons from their Japanese rivals. Instead of railing against the *keiretsu*, they started looking to them as a source of inspiration, forming partnerships that linked suppliers' and manufacturers' destinies. Seeing that in Japan suppliers shared manufacturers' interests and values, and manufacturers guaranteed business to worthy suppliers, the U.S. automakers gradually *established a context* that the same ideas could work for them.

Traditionally, automotive manufacturer-supplier relationships had been adversarial and disorganized. As recently as 1980, Ford's parts business included no fewer than 3,000 suppliers. Over the past decade, that number has been whittled down to just over 1,000, with predictions of a core supplier base consisting of just 750 suppliers by 1995. Choosing partnership did more than streamline the process; it saved money. The bidding process Ford and other automakers had long employed held only the illusion of cost control because inconsistent supplier quality and timeliness created huge hidden costs for every automaker.

Ford took an early lead in reforming its supplier relationships when it began cutting down the number of its suppliers. As Norm Ehlers, Ford's VP of Purchasing, summed up in an interview with *Purchasing* magazine, "It's hard to be a partner with thousands of suppliers." After creating a short list, Ford determined that for their suppliers to function as true partners, they must share Ford's values. Thus, when the company decided to pursue quality improvement, it required all of its suppliers to do so as well. After all, the ultimate quality of Ford's products would depend on the quality of the products it obtained from its suppliers. Rather than strong-arm suppliers,

Ford began to help them become better suppliers by establishing the American Supplier Institute and the Supplier Quality Improvement program to teach suppliers about quality-improvement techniques and to help them incorporate quality-improvement processes from the beginning of each new project. Ford created the Q1 award for its highest-quality suppliers, and gradually that award became the benchmark for all suppliers. Today, Q1 status is the minimum requirement for suppliers doing business with Ford, and the company has created a Total Quality Excellence award, similar to the Baldrige award, for its best suppliers; TQE winners are given preferential consideration for new projects. Ford *measured mission effectiveness* by including suppliers in the planning process and inviting their input on whether or not they thought that partnership could work. Though some suppliers debated the necessity of going along with Ford's directives on quality, most seized the opportunity to examine their own values and stake in the venture.

Another measure of the effectiveness of supplier partnerships occurred on GM's Saturn project. GM had set out to prove that American automakers could compete in the small car market, but in the end Saturn became much more than just a product for the company as it evolved into a learning laboratory on team play and supplier relations. GM's first new nameplate in over seventy years, Saturn has become a model for people in the auto and other industries, who today talk about ways to "Saturnize" their own operations.

Gradually, a new structure evolved in the auto industry. As automakers marshaled their new teams, they *identified opportunities for improvement* in the way they manufactured cars. The enlistment of suppliers to contribute as partners naturally led to their inclusion in the product teams. Chrysler, for example, gave its teams more leeway in choosing their suppliers, establishing four separate platform teams covering small and large cars, minivans, Jeeps, and trucks. Each team accepted "womb to tomb" responsibility for each car assigned to its platform. To fulfill that responsibility, the platform teams abandoned the low-bidder patterns of the past and instead employed cross-functional teams to choose the best suppliers available in each area. "Tier One" suppliers participated from the beginning of all new projects, even before the company completed its designs. This level of partnership culminated in the Neon project, where all major system and component suppliers were chosen three years before the start of production—six months before corporate approval for the Neon itself. Chrysler credits these platform teams for having introduced more new cars over the past three years than in the last twenty, and the company never hesitates to acknowledge the critical role suppliers played in that achievement.

Now, instead of endless rounds of specifications and bids, Chrysler works to *mobilize support* from its suppliers to achieve its vision. The Neon project involved such strict cost and time constraints that Chrysler found itself forced to push the evolution of supplier-customer relationships even further, to become co-creators on the project. The ambitions of the Neon team—building a new car in 31 months—bore fruit with a scant 287 suppliers, about half as many as would normally support a car program of that size. After the Neon team chose its suppliers, both sides signed a consensus agreement up front to define all parameters for investment, design assumptions, conformity, cost, and weight of each part. Key suppliers assigned representatives full time to the automobile product teams.

One supplier, United Technologies Automotive, even served as co-chair of the entire interior of the Neon. UTA coordinated the efforts of five other suppliers it would have considered competitors under more conventional circumstances. Yet, as one UTA team leader recalled, all six suppliers demonstrated commitment to the project and "went at it with an unselfish and singular purpose" in an effort to meet Chrysler's cost and quality targets. To assure a good color-for-color match between parts, all five suppliers even agreed to buy their resin from the same source. As co-creators, each invested as heavily in the success of the Neon as Chrysler itself.

The Mondeo team at Ford *took action* to strengthen its supplier partnerships by co-locating supplier engineers on site to work with project teams. Ford developed its first "world car" (the U.S. version will be nearly identical to the European version) on two continents, which required superhuman coordination. Since the Mondeo team had set a goal of sourcing as many parts as possible from single suppliers with facilities located close to the centers of production in Europe and the United States, several U.S. suppliers either formed joint ventures with European suppliers or built new plants overseas. As it turned out, 58 percent of the parts in the Mondeo share a common supplier, particularly impressive in light of the fact that the

European and American versions had to meet different safety and environmental standards set by their respective governments.

In designating suppliers, Ford had *evaluated the results* of relationships fashioned during the design of the Taurus, which pioneered cross-functional teams and supplier partnerships. Ford's earlier failure to create a world car in the Escort (produced in 1981, it shared only the water pump and front grill logo with its European cousin), also helped in designing supplier relationships on the Mondeo project. These experiences helped Ford create a "best expertise" criteria-based selection process when choosing suppliers for the Mondeo. With it, the Mondeo became a truly international collaboration, with four-cylinder engines built in England and Germany, six-cylinder engines manufactured in Cleveland, manual transmissions sourced from Europe, and automatic transmissions constructed in Ohio.

The Saturn project underscores Detroit's determination to achieve greater competitiveness through partnerships. Since the Spring Hills assembly plant opened in 1991, Saturn has relied on only 250 "Tier One" suppliers, and, as long as those suppliers continue to meet cost and quality needs, they can expect to enjoy Saturn's business for the life of the program. *Repeating the process continuously* means continually renewing the relationship through better service. The company trusts and empowers its suppliers continually, ever expanding the shared responsibility for results. Automakers expect their supplier partners to engage in continuing research and development work, to share their technological innovations, and to commit to continuous cost reduction in their own organizations.

The automakers do their share to help out suppliers in these areas as well. At Chrysler, more than 300 supplier personnel occupy offices at the Michigan Technology Center. In the interest of co-creation, partnering has begun to evolve from customer-supplier relationships to supplier-supplier ones, where the company encourages suppliers to work together on specific products. Chrysler's V.P. of Procurement and Supply arranges "marriages" between suppliers that enable them to share resources and thus cut costs. These supplier "marriages" have created Chrysler's suspension systems and Ram Pickup brake systems. The early time spent matchmaking pays off in lower costs for the company later.

Chrysler combines the advantages of a competitive open market with cooperation by always maintaining at least two or three suppliers per commodity; even if Chrysler single-sources an individual product, it always keeps alternative suppliers in mind should the partnership falter. The best supplier wins the business, but must remain the best choice or risk losing that business. Chrysler also sponsors a cost-reduction program for its suppliers called SCORE (Supplier Cost Reduction). The program, which focuses on helping suppliers identify opportunities for cost savings in their own systems, not on reducing margins, generated over $130 million in savings during its first two years in operation. While the program is voluntary, suppliers have responded to it enthusiastically; at no time has the program ignited the occasional bitterness that accompanied other automakers' demands for outright price cuts. At Chrysler, co-creation translates into co-prosperity for all.

By choosing partnership with suppliers, Detroit has woven together the best practices of cooperation and competition. The Big Three not only strive to choose the best suppliers, they share their own expertise to keep those suppliers stay constantly on their toes. At the same time, suppliers gain incentive to improve their own operations and a sense of balance in their organizations.

Choosing Heroism

Ford, Chrysler, and General Motors chose heroism in their supplier relationships by abandoning the industry's traditional adversarial stance and including suppliers in their organizational Medicine Circles. Automakers adhered to the three heroic principles by building heroic partnerships with suppliers, practicing strategic humility by letting supplier expertise take the lead when appropriate, and walking in a sacred manner by creating formal consensus agreements and by including suppliers as full-fledged team members on projects. Future projects hold the promise of even closer, more productive collaborations.

Build Heroic Partnerships

Donnelly Corporation applied the principle of building heroic partnerships at home before it extended it to its customers. To cut costs, Donnelly, a maker of rearview mirrors, modular windows, and lighting products for automobiles, reached out to its own workers.

Today, the company targets five suggestions per employee a year to improve efficiency and meet customer demands. The strength of all these "good little suggestions" cut overhead by 12 percent in just over two years.

The results of such employee involvement at Donnelly prompted Honda to form a partnership with the company to make exterior mirrors for all of Honda's U.S.-manufactured cars. Honda recognized that a company that knows how to foster collaborative relationships inside could apply that principle to outside relationships as well. Thus, on the strength of a handshake, Honda sealed a partnership with a company that had never made exterior mirrors and lacked a factory for making them. That didn't worry Honda, which assumed that Donnelly's values would get results.

As partners, Honda and Donnelly share cost-saving ideas. Donnelly began by participating in a mini-reengineering program that Honda had developed to strengthen its suppliers, whereby Honda engineers visited two Donnelly plants, scrutinizing processes and offering an objective outside opinion of the company's operations. Honda began the program with the hope that it would help Donnelly reduce costs by about 2 percent a year. The two companies split all cost savings that result from the effort.

Lead Through Strategic Humility

Organizations that lead through strategic humility eradicate the arrogance of the "not invented here" syndrome and take the opportunity to learn from their suppliers. Supplier partnership enables both companies to learn from each other, and thus become more competitive. Allied Signal learned how to cut costs when it tapped the knowledge of Betz Laboratories, a Pennsylvania-based maker of industrial water treatment chemicals.

Allied had long considered Betz merely a source of nutrients and not a potential partner who brought specialized knowledge to the relationship. Betz, in turn, just filled Allied's purchase orders. That changed when Betz came aboard as a supplier partner. Betz brought a new perspective to the water treatment systems at Allied: For the first time, Allied looked at water as an entire system. Betz and Allied engineers worked together to review every inch of the company's plants, looking for opportunities for improvement. In the past, a department manager might have seen ways to improve water usage efficiency, but since implementing those ideas would have provided improvement of the whole operation, rather than that manager's particular piece of it, he or she wasn't inclined to allocate any of the budget to achieve it.

Less than a year after working together on the water problem as a system, however, Allied and Betz engineers identified $2.5 million in potential annual cost reductions in one plant alone. In one case, at the cost of a few new valve controls, Betz ended up saving $100,000 a year by recycling water in a cooling tower. Betz added a level of expertise simply unavailable anywhere else. By making Betz a partner, Allied recognized its own limitations and by doing so learned and grew mutually stronger with its partner.

Walk in a Sacred Manner

Organizations can walk in a sacred manner with supplier partners by adopting a program of mutual prosperity and assuring the program's success with a protocol and standard for participation. Coleman Outdoor Products walks in a sacred manner with its supplier partners within an informal framework that the company nonetheless manages comprehensively with its Purchasing Department.

Coleman charges its Purchasing Department with a simple mandate: Develop strong supplier partnerships, which includes acting as the supplier's advocate within the company. Purchasing's chief customer is Coleman's Production Department; buyers visit the shop floors to talk to Production personnel and discuss their needs. There they can view the company's projects as whole systems, from raw material in the stock room through to the finished products on store shelves; this hands-on oversight enables them to make better decisions about which suppliers can best meet their needs. Purchasing actively participates in product development, attending product design meetings where they can begin thinking about the best sources to meet production needs. Purchasing also reaches out to supplier partners for design assistance. When the company needed to improve the quality of its coolers and camp stoves, Purchasing invited the company's steel supplier partner to invest in the technology necessary to produce embossed steel for the products.

Sometimes Purchasing finds more resistance at home than outside. Once, a supplier of valve cores used in the manufacture of propane cylinders suggested a component that would work better than the one Coleman currently used, a step that would both improve the product and reduce cost. But when Purchasing promoted the suggestion at the next product meeting, Engineering and Production turned their backs on it. As far as they were concerned, the current component worked well enough, so why fix it? It became Purchasing's job to win them over. Working as an advocate for the supplier, Purchasing won the argument and saved the company $50,000 a year.

Most Coleman suppliers sign exclusive contracts with the company, but to keep the process competitive, Purchasing keeps tabs on supplier quality and performance and compares them with their competitors. As part of the process, Coleman is putting together a formal program that will eventually include supplier certification. By walking in a sacred manner, Coleman stays competitive while maintaining the benefits of cooperation.

CONCLUSION

Organizations that choose competitive partnership with suppliers ensure their ability to permeate the organization with heroic self-improvement down to the very roots. With partnership, organizations can ensure quality from the first stages of product creation all the way to cost savings down the line. Competitive partnering derails the self-interest and adversarial motives of the past, replacing them with commitment to continuous excellence within the Medicine Circle. The basic heroic ethic of cooperation extends throughout the Medicine Circle to instill co-creation, with all partners serving a mutual interest: Serving the customer.

——13——
STAKEHOLDER:
International Partners

In his book *The Global Negotiator* (Harper Collins, 1990), attorney and author Trenholme Griffin tells this instructive story. A U. S. importer of bicycles had entered into negotiations with a Taiwanese manufacturer, expressing an interest in purchasing four distinctly different models in order to provide American buyers with the greatest possible selection. The Taiwanese company, on the other hand, insisted on delivering only two models because it could easily produce those with existing manufacturing processes. As the negotiators on both sides stiffened their respective positions, they reached a frustrating impasse. To conclude the deal, it seemed, one side or the other must offer a concession. As Griffin tells the story, someone on the American side stood back from the argument and posed an interesting question: "How can the higher cost of manufacturing be allocated between the American importer and the Taiwanese manufacturer?" This question dissolved the impasse as the two sides set about devising a formula that increased the unit cost of the different models to reflect the Taiwanese manufacturer's increased manufacturing cost. In the end, what had become a potential deal-breaking impasse evolved into a bridge-building activity aimed at achieving the interests of both sides. For the Taiwanese, profit per unit remained constant, while for the Americans, sales of more units at higher prices more than offset the increased manufacturing costs. Griffin draws a valuable lesson from this story: "When pressed to distill our international negotiating down to a single glib maxim, our response is immediate: When doing business internationally, think of the process as building a relationship, not doing a deal."

BUILDING GLOBAL BRIDGES

Any company engaged in the global arena, whether partnering with foreign firms or competing with foreign products and services, should keep this maxim in mind, viewing international partners and competitors as stakeholders in the organizational Medicine Circle. As with all other stakeholders, you must think in terms of relationships, building the sort of two-way bridges that promote and preserve the interests of all concerned. Given the constant acceleration of globalization, no other approach can possibly work in the long run.

The U.S. Department of Commerce reported that over half of the growth in the gross domestic product between 1988 and 1992 came from exports. During the same period, the number of jobs supported by exports grew from 5.03 million to 7.17 million, and by the beginning of 1994, over 10 percent of the U.S. economy depended on exports.

However, these figures tell only part of the story. America's export business has become a symbol of a resurgence in the confidence and competitiveness of not only U.S. business and industry, but of the society as a whole. As the global economy unfolds at an ever-escalating rate, the capacity of American society to expand its world view has become directly proportional to the capacity of U.S. businesses to export. America has always possessed a "world culture," home to the most ethnically and racially diverse population on the planet. Its people represent virtually every society on earth. More than making money, America's ability to build international bridges of cooperation will determine its existence, survival, and prosperity.

As the American economy increasingly globalizes, its health increasingly depends on its rate of exports. An analysis of the fastest growing sectors of the economy reveals some interesting facts:

U.S. TRADE FACTS

Excerpted from *Business America*, U.S. Department of Commerce:

The United States is the world's largest economy and the largest market.

In 1993, the United States retained the position as the world's largest exporter.

Goods Trade

U.S. two-way trade totaled over $1,045 billion in 1993, with exports of $465 billion and imports of $581 billion.

The 1993 U.S. trade deficit was $116 billion, 24% below the 1987 deficit peak.

U.S. goods exports fell to 7.3% of the nation's gross domestic product in 1993 from 7.4% in 1992. That compares with 1993 shares of GDP for Germany of 19.4%, and for Japan of 8.6%.

In 1992, the United States accounted for an estimated 12.3% of the world's goods exports.

In 1993, total goods exports were comprised of 84% manufactured goods; 9% agricultural goods; and 7% primarily mineral fuels and crude materials.

Total U.S. goods imports in 1993 were comprised of 82% manufactured goods; 10% mineral fuels; and 8% agricultural and other goods.

In 1992, U.S. exports of goods and services supported a total of 10.5 million U.S. jobs.

Capital goods, including aircraft, are the largest category of U.S. exports, followed by industrial supplies and materials, then non-automotive consumer products, automotive products, and, collectively, foods, feeds and beverages.

The Commerce Department estimates that over 37,000 U.S. manufacturing companies export—slightly more than one-third of all U.S. companies that export (104,564 firms).

Approximately two-thirds of U.S. goods exports are by U.S.-owned multinational corporations, with over one-third of these exports by the U.S. parent corporation shipped to foreign affiliates.

Business Services Exports

Exports of U.S. business services are over one-third as large as U.S. exports of goods.

Exports and imports of business services totaled over $174 billion and $116 billion, respectively, in 1993.

In 1993, U.S. exports of business services accounted for about 2.7% of the nation's GDP. Travel-service receipts and passenger fares accounted for over 40% of the total.

In such industries as machine tools, electronic components and accessories, surgical appliances, analytical instruments, plastics, X-ray technology, computers, and leather products, exports make up over 20 percent of all sales. For some areas, such as analytical instruments, the number rises to over 30 percent while for others, such as computers, exports will account for over 40 percent of the growth in sales. In the aerospace industry, the backlog of orders is rising faster for export markets than for domestic markets. Even industries whose growth prospects appear less robust, such as chemicals and aerospace, are finding that export markets figure ever more prominently in their growth.

Ten Fastest-Growing Manufacturing Industries in 1994
(percent change based on 1987-dollar shipments)

INDUSTRY	PERCENT CHANGE 1993–94
Machine tolls, metal cutting types	12.8
Electronic components and accessories	11.1
Surgical appliances	10.0
Mobile homes	9.4
Automotive parts and accessories	7.7
Surgical and medical instruments	7.0
Lighting fixtures	6.6
Mattresses and bedsprings	6.4
Leather tanning and finishing	6.0
Analytical instruments	6.0

Source: U.S. Department of Commerce, International Trade Administration

---

These statistics suggest that American manufacturing productivity has been reaching new levels of competitiveness in the global marketplace. A recent study by the McKinsey Global Institute found that American manufacturing companies led Japan in productivity by 17 percent and Germany by 21 percent. The McKinsey analysis also showed that American workers are more efficient than Japanese workers in 4 of 9 industries and more productive than German workers in 7 of 9. And even in some industries where Japan still leads the United States, such as steel and auto assembly, economists expressed their belief that the gap is narrowing.

On the other hand, the resurgence in the U.S. economy, especially in comparison to those of its trading partners, means that import growth in manufacturing goods will exceed export growth for the first time in the 1990s—exports rising an estimated 5.5 percent with imports up about 6.5 percent in 1994. By contrast, U.S. exports increased 7.5 percent and imports rose 6.5 percent in 1992, and both increased by 5 percent in 1993. The conditions abroad will thus require an intensified effort by U.S. firms to maintain the vital progress they have so recently won. For the American economy to continue its successful evolution into the new world economy, it must strengthen its capacity to build the international bridges of cooperation and reciprocity that make the whole system work for the benefit of all stakeholders.

APPLYING THE HEROIC PROCESS TO INTERNATIONAL PARTNERS

How do you go about building such bridges? In the midst of all the hype over the need for success on the global stage, one might easily overlook the fact that doing business overseas still comes down to a question of building relationships that can weather the threat of warring self-interests and worldwide conflict. On the most basic level, doing business on the world stage requires a special heroic commitment to practicing the principles of building heroic partnerships, leading through strategic humility, and walking in a sacred manner.

Building heroic partnerships on the international level requires a willingness to set aside one's biases and confront arrogance head-on. Overcoming the risks inherent in bringing cultures together requires an ability to assimilate a tremendous range of different perspectives to form the strong foundation on which bridges of empathy and understanding can be built. Such relationships demand exceptional self-discipline and a willingness to walk in a sacred manner of cooperation and interdependence, always strengthening the ties that bind disparate cultures for the benefit of all. Nothing can undermine a relationship more quickly than a failure to keep one's word and back up "faith" with appropriate action.

The complexity of doing business on the world stage requires a strong constancy of purpose. When so many factors, such as religion, history, and language, can disrupt and undermine a global relationship, walking in a sacred manner becomes the measure of integrity and trust. The Seven-Step Heroic Process can guide the building of global bridges because it enables competitors and partners to establish context clearly, to measure the appropriateness and effectiveness of the mission quickly, to identify risks and opportunities immediately, and to mobilize rapidly and take action with precision. In turn, it reminds partners to evaluate results constantly and improve continuously.

THE HEROIC PROCESS

1. Establish a Context for Action
2. Measure Mission Effectiveness
3. Identify Opportunities for Improvement
4. Mobilize Support
5. Take Action
6. Evaluate Results
7. Repeat the Process Continuously

Bill Shaw of World Wide Shipping demonstrated just how the Heroic Process sustains constancy of purpose in building international bridges.

CASE STUDY: WORLD WIDE SHIPPING

What do Simon Chacho in Dubai, Ian McLean in London, Sam Lien in Hong Kong, Harold Kim in Seoul, Sergio Enrico in Chile, Carmen Diaz in Madrid, Ken Graham in Johannesburg, and Robert Schneider and Ludwig Pohl in Frankfurt share in common? The answer: Bill

Shaw, Jr., president and founder of World Wide Shipping of Valley Stream, New York.

Shaw grew up near Kennedy International Airport, where his father served as a U.S. customs inspector. After leaving the Air Force in 1969, the younger Shaw began putting in place a plan he had been hatching since his boyhood. Brought up on stories about people and places from around the world, he had determined to make his fortune in international affairs. Shaw *established a context for action* that involved connecting an ever-shrinking world through a personal network of like-minded partners.

As a crucial first step, the young global entrepreneur joined British Airways to learn the craft of connecting people, places, and things that would one day lead him to fulfill his vision and start one of the most successful and respected freight forwarding and international logistics consulting organizations in the United States. Beginning in the air cargo warehouse at British Airways, he moved up the ranks to head the American labor management negotiating team. When deregulation hit the airline industry in 1970, he helped British Airways design the new systems that ended up achieving over 3,000 percent growth for the airline over the next ten years. After British Airways went private in 1979, Shaw joined the Japanese-based K Line Air Service, owned by Kawasaki, where he learned the intricacies of exporting to Asia firsthand, including the mechanics of selling "around" protectionist trade barriers.

After a succession of "fine-tuning" affiliations with Global Van Lines and the British-based Pandair Air Freight, Shaw *measured mission effectiveness* by sitting down and evaluating his chances at parlaying his international contacts into a viable business. Having worked on both the shipping and receiving end of the industry for nineteen years, he understood the business and had *identified opportunities for improvement* in international freight forwarding. While advances in technology had allowed people to communicate to the far corners of the earth at the speed of light, their products still moved the old-fashioned way, by train, truck, boat, and airplane. For clients with very special and urgent needs, mobilizing these resources quickly and efficiently, while managing the imponderables of cultural complexities on the world stage, was a tremendous challenge. Shaw knew that large freight forwarders simply could not mobilize the energy or resources to serve their special needs. Clearly, the world needed more individualized service, a company that could hand-hold shipments from packaging, through customs, to the client's front door, whether that be a small factory in the Thai countryside, an unnumbered apartment in the labyrinth of Tokyo, or a hotel in Beirut.

Shaw seized the opportunities, and he never shrank from risk, two components that proved to be exactly the right combination. With his wife, Ellen, the company's comptroller, Shaw began *mobilizing support* from his contacts, then *took action* to implement the strategic plan he had spent a lifetime developing. Shaw quickly claimed his niche in specialized shipping, taking on projects that other shippers shunned, either because of the technical complexity of the products or because of their own lack of shipping networks in certain countries. Overcoming such difficulties with his network of personal relationships, Shaw transported packages across warring borders in the Middle East and into the cauldron of confusion in Russia and her former satellites. His network enabled him to reach new countries in Eastern Europe before they had even clearly established their borders. In some cases, the names of destination countries changed even before packages arrived.

While his industry has become more volatile and unpredictable every year, the quality of his services has remained heroically constant. Shaw shared the credit when Bennett X-Ray of Long Island, New York, received the President's "E" Award from the U. S. Department of Commerce for "Export Excellence" in 1994. That company's success was due in large part to the friendly Irishman who, on the strength of a handshake, coached Bennett on how to make friends and sell to technology-hungry nations in the former Eastern Bloc. The awards ceremony dramatically affirmed Shaw's commitment to building bridges of trust and provided a tangible *evaluation of results.*

Shaw's success was also due to the formation of a U.S. network of independent logistics consultants and freight forwarding agents, called the Focus Group, composed of organizations in San Francisco, Chicago, Miami, Boston, and Atlanta. In cooperation with their international partners, the Focus Group walks clients through the complex minefields of tariffs, packaging, shipping, billing, collections, and customer service worldwide, from Angola to the Amazon, from Azerbaijan to Alaska. The power of this network became evident recently when a worldwide relief agency asked Shaw to help with the shipment of desperately needed supplies to war-torn Bosnia. Tapping his personal network of partners, he accomplished what standard shipping procedures could not. Interestingly, the first barrier the network scaled wasn't one of the obvious overseas obstacles. It turned out that the relief agency could not ship material directly to Bosnia from the New York Harbor because of possible interference by American-ethnic Serbs who hold influential positions in the longshoremen's union that dominates the docks.

Shaw circumvented the problem by employing a logistical delivery network centered in Amsterdam that he had used to ship computer peripherals into Eastern Europe and Yugoslavia before the civil war. Given the humanitarian nature of the cargo, Shaw's friends donated their services and helped build a bridge of over seventy-two connections in record time. Moving supplies from ships to trains to trucks, Shaw confidently relied on the unbending cooperation of associates to make the tenuous and complex connections across the Atlantic and into the war zone.

The success of efforts such as Shaw's provides tangible proof of the power of cooperation and reciprocity in the new global era. Recently, Shaw embarked on the seventh step of the heroic process, *repeating the improvement process,* by expanding his team to include his son William III. In an age when most companies focus on technology as the key to success, Bill Shaw and his family reaffirm the age-old truth that personal bonds of commitment create the greatest successes, whether on the local or the international level.

CHOOSING HEROISM

The complexities of exporting and importing demand nothing short of an heroic process of cooperation and continuous improvement. Shaw built his business on the three heroic principles in an arena where he sometimes found it necessary to make up rules as he went along. As nations converge into a global economy, the need for common understanding and ground rules grows ever greater. The principles of the Medicine Circle—build heroic partnerships, lead through strategic humility, and walk in a sacred manner—work together to provide a framework to meet this need. As international relationships increase in scope and number, the heroic path offers an opportunity for creating clarity of purpose and understanding.

Build Heroic Partnerships

When Chuck Neumann took over as President and CEO of the Hospital Corporation of America (HCA) for the United Kingdom and Europe, he knew that building bridges of understanding would provide the key to success. Neumann got the job because of a well-earned reputation as a man of impeccable integrity and tremendous energy. Under his leadership, European operations grew over 300 percent in less than five years. His founding of Rome-American Hospital, in particular, illustrates his ability to build global bridges of understanding.

In 1986, Neumann accepted an invitation to fly to Rome to meet with Stefano Falez, a prominent European businessman, regarding health-care business opportunities in Italy. Neumann arrived in Rome expecting to discuss technical issues relating to the financial feasibility of a joint venture; instead, he found himself immersed in an evening of thoughtful discussion of philosophy, values, and personal experiences.

Falez, as it turned out, was far more interested in the man than in his resume, and Neumann learned why after dinner when Falez invited him to meet the Holy Father for another "brief" discussion of health care. It turned out that Falez was a "gentleman of the Pope," one of a small handful of international advisers regarding worldly matters impacting the Vatican. While Neumann was a seasoned international negotiator, used to intense give-and-take with the likes of Margaret Thatcher and other European leaders, he was unprepared for the personal attentiveness and interest shown by Falez and the Holy Father. Both men barely touched on the topic of health care, probing instead into Neumann's personal background and his values as a business executive. What personal goals, they wanted to know, governed his life, and how did he measure success in others?

The first order of business for Falez and those committed to improving the quality of health care in Italy was the quality of the person they would ask to lead them. Only after Neumann's interview convinced the men that they were dealing with an individual of integrity committed to the well-being of others, did Falez invite Neumann to begin planning for a new state-of-the-art hospital, a joint venture between the Hospital Corporation of America, the Falez family enterprises, and a consortium of Italian banks. One caveat drove the negotiations. The project would go forward only if Neumann promised that he would personally guide the project to completion—regardless of the challenges that might arise or the time it might require.

Six years later, following the dismemberment of HCA, including the sale of its immensely successful British operations, Neumann understood why Falez had asked for his personal promise. Falez, his family, and many of Italy's financial leaders had invested heavily in Rome-American Hospital because they respected the integrity of the young American executive who said he would make the project work. When HCA decided to walk away from the venture as part of its corporate restructuring effort, Falez called Neumann to ask what would happen to their partnership.

Falez had chosen his partner well. Neumann immediately flew to Rome to find a way to honor his commitment. When he arrived, he expected to find a disappointed former business associate. Instead, he found a friend who responded with warmth and gratitude, as well as an offer to join him in continuing the venture they had started together. Stefano Falez, as Neumann had learned, was an astute judge of character. For Falez, character provided a far more important basis for building business relationships than anything else. As a former Slovenian freedom fighter during the Second World War, Falez had on more than one occasion put his life in the hands of those he trusted. He pursued the hospital project because, as he correctly judged, he could trust the word of Chuck Neumann. Neumann's integrity and commitment helped him to create one of the most progressive and successful hospitals in Italy. Today, he works with the Falez family in expanding the outreach of Rome-American Hospital to serve as a model for a whole new generation of health care organizations throughout Europe.

Lead Through Strategic Humility

Dr. Daniel Sudia, director of education at the Centers for Disease Control (CDC) and an internationally renowned scientist, ran into a thorny problem: The CDC was not disseminating its extensive library of medical and scientific reference materials because of cuts in the federal budget. Information that could save lives, especially in developing countries, had become bound and gagged by bureaucracy. After struggling with the problem without finding a way around the budget constraints, Sudia decided to ask for help. His opportunity came during a CDC conference, where he met Tom Paul, an educator and publisher.

Paul seemed at first blush a strange bedfellow. Neither a scientist, nor connected with the government, he operated outside Sudia's conventional circles. But after Paul independently expressed his concern to Sudia about the potential consequences of wasting the CDC's vast resources, Sudia asked Paul for his own ideas. They discussed the options, ruling out conventional publishing because the materials were too technical to appeal to a wide audience. Since Sudia had already exhausted such channels, the situation obviously required a new tack. During their conversation, Sudia became so impressed with Paul's commitment and interest that he decided to enlist his help, thinking that perhaps an entrepreneur would bring to the problem skills and resources that Sudia himself had been unable to muster.

Sudia had built the right bridge. Paul labored for the next year to create a coalition to establish a nonprofit international foundation for health science education that would distribute vital CDC educational and scientific research products to less developed countries. Urging friends and friends of friends to pull together corporate sponsors from technology and pharmaceutical businesses, Paul engaged in an arduous year of cold calls, fundraising, and calling in favors, until, at last, the nonprofit foundation came to life. The foundation not only published reference materials but acted as a forum for researchers and physicians to share ideas and findings via communication services such as the Internet. As a result, CDC materials have been distributed throughout the world because a creative partnership between a scientist and an entrepreneur translated mutual commitment into a service for others.

Walk in a Sacred Manner

Walking in a sacred manner, abiding by mutually understood and agreed-upon values, plays a particularly important role in the complex world of international relationships. Walking in a sacred manner helps people with different backgrounds, religions, social mores, and languages avoid misunderstandings and missteps. Doing so establishes a clear path everyone can follow when coping with inevitable conflicts.

Delta Airlines and British carrier Virgin Atlantic Airways walked in a sacred manner when they reached an alliance and joined services out of London's Heathrow Airport. Their bridge helped both airlines fill gaps in their competitive capabilities: Delta's desire to serve out of Europe's most lucrative destination, and Virgin's goal to offer a greater variety of frequent flyer services to its best customers.

Prior to the agreement, Delta could fly only into London's less popular Gatwick Airport, a restriction that severely hampered Delta's competitiveness, as rival carriers American and United both served Heathrow and could make connections from the popular hub. By allying with Virgin, Delta could put passengers directly on transatlantic flights through a "code sharing" arrangement that allowed the carriers to list connection services under one flight number.

In return, Virgin customers could now use their frequent flier miles on Delta's extensive U.S. and Eastern European routes—a big boost for both airlines' marketability. The alliance served a need for both partners, allowing each to more fully meet the challenge of global mega-carriers. The partners deepened their investment in their mutual success with plans for a stock swap if the initial program worked out. By choosing the partnership with care and moving with appropriate caution, both companies increased the likelihood of success.

CONCLUSION

As the global economy makes the world a smaller and more intimate place in which to live and do business, the need for building global bridges of cooperation becomes ever stronger. While the dialogue on international trade tends to include a lot of statistics and jargon, the stories of Shaw, Neumann, and Paul remind us that, at the heart of the matter, the issue remains one of relationship building. All three cut through the complexity of geographical, ethnic, and cultural differences to establish bonds by using the principles of cooperation and reciprocity.

—14—
STAKEHOLDER:
Competitors

Three African lakes, Tanganeeka, Malawi, and Victoria, contain a natural anomaly: A competitive species whose slight adaptation in eating mechanisms has enabled its members to coexist and thrive together in a confined environment. The chichilc fish have learned to break the rules of evolution, carving out specialized niches in their environment that allow the whole population to thrive. Each of the 200 variations of this unusual fish displays subtle differences in their jaws and mouths, allowing them to feed on different plants than their cousins do. As a result, all variations thrive together, defying both common wisdom and the "law" of nature in their ability to coexist through cooperation.

Normally, 200 varieties of all of the same creature would constantly battle one another to dominate the habitat. The "law" of nature—survival of the fittest, and the fittest alone—usually designates only one winner in such contests, as the fate of the English brown squirrel, which lost its native home to the aggressive imported American gray squirrel, proves. However, the chichilc has triumphed by adhering to another natural law: strength through diversity.

Strength Through
Competition

Many organizations behave as though their world must obey a natural "law," that dominance can come only through head-to-head competition that forces the strong to eliminate the weak. Any attempt at cooperation, or even at recognizing competitors as respected stakeholders in the business environment, runs counter to survival of the fittest. Consequently, most organizations view all others as potential competitors, as a threat to their success, and they define every other's gain as their own loss. Such organizations forget, however, the lessons of the chichilc. While competitors do pose real threats, they do so only to the extent that an organization itself allows. Too many organizations waste more time trying to destroy competitors than striving to improve themselves and their service to the customer. Pepsi battles Coke in an ongoing grudge match; MCI and AT&T spend millions struggling to out-advertise each other; and giant Microsoft, which simply can't bear to run in second place, has gone so far as to abandon its European market drive to concentrate its energy instead on battling tiny Intuit, maker of the number-one check-writing software, Quicken.

Combative organizations focus on the single goal of "winning the battle." However, today's global economy makes it harder for any one competitor to support such battles; the competition sports surprising new faces, more and more countries compete with world-class products, and the service-oriented economy welcomes small upstarts able to fill specific niches, as the success of companies like Snapple, Ben & Jerry's, and Intuit reveals. History has proven that one-winner scenarios not only hurt the customer and other stakeholders in the Medicine Circle, but ultimately prove unsustainable. A state of monopoly inherently slows progress, creating a static culture that nullifies the true natural order of competition that makes all stakeholders stronger.

Instead of defining competitors as alien and hostile forces to be crushed at all costs, the Heroic Organization includes them as part of the organizational Medicine Circle, a view that reflects the reality that all stakeholders share the impact of competition. In an evolving system such as the Medicine Circle, competition holds a vital place as the spur of progress, forcing organizations to strive continuously to improve their own ability to serve the customer.

That the Sioux valued fortitude—bravery—as one of the Four Sacred Virtues gives evidence to the prominence of competition in their society. For the Sioux, competition was a constant way of life. Enemies surrounded them, and rarely did they enjoy a time of complete peace. Competition eventually led the various tribes to hone their skills to the point where war skills became cultural symbols. As tribes became more established on the plains, the Sioux created a strategy of symbolic victory, a system of "counting coup" that demonstrated an individual's bravery in battle and won social status for that individual. A coup did not necessitate killing an enemy; a warrior gained more prestige by simply touching a hostile enemy with a coup stick or with his hand than by killing him from a distance with an arrow, because by doing so he had endangered himself and proven his bravery. The great chief Sitting Bull counted coup by deliberately sitting in the line of fire during a conflict with U.S. soldiers and smoking a pipe. Like all peoples, the Sioux strayed from their ideals of harmony during warfare, but they did not seek to obliterate their enemies, nor did they delude themselves that war represented a worthy end unto itself.

Organizations that focus so intently on defeating competitors that the "war" does, in fact, become an end unto itself, ultimately unbalance the organization's energy and bankrupt their own values. In contrast, Heroic Organizations learn to include competitors in their circle of stakeholders, neither underestimating their effect on the Medicine Circle, nor engaging exclusively in a head-to-head contest. Heroic Organizations value their competitors for the opportunities they bring to the Medicine Circle, recognizing that their closest competitors actually share their own journey. They share the same struggles and seek the same quest, and, as such, they provide a benchmark and stimulus for change and growth. Warriors throughout the ages, from the Sioux, to the Samurai, to the Knights in the Age of Heraldry, have recognized this value in their competitors. Rather than loathe their competitors, Heroic Organizations honor competitors for enabling them to realize their own potential.

This attitude has yielded corporate practices such as benchmarking and competing for the Baldrige National Quality Award. With these tools, organizations gain from the power of strategic humility, learning from competitors and adopting their best strategies. With the wider perspective of the Medicine Circle, organizations can also learn to see their competitors not just as rulers by which to measure achievement, but as co-creators toward an ultimate goal of customer service.

Competition has brought great benefits to the world—from Kennedy's vision of placing a man on the moon within a decade to the amazing increase in the power of computers. Clearly, competition toward such goals enables everyone to win, and when it does so it argues against the traditional view of competition as a zero-sum game of winners and losers. As a linear, goal-oriented process, head-to-head competition can, and does, waste enormous amounts of money, time, and energy, but as part of circular, encompassing process, competition can earn a huge return on a company's investment in it. Organizations that choose to create together or that choose to compete in niche markets can take heroic advantage of competition. Whether in the form of competitive alliances, partnerships, or subcontracting, companies can profit from competitors' strengths and enhance their own ability to serve the customer.

The case for competitive partnering has never been stronger. New ventures require so much capital, especially in technology fields, that few companies can go it alone in every situation. Partnerships have grown particularly important on the international front; today even the largest American corporations can no longer simply outspend their international rivals. Alliances can provide shortcuts for companies developing new products or entering new markets as they use "competitive collaboration" to enhance internal skills and technologies, to make up for weaknesses, and to learn new methods for manufacturing and marketing their products. Such collaboration redefines competition in a way that permits companies to alter their competitive tactics without losing sight of their competitive goals.

Even in the complex field of health care, competitors have begun transforming their former adversaries into partners. The recently formed Universal Cardiac Care Consortium has bound former competitors in a strategic alliance that enables each partner to compete more effectively for the $100 billion Americans spend each year for heart care, by far the largest slice of the health-care market. In response to the threat of losing business to lower-cost community hospitals, the UCCC unites some of the country's leading teaching hospitals—the Mayo Clinic, Stanford University Medical Clinic, Mt.

Sinai, Massachusetts General, and six other world-class teaching hospitals. Despite their reputations, these providers were losing business because of their high cost structures. Their leading-edge technological capabilities, it turned out, could not overcome the fact that patients and their insurers were choosing more economical community hospitals for heart care. Since they knew that the spotlight on health care costs would only grow more intense, the UCCC hospitals realized that they must cut costs or continue losing business. Rather than compromise their level of care by cutting research budgets or staff, they concentrated instead on finding a way to share the burden of leading-edge research by uniting forces with those with whom they had the most in common: their traditional competitors, who were suffering the same malaise in their own communities.

Together, the hospitals could unite forces on the forefront of cardiac and cancer research, lowering their individual costs while at the same time increasing their collective talent and expertise. Their rivals, community hospitals, which currently operate more cost effectively, must now increase the value of their services, either through more effective cost structures or increased quality of care. They, too, might choose to pool resources and technologies in order to compete, but however this competition scenario plays itself out, the true winner will be the customer.

Learning to change deeply ingrained assumptions about competitors will surely test most organizations, which will find it hard to break old habits, choosing instead to continue trying to crush and dominate every competitor in sight. However, history has proven that those who compete with the most integrity ultimately win. Just as stakeholders linked corporate ethics to corporate longevity, rapacious and morally bankrupt organizations tend to destroy themselves in the long run. An example of the positive results of learning to live with, respect, and learn from competitors has occurred in Sweden, where businesses have established a history of connecting destinies and learning to prosper together. The path they have followed adheres to the precepts of the Heroic Process.

THE HEROIC PROCESS

1. Establish a Context for Action

2. Measure Mission Effectiveness

3. Identify Opportunities for Improvement

4. Mobilize Support

5. Take Action

6. Evaluate Results

7. Repeat the Process Continuously

CASE STUDY:
SWEDEN

Sweden displays a long history of striking a balance among social and economic relationships. Charles Hampden-Turner and Alfons Trompenaars recount an interesting example in their book, *The Seven Cultures of Capitalism*: When the early Vikings passed around the drinking horn in a circle, a dilemma arose concerning drinking too much or too little. To drink too little would deprive you of intoxicating pleasures, but to drink too much would attract the ire of the warriors who drank after you. The answer? To imbibe *lagom*, just the right quantity to satisfy yourself as well as the others. *Lagom* represents the mean between self and others that governs Swedish relationships on the individual and organizational level.

The ideals and values that led the country down the socialist political path remain an intrinsic part of its culture. For decades, Sweden successfully managed to unite the values of humanitarianism, social conscience, egalitarianism, and environmental concern with one of the most prosperous economies in the world, defying the conventional wisdom that businesses must swim like sharks to succeed. The country's extraordinarily rapid industrial development, beginning only a few years before the turn of the century, and its defiance of conventional attitudes toward creating wealth present a unique model that parallels the ideals of *Cangleska Wakan*. While Sweden, like the rest of the world, must wrestle with the need to change in order to prosper in a global economy, shifting from labor to service intensive, it possesses unique qualities that enable it to compete in an era where cooperation and connection have become increasingly important to success.

In its choice of government and model for business, Sweden *established a context* of mutual prosperity. From the earliest times, when a factory paid the salary of the priest and the schoolmaster serving the township, to the modern-day company BAHCO, which found new jobs for every person it laid off in a major corporate restructuring, business has demonstrated its determination to share responsibility and prosperity. This point of view has extended to the concept of competition, where Swedish businesses have followed the tenets of the Medicine Circle by including their competitors in their world view. In doing so, they have engineered a system that promotes alliance as well as competition.

Sweden's economic success provides a promising *measure of mission effectiveness.* The ethic of inclusion has helped it become one of the most highly developed countries in the world. Now facing a downturn in industrial growth, the country's policymakers are concentrating on methods of new business creation while maintaining Sweden's unique social contract. Swedish companies use a variety of ways to innovate and grow new industry, including nurturing partnerships with would-be competitors. Companies cultivate innovation by challenging themselves and opening their eyes to the competition's point of view. For example, Volvo, Sweden's largest company, generates new ideas and spin-off businesses by working with Euroventures Nordica, a European version of a venture capital fund. Euroventures Nordica helps link companies to fellow corporate members, sometimes traditional rivals, to work together on a project. The fund itself provides the money, while the new partners add their expertise to the new venture.

Sweden works to balance competition and alliance in the country's best interests. The formation of the European Community, to which Sweden does not belong, created a major challenge. Recognizing that the EC had rewritten the rules of competition, and that global competitiveness begins at home, the Swedish government *identified opportunities for improvement* by deregulating its airline industry. Previously, air routes were awarded to individual carriers on a five-year basis, with competition allowed only on routes that carried more than 300,000 passengers. If a carrier served a route well, renewal was virtually automatic. Domestic carriers faced almost no competition from other airlines, and they could grow only by buying other carriers or their routes. Large carriers could own all or portions of smaller carriers without competing against themselves. The end of this comfortable arrangement signaled the country's commitment to balancing its national competitiveness in the emerging global economy. Choosing competition over comfortable alliances made the airline industry both more self-reliant and more competitive at home and abroad.

Swedish companies *mobilize support* to compete in an increasingly globalized market by relying on an infrastructure that supports innovation and partnerships between small and large companies. Swedish companies encourage their employees to innovate by allowing them to work on new ventures while holding onto their present jobs. Employees can spend six months developing a new idea; if successful, they go full time on the new job, usually with a promotion, and if unsuccessful, they simply go back to their old job. The practice provides not only financial support and resources for individuals and new ventures, but security for the company's most entrepreneurial souls. In turn, the company wins by retaining the energy of its talent instead of spinning off new competitors.

Large Swedish companies also mobilize support for innovation by linking with smaller companies in entrepreneurial partnerships. Perstorp, a producer of specialty chemicals, has established a corporate incubator at a university research park dedicated to investing in promising new businesses that can eventually become Perstorp's partners. Perstorp links up with these companies, providing marketing support, patenting knowledge, and networking power. Today, the companies that Perstorp has supported over the years account for over 20 percent of the company's sales. By linking efforts with would-be competitors that would either threaten its business or be crushed by its own marketing power, Perstorp helps everyone, customers especially, reap the rewards of co-creation.

Swedish organizations have learned that working with competitors presents an opportunity to learn and rectify a company's own weaknesses. While partnerships necessarily entail a level of risk, Heroic Organizations take the opportunity to improve their own processes and strengthen themselves from the partnership. The most lucrative aspect of partnership, and the one most frequently ignored by American organizations, comes in the form of learning. Most American organizations use competitor partnerships, particularly international ones, as expedient ways to break into new markets or to develop products. More interested in reducing the costs and risks involved in entering new businesses or markets than in acquiring new skills, they adopt a posture of avoidance, and, as a result, they lose the greatest benefit of competitive collaboration: self-improvement.

Successful competitive partnerships erect a learning platform for both organizations. An organization that partners with a competitor out of a desire to benefit from the other's quality manufacturing expertise does itself a great disservice if it simply borrows that expertise and avoids working it into its own plants. The tremendous success of Japanese and Korean collaborative efforts with U.S. companies after World War II teach a vital lesson. Japan and Korea entered alliances with Western rivals from weak positions, but they worked steadfastly toward independence by learning from their competitors. In the early 1960s, NEC's computer business was only one quarter the size of Honeywell's, its primary foreign partner. However, in only two decades, NEC grew large enough to buy out Honeywell's computer operations. The NEC experience demonstrates that dependence on a competitor-partner doesn't automatically condemn a company to also-ran status. A smart company makes the most of a partnership, regardless of the size of its stake in the arrangement.

Sweden has institutionalized another unique form of competitive partnering: Certain companies act as entrepreneurial managers, speeding the process of growth for small companies. Incentive, Inc., for instance, acquires small companies and then invests capital, provides management consulting, and taps into its own network of sales and distribution channels to help grow its acquisition. The combination of professional management, a seasoned board of directors, fresh strategy, capital for expansion, and introduction into new markets, including those abroad, enable Incentive to turn around sleepy family firms and transfer them into international powerhouses. An Incentive venture differs from a more traditional acquisition typical in the United States because Incentive treats the new acquisition as a partner, respecting the integrity of the product that attracted it to the company in the first place, and concentrating on growing its strengths. Incentive provides the capital and the marketing muscle, while the new partner supplies the talent and experience in its field. When Incentive courts promising companies, the targets know from the company's reputation that the prospect will enable all concerned to *take action* on a promising new venture.

Compare that attitude with a classic "benign" takeover in the U.S.—Kraft's acquisition of Celestial Seasonings herbal tea company. Celestial Seasonings joined Kraft in 1984 with high hopes all around. The company had started as a one-man operation, and, after fifteen years of wild growth it had climbed to the top of the herbal tea market, racking up more sales than all of its competitors combined. But the company had run into trouble as it tried to break out of health food stores and into the mainstream market. The cyclical nature of the herbal tea business, which sees three quarters of all products consumed in winter, so fully consumed the company's resources it could not gain the funds it needed to grow further.

A buyout seemed a smart move, but under Kraft's heavy bureaucratic hand the company soon began to lose the individualistic innovative edge that had made it so popular from the outset. Bland product names like "Herb and Spice Blend" didn't play well to a customer base used to "Red Zinger" and "Morning Thunder." Worse, Kraft executives lacked experience in the tea industry and remained inflexible when the company needed to make changes in tea formulas or quantities based on herbal crops. Kraft strayed from Celestial's commitment to using only the very finest ingredients, choosing more generic sources, and then began to use the Celestial Seasonings name on a variety of unrelated spin-offs, such as salad dressings and spices, draining millions of the company's resources on dead-end product testing that ignored the company's core customers. Finally, Celestial put together a costly LBO to divorce itself from Kraft. Though the process saddled the company with debt, Celestial felt compelled to remove itself from the clutches of a disinterested partner that was ruining the company.

In contrast, Swedish businesses' cultural ethic of *lagom* enables companies to share resources and mutually profit rather than overextend themselves trying to dominate a market. This attitude particularly benefits small companies ready to take on more growth but unable to finance it. In Sweden, small companies partner in semi-independent business arrangements to add the power of big company networks and marketing to their businesses while retaining control of their own destinies. SAS Intercultural Communications, a training company, chose just such a partnering relationship. The company, started by owner Lena Ahlstrom as a small service company offering training to managers on international assignments, began soaring when Ahlstrom formed a partnership with Scandinavian Airlines (SAS). The unique arrangement guarantees Ahlstrom 50 percent of her business with SAS, and sends a steady stream of clients to Scandinavian Air as well. Ahlstrom pays rent for offices at SAS headquarters; SAS pays for the phones and salaries and shares the company's profits. Ahlstrom has gained a steady lifelong client stream, and SAS enjoys an in-house training facility and a marketing edge in offering intercultural training to large corporations it wants to attract as clients. While Ahlstrom cannot do business with direct competitors of SAS, the relationship with SAS as a parent partner guarantees the company's fiscal well-being.

Swedish businesses can *evaluate the results* of the partnering ethic by looking at the success of partnerships such as SAS Intercultural Communications, where both companies gained. Such partnering enables Swedish businesses to take the best advantage of its inventors' ideas, which will play a significantly increasing role in their futures as the global economy evolves from concentrating on large industry to dependence on information and service.

Sweden will surely encounter its share of change ahead as it strives to keep pace with the demands of the global economy, and though it no longer operates as a socialist country, it retains its ethic of *lagom*, a rare holistic approach to business that includes all stakeholders in the Medicine Circle. By *repeating continuously* this commitment in all of its transitions, Sweden has uniquely positioned itself to compete in a world where technologies subsume each other to grow and where those who know how to cooperate will win in the long run.

Choosing Heroism

Swedish businesses consistently apply the three heroic principles to their relationships with competitors. They practice strategic humility to learn from competitors and improve; they build heroic partnerships with small businesses and would-be competitors for mutual benefits; and they walk in a sacred manner by supporting partnership and mutual prosperity in all undertakings. By supporting partnership-building enterprises such as Euroventures Nordica and Incentive, Inc., Sweden makes the most of its business resources by combining its companies' strengths rather than by pitting them ruthlessly against one another.

On this side of the Atlantic, the story of longtime rivals Apple Computer and IBM, who ventured into a partnership to become more competitive, demonstrates an American commitment to these same heroic principles.

Lead Through Strategic Humility

In the last few years, both Apple and IBM have seen their market shares erode and their profits wane. Apple, long a proprietary outfit that relied on its superior user interface to sell its machines and software, found its appeal dwindling as DOS-based machines grew more capable of imitating its own strengths. At the same time that Apple's machines were losing their quality advantage, they also failed to compete on the software front. Its lack of resources kept its own offerings limited, and those limited offerings could not run the variety of DOS software products available.

If Apple wrestled with the problem of exclusivity, IBM struggled with just the opposite. Having built its machines around Microsoft's DOS operating system, IBM had no exclusive hold over its PC market. Any company that bought DOS-based chips, mostly made by IBM's own supplier, Intel, could clone its products, and upstarts such as Dell, Compaq, DEC, and others were eating away huge chunks of IBM's market.

The two companies, head-to-head rivals for years, had both run aground in the sea of changes buffeting their businesses. Both shared weaknesses in meeting the demands of the new market, and both companies needed a strong dose of strategic humility to come to grips with their respective deficiencies. Their complementary needs eventually led them into each other's camps. By respecting each other as rivals with something to share, they moved to the next step and built an heroic partnership.

Build Heroic Partnerships

The two companies met in Austin, Texas, each bringing ideas and products to the table. IBM offered its newly developed RISC (Reduced Instruction Set Computing) chip, a breakthrough designed to compete with Intel's latest processor, and Apple presented its new operating system, code-named Pink. From that starting point, the two competitors worked together to modify their products so that they would support each other. The resulting PowerPC chip was not only one of the fastest chips ever made, it could run both Apple and DOS software. Apple further committed to tailor its software to run on the PowerPC. The project led the companies to the joint creation of Taligent, a firm that will develop operating systems for the next generation of microcomputers, IBM's strength, and of Kaleida, which will borrow from Apple's superiority in graphics software to develop and license technologies for the fast-growing multimedia computing market.

Walk in a Sacred Manner

Despite their common interests, Apple and IBM possessed radically different corporate cultures that inevitably clashed at Taligent. On the face of it, dress codes told the story. Taligent's CEO Joe Guglielmi found it necessary to negotiate a median between IBM's pinstripe-suit-and-power-tie types and Apple's denim-and-sneakers crowd. Wisely adopting a spirit of compromise in this area, Guglielmi abandoned strict dress codes and allowed individuals to dress as they wished. Had he favored one uniform or the other, this mundane aspect of the partnership could have fragmented the cultures. Understanding that only by creating a protocol for cooperation could the partnership hold together, he struck a balance by evaluating the needs of the partnership and walking in a sacred manner to accomplish them.

In one instance, Guglielmi met some resistance when he wanted to implement IBM's method of day-to-day project accountability. Using the precepts of the Seven-Step Heroic Process, he established the context: The company needed solid, verifiable record keeping of its work so that others could replicate projects later as necessary. Since the organization could not rely on "folklore" surrounding a project, Guglielmi invited all of the stakeholders to come up with a better method for benchmarking themselves; if they could not, then they would adopt the IBM method. Eventually, the stakeholders decided to use the IBM method. While the process took longer than a top-down ultimatum, by including the stakeholders in the process, Guglielmi mobilized all the participants' support behind a common goal and guaranteed their investment in the ultimate decision. By walking in a sacred manner, he successfully created a balance between stakeholders' desires and the needs of the organization.

Conclusion

As noted biologist Lewis Thomas observed, survival of the fittest does not mean that "nature is red in tooth and claw," as nineteenth century evolutionary theory argued. Nor does it mean that only the strongest and most ruthless will win. Those who survive, Thomas suggested, cooperate best with other living things. Although the relationship between Apple and IBM still simmers in its earliest stages, these two very different companies have put aside their fears and embraced cooperation. Together they are striving toward improved customer service as they attempt to create a product that incorporates the strengths of both organizations and allows both to become more competitive. Organizations that choose to include their competitors in their circle of stakeholders, learning from them when they can and respecting their input in the ongoing cycle of improvement, best position themselves to cope with the changes being played out the world over. As every organization's competitors grow more numerous on the international playing field, organizations that learn to cooperate for survival by carving their own niches and protecting their market shares with learning partnerships will avoid the fate of the Brontosaurus.

PART THREE

THE HEROIC GUIDE TO ACTION
Tools for Forging the Heroic Organization

The invasion of Normandy. The Battle of the Little Big Horn. The quest for Total Quality. Reengineering and Redesigning the Corporation. The competition for Global Customers. The outcome of every major endeavor hinges on meticulous planning, but even the best laid plans will go awry if actions fail to carry those plans through to victory. Every organizational case study we've explored in this book achieved victory through a dual commitment: to the three principles of heroic behavior—lead through strategic humility, build heroic partnerships, and walk in a sacred manner—and a Seven-Step Heroic Process that translates those principles into action: establish a context for action, measure mission effectiveness, identify opportunities for improvement, mobilize support, take action, evaluate results, and repeat the process continuously.

The Heroic Guide to Action provides four tools that enable you to apply these principles and that process to your own organization and its relationships with all of the stakeholders in your organizational Medicine Circle—the leadership team, frontline managers, the workforce, customers, suppliers, competitors, shareholders and the board, the community, the environment, government, and international partners and competitors.

TOOL 1: MISSION DEVELOPMENT will help you identify crucial challenges, the visionary response, and develop a mission statement to establish a leadership plan of action.

TOOL 2: MISSION EFFECTIVENESS ASSESSMENT provides means for imaging the way in which people actually perform work in your organization and measuring the results of that work. This tool is a mini-version of a comprehensive Work Imaging™ Assessment that teams can use diagnostically and/or as preparation for a more comprehensive Mission Effectiveness Assessment of the full continuum of the work and service process. For copies of this instrument, or to compare your team's evaluation of organizational effectiveness with the National Benchmarking Database of Heroic Organizations, contact the Center for Heroic Leadership, c/o E. C. Murphy, Ltd., at 800-922-5005.

TOOL 3: WORK REDESIGN ACTION PLANNING GUIDE will aid you in identifying opportunities for improvement and mobilizing support throughout your organization.

TOOL 4: CONTINUOUS APPLICATION OF THE SEVEN-STEP HEROIC PROCESS will ensure that you repeat the heroic process steadily. Like *Cangleska Wakan,* the work never stops but flows continuously through an ever changing array of stakeholders and relationships.

Together, these four tools can launch an organization on the path toward heroism. While they will not guarantee success—only your creative imagination and tireless effort can do that—they will help you focus on the key elements for success in the future.

TOOL 1:
MISSION DEVELOPMENT EXERCISE

This tool supports Step 1 of the Heroic Process: Establish Context.

GOAL: To identify the organization's challenges and develop a mission statement to meet those challenges. The mission statement establishes a leadership context for action. It is a practical exercise for translating vision and values into reality by defining an objective for action. The mission statement will also facilitate Strategic Planning, Product Line Development, Image Development, and overall corporate communications. Review each of the components of your own platform in terms of their function, content, and utility.

Components of an Effective Mission Statement

Vision Statement

Values Statement

Objective Statement

Vision Statement

- Function

  To describe the reason for which the organization exists, the intention of its beliefs and the focus of its service.

- Content

  Why are we here?

  What do we do?

  Whom do we serve?

- Utility

  Corporate Image Collateral, Product Line Literature, Employee Orientation Materials, Community Education Flyers

Values Statement

- Function

  To establish a social contract for acting on the mission and expectations for service performance and accountability to those that are served.

- Content

  How should we act on our belief?

  How should we serve as individuals/teams?

  To what performance criteria will we hold ourselves accountable?

- Utility

  Employee Orientation Materials, Job Descriptions, Performance Evaluations, Management Education, Performance/Service Measurement

Objective Statement

- Function

  To explain the organization's philosophy of management, provide a common goal for day-to-day operations, and challenge the status quo.

  (continued on next page)

Objective Statement
(continued)

- Content

  How will we manage the organization?

  What should we strive for?

  How will we continually improve?

- Utility

  Employee Orientation Materials, Continuing Education, Employee Communications

How will the organization apply the mission statement? Which groups will use it? To what ends will they use it? The answers to these questions involve once again considering the mission statement: Vision, Values, and Objective.

Applying the Mission Statement

What Ends?	*How?*
Protecting and Assuring *Vision*	Board/CEO Leadership, Community Outreach, Cost-Containment
Building and Maintaining *Values*	Constancy of Purpose, Organizational Development, Performance Evaluation, Continuing Education
Measuring and Improving *Objective*	Ongoing Marketplace and Operational Assessment, Integrated Work Redesign Action Process, Team Learning Environment, Educated and Involved Workforce

After reviewing each of the components of the mission statement, you can set about developing your own. You and your team can further focus the organization's Mission Statement with the

Mission Statement Evaluation Worksheet, a tool for fine tuning the language used to define the organization's challenge and the proper response. The following questions concern the mission statement's effective representation of Vision, Values, and Objective.

Mission Statement Evaluation Worksheet

Components	*A* Write the exact words from your mission statement that support the components listed in the left column.	*B* What words are missing, awkward, unclear, or hard to understand?	*C* What revisions could be made to make the mission statement a simpler, clearer, more practical working tool?
Vision • Why are we here? • What do we do? • Whom do we serve? • What kind of organization do we want to become?			
Values • How should we act on our beliefs? • How should we serve as individuals/teams? • To what performance criteria will we hold ourselves accountable?			
Objective • How will we manage the organization? • What should we strive for? • How will we continually improve?			

This chart includes the specific words you can use when writing your organization's mission statement.

Mission Statement Word List

Vision Statement	Values Statement	Objective Statement
Teach	Sensitivity	Customer Focused
Learn	Integrity	Leadership
Live	Reverence	Empowerment
Lead	Responsibility	Teamwork
Guide	Ethical	Education
Protect	Fairness	Continuous
Provide	Justice	Measurement
Promote	Respect	Data Driven
Maintain	Dignity	Evaluation
Comply	Expertise	Performance
Strive	Excellence	Problem Solving
Research	Knowledge	Innovation
Develop	Competency	Creativity
	Timeliness	Process
	Responsiveness	Workflow
	Accuracy	Prevention
	Effectiveness	Achievement
	Efficiency	Recognition
	Productivity	
	Coordination	
	Collegiality	
	Stewardship	
	Diversity	
	Thoroughness	
	Follow-Through	
	Commitment	
	Accessibility	
	Comprehensiveness	

Consider this example of how an organization formulated its mission statement using Tool 1.

Sample Mission Statement

- Our Vision

    We will provide the highest quality, most reasonably priced computer microprocessor chips in the world.

- Our Values

    We view participation and teamwork necessary for excellence.

    We recognize diversity and creativity as sources of strength.

    We hold in reverence the desires of the customer.

- Our Objective

    We will continually learn, seek, and improve.

    We will listen to and act upon the needs of our customers.

    We will meet expectations with the right resources, at the right time.

    We will relentlessly pursue quality.

TOOL 2:
MISSION EFFECTIVENESS ASSESSMENT

This tool relates to Step 2 of the Heroic Process: Measure Mission Effectiveness.

GOAL: To capture feelings and opinions about an organization's mission effectiveness and service to the customer. Read and answer the following questions. If you "Strongly Agree" with a statement about the organization, mark circle #4. If you agree, but do not have strong feelings, mark circle #3. If you disagree but do not have strong feelings, mark circle #2, and if you "Strongly Disagree" mark circle #1. If you cannot answer a question, mark circle #0. Answer each question based on your personal experience. When finished, use the scoring sheet to calculate your results.

I. THE CUSTOMER Customer Empowerment	*Strongly* *Disagree*		*Strongly* *Agree*		*Don't* *Know*
1. We provide customers with all the information they need to make a thoughtful decision.	1	2	3	4	0
2. We respond to customer complaints promptly and courteously.	1	2	3	4	0
3. We routinely assess customer needs.	1	2	3	4	0
4. We routinely evaluate customer satisfaction.	1	2	3	4	0

Overall Quality of Service

5. Customers receive the best professional and technical service the organization can offer.	1	2	3	4	0
6. The customer's needs come before personal, financial, or procedural concerns.	1	2	3	4	0
7. Customers are treated with understanding.	1	2	3	4	0
8. Customers receive service that is careful and exact, free from errors.	1	2	3	4	0
9. Customers receive timely attention to their needs.	1	2	3	4	0
10. Customer service is well-organized and delivered in proper sequence.	1	2	3	4	0
11. Customers receive all services appropriate to their needs.	1	2	3	4	0

II. THE ORGANIZATION
The Mission

12. We have clearly stated our mission.	1	2	3	4	0
13. All our stakeholders clearly understand our mission.	1	2	3	4	0
14. We effectively translate our mission into action on a daily basis.	1	2	3	4	0

	Strongly Disagree	Strongly Agree	Don't Know

Organizational Values

15. We recognize the needs and rights of customers regardless of race, religion, gender, or age.

1	2	3	4	0

16. High-quality customer service is our number-one priority.

| 1 | 2 | 3 | 4 | 0 |

17. We respect the contributions of individual employees.

| 1 | 2 | 3 | 4 | 0 |

Quality of Organizational Teamwork

18. Employees treat one another with courtesy and respect.

| 1 | 2 | 3 | 4 | 0 |

19. Employees share information and resources with co-workers.

| 1 | 2 | 3 | 4 | 0 |

20. Employees take responsibility for their own actions.

| 1 | 2 | 3 | 4 | 0 |

21. Employees work together to solve problems.

| 1 | 2 | 3 | 4 | 0 |

22. Departments do not let conflicts between them interfere with service.

| 1 | 2 | 3 | 4 | 0 |

23. Employees take the initiative to help others.

| 1 | 2 | 3 | 4 | 0 |

24. Employees welcome suggestions for improvement.

| 1 | 2 | 3 | 4 | 0 |

25. Employees remain calm and supportive under stress.

| 1 | 2 | 3 | 4 | 0 |

26. Employees discuss confidential issues only in an appropriate setting.

| 1 | 2 | 3 | 4 | 0 |

27. Employees willingly perform more than their minimum job requirements when helping customers.

| 1 | 2 | 3 | 4 | 0 |

28. Employees speak in a positive, professional manner about their co-workers.

| 1 | 2 | 3 | 4 | 0 |

	Strongly Disagree		Strongly Agree		Don't Know

Physical Environment

29. The layout of facilities promotes quality customer service.

1	2	3	4	0

30. Facilities are attractive and up-to-date.

1	2	3	4	0

31. Equipment is in good condition and up-to-date.

1	2	3	4	0

32. Employees maintain a professional appearance on the job.

1	2	3	4	0

33. Facilities are kept very clean.

1	2	3	4	0

34. The layout of facilities enables access for the disabled.

1	2	3	4	0

Community & Market Relations

35. The organization enjoys a strong, positive reputation in the community.

1	2	3	4	0

36. Customers refer their families and friends to the organization.

1	2	3	4	0

37. Employees refer their families and friends to the organization.

1	2	3	4	0

III. THE SERVICE TEAM
Self

When providing service to internal and external customers, I . . .

38. Possess the *knowledge and skills* necessary to do my job.

1	2	3	4	0

39. Act *responsibly.*

1	2	3	4	0

40. Remain *sensitive* to others' emotional needs.

1	2	3	4	0

41. Am *accurate* and attentive to detail.

1	2	3	4	0

	Strongly Disagree		Strongly Agree		Don't Know
42. Act in a *timely* fashion.	1	2	3	4	0
43. Am *organized and efficient.*	1	2	3	4	0
44. Pay *attention to details.*	1	2	3	4	0

Frontliners (people who serve on the frontlines of service)

When providing service to customers, frontliners . . .

45. Possess the *knowledge* necessary to do their jobs.	1	2	3	4	0
46. Act *responsibly.*	1	2	3	4	0
47. Remain *sensitive* to the emotional needs of others.	1	2	3	4	0
48. Are *accurate* and attentive to detail.	1	2	3	4	0
49. Act in a *timely* fashion.	1	2	3	4	0
50. Are *organized and efficient.*	1	2	3	4	0
51. Pay *attention to details.*	1	2	3	4	0

Please indicate your overall level of agreement or disagreement with the following statement: The following groups or departments provide high levels of quality in their service to customers . . . (List core departments in your organization. These may include manufacturing, marketing, frontline customer service, financial services, administrative services, etc.)

52. _____	1	2	3	4	0
53. _____	1	2	3	4	0
54. _____	1	2	3	4	0
55. _____	1	2	3	4	0
56. _____	1	2	3	4	0

IV. CHALLENGE ASSESSMENT

	Strongly Disagree		Strongly Agree		Don't Know

57. The organization is facing increased pressure to reduce costs and increase quality.

    1   2   3   4   0

58. The organization is responding well to these challenges and changes.

    1   2   3   4   0

59. Employees understand the pressures to change.

    1   2   3   4   0

60. Employees feel prepared to meet these challenges.

    1   2   3   4   0

61. Customers receive better service now than they did a few years ago.

    1   2   3   4   0

V. WORK EFFICIENCY

62. We do the right work at the right time.

    1   2   3   4   0

63. The way we organize work makes it possible to deliver quality service to our customers and co-workers.

    1   2   3   4   0

64. Work between departments is performed efficiently.

    1   2   3   4   0

65. In my department, we distribute work properly among individuals.

    1   2   3   4   0

66. Compensation and rewards relate directly to work performance.

    1   2   3   4   0

VI. ROADBLOCK ASSESSMENT

Please estimate the *percentage* of your time during a normal work week you spend in overcoming roadblocks to the delivery of quality service (i.e., how much of your time is wasted) in the blanks provided.

Percentage of Time Wasted

67. Communication:

    Examples: junk mail, telephone interruptions, duplicate paperwork, inefficient meetings.

    ———————————————

68. Work Procedures:

    Examples: confusing procedures, insufficient training, redoing work, poor organization.

    ———————————————

69. Equipment:

    Examples: equipment breakdowns, scheduling conflicts, equipment not suitable for the task.

    ———————————————

70. Materials:

    Examples: materials not available when needed, substandard materials.

    ———————————————

VII. COMMENTS

Please elaborate on issues of special concern:

———————————————————————————————

———————————————————————————————

———————————————————————————————

———————————————————————————————

———————————————————————————————

———————————————————————————————

———————————————————————————————

VIII. SCORING

This section provides a general interpretation of your scores on the Mission Effectiveness Assessment. To receive a more comprehensive scoring evaluation, contact the Center for Heroic Leadership, c/o E. C. Murphy, Ltd., at 800-922-5005.

Directions: Average the scores for each section by first counting each item in each section for which there is a nonzero score marked. Then, total the scores and divide by the number of nonzero scores, rounding to one decimal point. For example:

Scores for Section IV= 4, 3, 2, 0, 4
= Four nonzero items
= 4 + 3 + 2 + 4
= 13
= 13 ÷ 4
= 3.25
= 3.3

Using the following chart, plot your scores for each section to obtain an overall picture of the scores. The items in each section of the assessment have been normed to fit within the given ranges. Once completed, proceed to the next section to examine the data to identify opportunities for improvement.

	Low [1.0–1.7]	Moderately Low [1.8–2.5]	Moderately High [2.6–3.4]	High [3.5–4.0]
Section I				
Section II				
Section III				
Section IV				
Section V				

TOOL 3:
WORK REDESIGN ACTION PLANNING GUIDE

This tool implements Step 4 of the Heroic Process: Mobilize Support
Managers and cross-functional work redesign teams can use this guide to translate the data from the comprehensive Mission Effectiveness Assessment into opportunities and concrete plans for improvement. The *Work Redesign Action Planning Guide* enables teams to gather observations about the organization, select those opportunities that will most greatly impact quality and financial results, and create action plans for key opportunities following a ten-step heroic redesign process.

Step 1: Establish Goals

Step 2: Focus on the Data

Step 3: Identify Opportunities

Step 4: Research the Opportunity

Step 5: Create a Plan

Step 6: Evaluate the Plan

Step 7: Submit the Plan

Step 8: Authorize the Plan

Step 9: Execute the Plan and Evaluate Results

Step 10: Improve Continuously

The first four steps eliminate those observations that do not substantiate opportunities, or those opportunities that will not lead to significant improvements. The remaining steps allow teams to formulate plans to address key opportunities and develop ways to evaluate their degree of success.

Once teams are authorized to execute a plan, the problem-solving techniques used in the Work Redesign Action Planning process can be used to take action that will drive toward fulfillment of the organization's goals and objectives.

Step 1: Establish Goals

OBJECTIVE: Establish mission-based goals for your area of responsibility.

Based on the organization's mission, can you define goals for the work redesign and customer-focused restructuring process in your area of responsibility, whether as a manager responsible for a particular cost center, or as a member of a cross-functional work team?

List goals below.

#	*Goals*
ex.	*To improve responsiveness to customer and associate needs by improving team focus.*
ex.	*To reduce procedural inefficiency both within and between departments through the redesign of work processes.*

Step 2: Focus on the Data

OBJECTIVE: As a team, review the results from the Mission Effectiveness Assessment and list observations regarding the values of the organization, quality of organization's teamwork, community and market relations, the service team, frontline workers, work efficiency, and customer empowerment.

#	*Observations*
ex.	*A low score of 2.2 for the teamwork section of the Mission Effectiveness Assessment indicated an opportunity for improvement. A review of particular items revealed scores of 1 for both interdepartmental sharing and interdepartmental cooperation.*
ex.	*The percentage of time wasted in overcoming roadblocks to work procedures was 14%.*

Step 3: Identify the Opportunities

OBJECTIVE: As a team, consolidate observations into a list of dominant issues and create Opportunity Statements for each by completing the following sentence.

We can seize the opportunity to ___(issue)___ *by/through* ___(possible action)___.

#	*We can seize the opportunity to*	*by/through*
ex.	*improve teamwork and operational responsiveness*	*reducing complexity and disconnection between and within service units*
ex.	*reduce inefficiency*	*removing roadblocks to work procedures*

Step 4: Research the Opportunity

OBJECTIVE: To pinpoint areas where you need to obtain more data and information before creating plans to address the opportunities you have identified.

We should research ___(need)___ by/through ___(action)___.

#	*We should research*	*by/through*
ex.	the areas where teamwork breaks down both within and between departments	holding team discussion sessions about how to redesign the work to improve information sharing.
ex.	the specific work procedures where roadblocks occur	holding team discussion sessions to outline inefficient processes.

Step 5: Create a Work Redesign Plan

OBJECTIVE: To consolidate Research and Opportunity Statement Lists using the Improvement Planning Form. This form will assist you in organizing the:

1. Opportunities identified

2. Action recommended (inter or intradepartmental, existing committee, individual, etc.)

3. Activities recommended (research, workflow analysis, work restructuring, etc.)

4. Due date for the completed plan

5. Potential leaders who can guide the Work Redesign Action Planning Team

#	Opportunities	What Kinds of Action . . . (Research, Plan, Analysis, etc.)	Will Need What Resources . . . (People, Space, Time, Equipment, etc.)	By When . . . (Due Date)	Under Whose Leadership . . .

Step 6: Evaluate the Plan

OBJECTIVE: To evaluate the likely cost/benefit impact of each plan you have developed.

Using the following four-point scale, fill in a score for each item on both the Benefits and Costs charts. Once you have filled in each item, total all items and mark your score in the *Total* space provided on each form. (You will want to make copies of this form for each plan.) Once you have completed both forms, input the totals into the Return on Investment form and calculate your level of investment return. This will guide you in discerning which plans are likely to be successful and worthwhile and which plans will likely produce few results.

1	2	3	4	0

Low Benefit/Cost   High Benefit/Cost

BENEFITS
Opportunity #:_____

Item	*Score*	*Example*
Impact on Quality		4
Probability of Success		3
Importance of Result		3
Timeliness of Benefits		2
Cost Savings Realized		4
Benefit Total Score		16

COSTS
Opportunity #:_____

Item	Score	Example
Time Investment		2
People Investment		3
Dollar Investment		3
Cost Total Score		8

RETURN ON INVESTMENT

Item	Score	Example
Benefit Total		16
Cost Total		8
Return on Investment (ROI) (Benefit Total-Cost Total)		8

SCORING

Low ROI	Medium ROI	High ROI	
-7–0	1–10	11–17	Scale
	✓		Example
			Your Score

Step 7: Submit the Plan

OBJECTIVE: To select those plans you feel warrant full consideration by the Leadership Team. Complete one form for each of the opportunities selected. When finished, move to Step 8, completion of the Authorization Form by the Leadership Team. Both forms will combine to become a plan for Team Action.

PLAN SUBMISSION FORM

Please Check One

___ Authorization Requested   ___ Information & Awareness

_____   _____
Name   Department Name

Name of Work Redesign Action Plan: _____

Starting Date: _____   Completion Date: _____

Work Redesign Action Plan Team Leader: _____

Team Members: _____   _____

_____   _____   _____

Description of identified opportunity and anticipated resources:

_____

_____

_____

Anticipated Financial Savings: _____

ROI (Total and Scoring Range): _____

Who Should Do What by When?

Action(s):	Responsible Person(s)	Start Date/End Date

Step 8: Authorize the Plan

OBJECTIVE: For the Leadership Team to communicate its decision to set clear parameters for action and ensure alignment and consistency with strategic priorities and fiscal realities. Attach this form to the Plan Submission Form to create a plan for Team Action.

AUTHORIZATION FORM

Magnitude of Improvements Expected:

_____

_____

_____

Limitations or Boundaries (Time, Money, Authority, etc.):

_____

_____

_____

Assigned Adviser: _____

Assigned Coaching Team: _____

Report to: _____   Frequency: _____

Authorization Signature:_____

Step 9: Execute the Plan and Evaluate Results

OBJECTIVE: To utilize the problem-solving process and quality tools and techniques from the Work Redesign Action Plan to execute the plan and attain goals and objectives.

Measure results of the plan against the goals put forward in Step 1 and the Cost/Benefit analysis undertaken in evaluating the plan's potential in Step 6. Also retake the Mission Effectiveness Assessment to identify the plan's effectiveness in specific areas.

Step 10: Improve Continuously

OBJECTIVE: To repeat and improve the process continuously.

TOOL 4:
CONTINUOUS APPLICATION
OF THE SEVEN-STEP HEROIC PROCESS

*This tool initiates Step 7 of the Heroic Process: Improve Continuously.
It summarizes the essential elements of the Seven-Step Heroic Process,
providing a check list for leadership and team planning.*

Step 1: Establish Context

WHY? Need a leadership platform that cuts through complexity,
establishes common ground, and provides a social contract for all
stakeholders.

HOW?

- Focus on the customer
- Define customer-centered values and mission
- Outline a Work Redesign Action Plan
- Invite all stakeholders to assess commitment to customer-centered values and mission

Step 2: Measure Mission Effectiveness

WHY? Need a data-driven process to minimize subjectivity, overcome
resistance, and reinforce customer-focused values

HOW?

- Involve all stakeholders in a global Mission Effectiveness Assessment of . . .

  Quality of work—Is customer service expert, responsible, sensitive, accurate, timely, coordinated, and thorough?

  Efficiency of work—Are the right people, in the right place, at the right time, for the right reason, at the right cost, for the mission of the organization?

Step 3: Identify Opportunities for Improvement

WHY? Need to establish customer-focused priorities, build consensus for work redesign, and protect the organization's mission.

HOW?
- Focus on the whole system, not individual people or departments
- Examine individual work roles, service structures, cross-functional processes, and levels of the hierarchy
- Diagnose organizational complexity and waste
- Reference benchmarks from like organizations
- Target opportunities for simplification, integration

Step 4: Mobilize Support

WHY? Need to prepare the organization for change, build frontline accountability, and harness energy for work redesign

HOW?
- Share the diagnosis globally
- Develop and announce an organization-wide action plan
- Reaffirm customer-focused priorities
- Empower stakeholders with responsibility for work redesign
- Provide work redesign skills, tools, and processes
- Commission customer-focused work redesign teams
- Create data-driven improvement plans

Step 5: Take Action

WHY? Need to evaluate appropriateness of work redesign plans, prioritize for biggest returns, and redistribute resources where necessary

HOW?
- Connect work redesign to capital and operating budget process
- Establish customer-focused criteria to evaluate work redesign plans

- Approve and implement plans that are do-able and cost-effective
- Encourage frontline accountability for restructuring goals and timeliness
- Build on and integrate existing investments wherever possible

Step 6: Evaluate Results

WHY? Need to hold the organization accountable to its mission, identify performance improvements, and celebrate work redesign accomplishments

HOW?
- Repeat the global assessment
- Analyze trends in the data
- Identify best practices in terms of quality and cost
- Compare results to national norms
- Establish benchmarks for future improvement

Step 7: Repeat the Process Continuously

WHY? Need to "hold the gains," strengthen resolve, and assure the organization's capacity to improve continuously

HOW?
- Develop a yearly cycle for ongoing mission assessment and diagnosis, work redesign, and evaluation
- Reinforce customer-focused mission and process through continuing education for all staff
- Increase involvement of all stakeholders

BIBLIOGRAPHY

Allen, Paula Gunn, *The Sacred Hoop*. Boston: Beacon Press, 1986.

Avery, Susan, "Using Suppliers to Drive Change: Coleman Outdoor Products, Inc. Optimizes Supplier Partnerships," *Purchasing,* March 18, 1993, p. 54.

Bennett, Lynne, "Kings of Know-How: Transferring Technologies from Research Laboratories to Business," *California Business,* April 1993, p. 33.

Benson, Tracy E. "Robert Haas' Vision Scores 20/20," *Industry Week,* April 2, 1990, p. 19.

Biesada, Alexandra, "Fed Ex: Pride Goeth . . . ," *FW,* Sept. 4, 1990, p. 38.

Block, Peter, *Stewardship: Choosing Service Over Self-Interest.* San Francisco: Berrett-Koehler Publishers, Inc., 1993.

Botkin, James W., and Jana B. Matthews, *Winning Combinations: The Coming Wave of Entreprenurial Partnerships Between Large and Small Companies.* New York: John Wiley & Sons, Inc., 1992.

273

Boyadjis, George and Earl Merkel, "Empowerment: Managers Promote Employee Growth," *Healthcare Financial Management.* March 1990, p. 58.

Boyett, Joseph H., and Henry P. Conn, *Workplace 2000: The Revolution Reshaping American Business.* New York: Dutton, 1991.

Bradley, Peter, "Making Quality Fly," *Purchasing,* Jan. 17, 1991, p. 100.

Braham, James, "The Billion-Dollar Dustpan." *Industry Week,* Aug. 1, 1988, p. 46.

Burrows, Peter, "Forget the Nitpiks! The Baldrige Is Working," *Electronic Business,* Oct. 1992, p. 34.

Cordtz, Dan, "Corporate Citizenship: No More Soft Touches," *FW,* May 29, 1990, p. 30.

Covey, Stephen R., *Principle-Centered Leadership.* New York: Simon & Schuster, 1990.

Davenport, Thomas H., *Process Innovation: Reengineering Work Through Information Technology.* Boston: Harvard Business School Press, 1993.

DePree, Max, *Leadership Is an Art.* New York: Doubleday, 1989.

Dillon, George C., "Does It Pay to Do the Right Thing?" *Across the Board,* July-August 1991, p. 15.

Driben, Louise I., et al., "Sales & Marketing Management's 1992 Marketing Achievement Awards," *Sales & Marketing Management,* August 1992, p. 40.

Dwek, Robert, "Doing Well by Giving Generously," *Marketing,* July 23, 1992, p. 16.

Etzioni, Amitai, *The Spirit of Community,* New York: Crown Publishers, 1993.

Everett, Martin, "Court of Last Resort," *Across the Board,* Nov. 1991, p. 49.

Farber, Barry, and Joyce Wycoff, "Customer Service: Evolution and Revolution," *Sales & Marketing Management,* May 1994, p. 44.

Forbes, Christine, "Creating the Super Supplier," *Industrial Distribution,* Sept. 1993, p. 30.

Gabor, Andrea, "Rochester Focuses: A Community's Core Competence," *Harvard Business Review,* July-August 1991, p. 116.

Gerlach, Michael L., *Alliance Capitalism.* Los Angeles: University of California Press, 1992.

Gingold, Diane, "American Corporate Community Service," *Fortune,* Nov. 30, 1992, p. 127.

Hamel, Gary, Yves L. Doz, and C. K. Prahalad, "Collaborate with Your Competitors—and Win," *Harvard Business Review,* Jan./Feb. 1989, p. 133.

Hammer, Michael, and James Champy, *Reengineering the Corporation: A Manifesto for Business Revolution.* New York: Harper Collins Publishers, Inc., 1993.

Hampden-Turner, Charles, and Alfons Trompenaars, *The Seven Cultures of Capitalism.* New York: Currency/Doubleday, 1993.

Handy, Charles, *The Age of Unreason.* Boston: Harvard Business School Press, 1989.

Hasell, Nick, "The Intelligence of Intel," *Management Today,* Nov. 1992, p. 76.

Hassrick, Royal B., *The Sioux.* Norman, OK: University of Oklahoma Press, 1964.

Hawken, Paul, *The Ecology of Commerce.* New York: Harper Collins Publishers, Inc., 1993.

Hawken, Paul, and William McDonough, "Seven Steps to Doing Good Business," *Inc.,* Nov. 1993, p. 79.

Ibrahim, Nabil A., "Corporate Responsibility: A Comparative Analysis of Perceptions of Top Executives and Business Students," *Mid-Atlantic Journal of Business,* December 1993, p. 303.

Impoco, Jim, "The Sultan of Silicon Valley: Andrew Grove's Intel Is the World Leader in Chips," *U.S. News & World Report,* March 1, 1993, p. 56.

Kathawala, Yunus, Dean Elmuti, and Laura Toepp, "An Overview of the Baldrige Award: America's Tool for Global Competitiveness," *Industrial Management,* March-April 1991, p. 27.

Keenan, William, Jr.,"What's Sales Got to Do with It?" *Sales & Marketing Management,* March 1994, p. 66.

Krause, Reinhardt, "FPD Directive Imminent; IBM Making License Bid," *Electronic News,* Jan. 31, 1994, p. 1.

Lame Deer, Archie Fire, and Richard Erdoes, *The Gift of Power.* Santa Fe, NM: Bear & Company Publishing, 1992.

Levering, Robert, and Milton Moskowitz, *The 100 Best Companies to Work for in America.* New York: Doubleday/Currency, 1993.

Liebeck, Laura, "Schmitt's Success: Reinventing the Wheel," *Discount Store News,* Sept. 21, 1992, p. 127.

Loden, Marilyn, and Judy B. Rosener, *Workforce America! Managing Employee Diversity as a Vital Resource.* Homewood, IL: Business One Irwin, 1991.

Long, Felicity, "Who's Minding the Store? Everybody," *Travel Weekly,* Sept. 23, 1993, p. 35.

Main, Jeremy, "Is the Baldrige Overblown?" *Fortune,* July 1, 1991, p. 62.

Maital, Shlomo, "When You Absolutely, Positively Have to Give Better Service," *Across the Board,* March 1991, p. 8.

Mander, Jerry, *In the Absence of the Sacred.* San Francisco: Sierra Club Books, 1991.

Mangelsdorf, Martha E., "Inc.'s Guide to 'Smart' Government Money: How Small Companies Are Profiting from New Economic-Development Programs," *Inc.,* August 1989, p. 51.

Melohn, Tom, *The New Partnership.* Essex Junction, VT: Oliver Wight Publications, 1994.

Moskal, Brian S., "Is Industry Ready for Adult Relationships? Among Top Executives, Optimism Abounds About Employee Involvement and Participative Management, Indicates an Industry Week/Wyatt Co. Survey," *Industry Week,* Jan. 21, 1991, p. 18.

Moskowitz, Levering, and Katz, *Everybody's Business.* New York: Doubleday/Currency, 1990.

Naisbitt, John, and Patricia Aburdeen, *Megatrends 2000: Ten New Directions for the 1990s.* New York: William Morrow and Company, Inc., 1990.

Nirenberg, John, *The Living Organization.* Homewood, IL: Business One Irwin, 1993.

Panchak, Patricia L., "How to Implement a Quality Management Initiative," *Modern Office Technology,* Feb. 1992, p. 27.

Pinchot, Gifford and Elizabeth, *The End of Bureaucracy and the Rise of the Intelligent Organization.* San Francisco: Berrett-Koehler Publishers, 1993.

Plumb, Stephen E., "Supplier Joint Ventures: A Look at Who's Marrying Whom, Why, and Who's Steering," *Ward's Auto World,* July 1990, p. 29.

Quinn, James Brian, *Intelligent Enterprise: A Knowledge and Service Based Paradigm for Industry.* New York: The Free Press, 1992.

Raia, Ernest, "Teaming in Detroit," *Purchasing,* March 3, 1994, p. 40.

Ray, Michael, and Alan Rinzler, *The New Paradigm In Business.* New York: Perigee Books, 1993.

Reynolds, Larry, "Business and Government Join Hands," *Management Review,* Dec. 1993, p. 19.

Roddick, Anita, *Body and Soul.* New York: Crown, 1991.

Schlesinger, Arthur, *The Disuniting of America.* New York: W. W. Norton & Co., 1992.

Scott, Mary, and Howard Rothman, *Companies with a Conscience.* New York: Birch Lane Press, 1992.

Senge, Peter, *The Fifth Discipline: The Art and Practice of the Learning Organization.* New York: Doubleday/Currency, 1990.

Teresko, John, "Andy Grove's Vision for Intel," *Industry Week,* Dec. 4, 1989, p. 27.

Tichy, Noel M., and Stratford Sherman, *Control Your Own Destiny or Someone Else Will.* New York: Doubleday/Currency, 1993.

Trimble, Vince, *Overnight Success.* New York: Crown, 1993.

Troy, Terry, "Stacking the Deck: Rubbermaid Hones New Marketing Campaign to Heighten Brand Awareness," *HFD-The Weekly Home Furnishings Newspaper,* Jan. 20, 1992, p. 59.

Tucker, Robert B., *Managing the Future: 10 Driving Forces of Change for the 90s.* New York: G. P. Putnam's Sons, 1991.

Weidenbaum, Murray L., "The Shifting Roles of Business and Government in the World Economy," *Challenge,* Jan.-Feb. 1993, p. 23.

INDEX